World labour report

3

Incomes from work: between equity and efficiency

International Labour Office   Geneva

ISBN 92-2-105951-0

ISSN 0255-5514

First published 1987

Printed in Switzerland   POP

Preface

This third volume of our *World Labour Report* – one of a series dealing with labour problems – takes as its theme: "Income from work: Between equity and efficiency". Part 1 contains an analysis of recent trends in employment, labour relations, social security and training for skills – all subjects closely linked to the main theme. Part 2 reviews the broad trends affecting the income of workers, whether employed or self-employed, and attempts to explain them. A fourth volume, now in preparation, will deal mainly with labour in the public sector, and will be published before the end of this decade.

The world labour situation has deteriorated further since the first two volumes of the *World Labour Report* were published in 1984 and 1985. Real incomes from work, the principal source of income for most households, have fallen in many countries. The great majority of workers in sub-Saharan Africa and Latin America, both wage workers and the self-employed, have suffered a drop in real income of as much as 30 to 40 per cent or more since the beginning of the 1980s. This trend has also affected a smaller but still significant proportion of workers in some Asian countries and in certain industrialised market economies (IMECs).

Employment trends present an equally disturbing picture. In the rural areas of many developing countries, with unsuitable systems of land tenure, mechanisation and the introduction of modern agricultural techniques have led millions of people to join the ever-increasing flight from the countryside. Many have gone to swell the ranks of the unemployed and the casual workforce, or have found only part-time or temporary employment in small urban enterprises. Few have found steady employment in large-scale enterprises or in the public sector. In many industrialised market economies, unemployment has remained high, with few countries managing to offset job losses by creating new jobs in sufficient numbers.

Furthermore employment and income have become more vulnerable and more precarious. In the developing countries, large numbers of workers have little or no job security. Many jobs are dead-end jobs, providing almost no chance of moving to something better. Certain groups, such as itinerant or migrant workers and women, are especially vulnerable to low incomes and poor working conditions. In the industrialised market economies, too, an increasing number of workers are now in precarious or casual employment.

One of the recurrent themes of this *Report* is the increasing emphasis being given to considerations of efficiency in all work-related matters. In most countries, for example, wage determination has been harnessed to achievement of macro-economic objectives such as reduced inflation, economic growth and a healthy balance of payments.

In the industrialised market economies the moderation of real wages, combined with other measures, has helped to check inflation, but has not reduced unemployment. In the private sector of many developing countries, wage adjustments have only a limited impact because wages represent a relatively small share of production costs. On the other hand, they have a substantial impact in the public sector, which accounts for the bulk of regular paid employment and spends a large proportion of its budget on wages and salaries.

Many countries, especially the centrally planned economies (CPECs), are giving particular encouragement to new forms of financial incentive and worker participation so as to increase labour productivity. In the industrialised market economies, collective bargaining on wages has become more pragmatic and more attuned to economic conditions, structural changes and the needs of the enterprise.

The same concern with efficiency has increasingly influenced governments' social expenditures. In the social security field, governments are trying to target benefits more accurately at groups most in need. In the industrialised market economies, there has been a rapid increase in social welfare expenditure to assist those, such as the long-term unemployed or single-parent families, who are no longer, or not adequately, covered by social insurance benefits. Meanwhile, governments have tried to hold down the costs of social insurance through a variety of measures and reforms.

The increasing weight being given to efficiency considerations in labour matters inevitably raise problems of equity. While more flexible forms of employment and remuneration have made it possible to increase efficiency and promote economic growth, they have very often helped to relegate to the margins of the labour market large groups of workers who survive only through precarious employment. At the same time, the reduction in government spending on training and social security has reduced opportunities for the most vulnerable social groups. Yet those very groups are often denied the protection afforded by

collective bargaining. New forms of economic and social organisation are needed in order to guarantee their rights and defend their interests.

In the last few years, governments and the social partners have largely been compelled to tackle immediate problems. Many debtor countries have had to restore their finances to order, enterprises have struggled for survival, and trade unions have given priority to the defence of their members' interests.

To reverse the adverse trends in employment and income will require the rethinking of many of our ideas in the economic and social sphere and in the world of work, the formulation of long-term economic and social policies, and their adoption with vigour and resolution at both the national and the international level.

It is in no way the purpose of this *Report* to outline such policies. Its aim is to provide appropriate analysis for all those concerned with labour problems and to inspire their thought and action.

Francis Blanchard

Contents

Preface   III

Part 1   Background: Recent trends and issues

Introduction   3

Chapter 1   Developing countries: Employment,   1. The economic context   *5*
                   skills and the state of labour   2. Employment   *8*
                   relations   **5**   3. Meeting the need for skills   *16*
                                                             4. The state of labour relations   *22*
                                                             5. Concluding remarks   *25*

Chapter 2   Industrialised market economies: Jobs,   1. Employment and hours of work   *27*
                   collective bargaining and social   2. Collective bargaining   *34*
                   security   **27**   3. Social insurance and social assistance   *38*
                                                             4. Concluding remarks   *43*

Chapter 3   Centrally planned economies: 1. Employment and labour productivity   *45*
                   Employment, productivity and   2. Reforms in workers' participation   *51*
                   participation   **45**   3. Social security   *53*
                                                             4. Conclusions   *56*

*Part 2   Incomes from work: Between equity and
                   efficiency*

Introduction   59

Chapter 4   Incomes from rural work in developing   1. Africa   *64*
                   countries   **63**   2. Asia   *74*
                                                             3. Latin America   *81*

Chapter 5   Wages from regular urban employment   1. Wage levels   *92*
                   in developing countries   **91**   2. Wage adjustments   *100*
                                                             3. Wage structures   *104*

Chapter 6   Other urban incomes: Vulnerable   1. Vulnerability by sector   *114*
                   groups in developing countries   **113** 2. Vulnerability by labour status   *118*
                                                             3. Vulnerable groups: Segmentation and
                                                                stratification   *123*
                                                             4. Concluding points   *131*

Chapter 7   Wages in the industrialised market economies   **133**

1. Wage levels and employment   *133*
2. Wage adjustment   *137*
3. Wage adjustment policies   *139*
4. Wage structures   *144*
5. Pay systems   *147*
6. Conclusions   *149*

Chapter 8   Wages in the centrally planned economies   **151**

1. The level of wages and incomes   *151*
2. Wage adjustment   *153*
3. Changing wage structures   *156*
4. Adapting enterprise wage systems   *161*
5. Conclusion   *164*

Bibliographical note   **165**

Text tables

1.1   Non-fuel exporting developing countries: External shocks, 1978-86   *6*

1.2   Export and import volumes: Developing countries, 1978-86   *8*

1.3   Trends in regular urban wage employment and the non-agricultural labour force: Africa, 1978-85   *10*

1.4   Unemployment rates: Asia, 1979-85   *14*

1.5   Percentage distribution and growth rates of the urban labour force: Latin America, 1980-85   *15*

1.6   Urban unemployment: Latin America, 1980-86   *15*

1.7   Percentage of agricultural employment in total employment: Latin America, 1980-85   *17*

1.8   Rates of return in secondary education: Developing countries, 1970s and 1980s   *18*

2.1   Percentage of the unemployed out of work for over one year: Industrialised market economies, 1981-86   *28*

2.2   Average actual hours worked: Industrialised market economies, 1980-86   *29*

2.3   International comparison of weekly and annual hours of work in collective agreements for workers in manufacturing: Industrialised market economies, 1985   *30*

2.4   Civilian employment in industry and services: Industrialised market economies, 1981-86   *31*

2.5   Growth of world import volumes, 1980-86 (annual percentage change)   *32*

2.6   Real interest rates: Industrialised market economies, 1980-86   *32*

2.7   Real hourly labour costs: Industrialised market economies, 1973-85 (annual growth rates)   *33*

2.8   Compensation of employees as a percentage of GDP: Industrialised market economies, 1973-85   *28*

3.1   Annual labour force growth rates: Centrally planned economies, 1960-90   *45*

3.2   Labour productivity, capital productivity and energy intensity: Centrally planned economies, 1975-86   *46*

3.3   Distribution of employment in the material and non-material sphere: Centrally planned economies, 1985   *47*

3.4   Expenditure on pensions and grants, as a percentage of total social consumption fund outlays: Centrally planned economies, 1975-84   *54*

3.5   Pensions paid as a percentage of national income: Centrally planned economies, 1975-84   *55*

3.6   Family allowances for two children as a percentage of the average wage: Centrally planned economies, 1980s   *56*

4.1   Agricultural workers in the labour force; women in the agricultural labour force, 1970-85   *63*

4.2   Characteristics of agriculture in Africa and other developing regions, 1978-80   *65*

4.3   Rates of growth of GNP per capita: Africa, 1965-85   *67*

4.4   Rates of growth of GNP and agriculture, and per capita food production in SSA countries, 1965-84   *67*

4.5   Ratio of producer prices received to rural consumer price index: African countries, 1972-85   *69*

4.6   Rate of growth of agricultural production and labour productivity and food production: African countries, 1970-84   *70*

4.7   Average rural income in real terms for four SSA countries, 1970-83   *71*

4.8   Real wages of agricultural workers in SSA countries, 1971-85   *71*

4.9   Incidence of rural poverty in African countries, 1970s and 1980s   *72*

4.10   Rural-urban income differentials in selected SSA countries, 1970-83   *72*

4.11   Composition of employment in agriculture by employment status: Asia, 1972-85   *74*

4.12   Land availability: Asian countries, 1969-84   *75*

4.13   Percentage distribution of labour hired and sold, by type of contract and farm size; Dinajpur villages, Bangladesh, 1982/83   *79*

4.14   Work done by family labour as a percentage of total labour input: Asian countries, 1970s and 1980s   *79*

4.15   Labour intensity per unit of land: Asian countries, 1970s and 1980s   *79*

4.16   Productivity of land and labour in Bangladesh, 1982/83   *80*

4.17   Productivity of land and labour incomes in Indonesia and Malaysia, 1975   *80*

4.18   Percentage of the traditional sector in the labour force: Latin America, 1970 and 1980   *83*

4.19   Structure of employment in agricultural and rural sectors: Latin America, 1960-80   *86*

4.20   Trends in real agricultural and non-agricultural wages: Latin America, 1965-84   *87*

4.21   Implicit remuneration of family labour: Brazil and Chile, 1970-80   *88*

5.1   Average annual growth rates of real wages and GDP per capita: Developing countries, 1971-85   *99*

5.2   Private/public wage ratios in selected industries and occupations: Developing countries, October 1985   *111*

6.1   Different categories of the surplus population (or the labour reserve)   *116*

6.2   Unemployment rates of non-farm service and production workers in the current labour force by expenditure classes in urban West Bengal, 1977-78   *117*

6.3   Costa Rica: Urban poverty profile by household head's sector of employment, 1982   *118*

6.4   Wage rates for non-farm service and production workers by general education categories, urban West Bengal, 1977-78   *119*

6.5   Employment in construction, Peninsular Malaysia, 1975-83   *121*

6.6   Composition of urban non-agricultural employment, by work status, Brazil, 1981-83   *122*

6.7   Incidence of poverty among urban workers, by work status, Brazil, 1981-83   *122*

6.8   Individual and household incomes by employment status, Montevideo, 1984   *123*

6.9   Income differentials by sectors in three developing countries   *123*

6.10   Distribution of types of labour combination, Jakarta, 1980   *124*

6.11   Typical subcontracting chain, Mexico City   *130*

7.1   Estimates of real capital costs relative to real labour costs: Industrialised market economies, 1970s and 1980s   *136*

8.1   Wage differentials between industrial sectors: Centrally planned economies, 1980   *158*

8.2   Earnings differentials by occupation and sex: Centrally planned economies, 1980   *158*

8.3   Wage differentials between occupations: Centrally planned economies, 1956-80: Industrial employees   *159*

Text figures

1.1   Share of employees in total employment: Developing countries, 1970s and 1980s   *9*

1.2   Real monthly earnings of wage earners outside agriculture: Africa, 1979-85   *11*

1.3   Real earnings of employees outside agriculture: Asia, 1979-85   *13*

1.4   Real earnings of wage earners in manufacturing: Latin America, 1980-86   *16*

2.1   Labour income-earning opportunities for rural and urban households   *61*

4.1   Yields in cereal production: Asia, 1974-85   *76*

4.2   Real daily wage rates in agriculture: Asia, 1971-85   *81*

5.1   Real earnings of employees outside agriculture: African countries, 1971-85   *96*

5.2   Real earnings of employees outside agriculture: Asian and North African countries, 1971-85   *97*

5.3   Real wages of wage earners in manufacturing: Latin American countries, 1971-86   *98*

5.4   Ratio of wages between selected occupations and unskilled construction workers in major cities: Developing countries, 1985   *108*

5.5   Average ratios of wages between selected occupations and unskilled construction workers : Cities in DCs and IMECs, 1985   *109*

7.1   Real hourly earnings, wage earners in manufacturing: Industrialised market economies, 1971-86   *134*

7.2   Hourly earnings and inflation in the United States, 1971-86: Wage earners in manufacturing   *139*

7.3   Female earnings as a percentage of male earnings: Industrialised market economies, 1971-85: Wage earners in manufacturing   *145*

8.1   Consumption as a percentage of national income: Centrally planned economies, 1970-86   *152*

8.2   Monthly real earnings in the non-agricultural economy: Centrally planned economies, 1971-85: Employees in the socialised sector   *153*

8.3   Wage differentials in the socialised sector: Centrally planned economies, 1970 and 1985   *157*

Text boxes

1.1   Remittance inflows to labour-sending developing countries   *7*

1.2   The pitfalls of audio-visual training material   *22*

2.1   Part-time work: Advantages and problems   *32*

2.2   More co-operative labour relations in IMECs during the 1980s   *36*

2.3   Flexibility of working time   *39*

2.4   Reform of the Japanese pension scheme   *41*

3.1   Employment incentives for pensioners   *49*

3.2   The scope of collective agreements and workers' participation   *52*

3.3   Production brigades in the USSR   *53*

p2.1   Statistics on labour incomes and prices   *60*

4.1   China's policy of encouraging peasants "to leave the land but not the village"   *75*

4.2   Distribution of land and rural development in the Republic of Korea   *78*

4.3   Cuba: A declining proportion of peasants in the agricultural labour force   *84*

4.4   The accumulation of marginal labour in the peasant sector: The case of Brazil   *85*

5.1   Wages and structural adjustment in the Sudan   *102*

5.2   Economic and wage stabilisation in Israel   *103*

7.1   Concession bargaining in the United States   *138*

7.2   Indexation and inflation   *140*

7.3   Australia: The Prices and Incomes Accord (1983-87)   *142*

8.1   Yugoslavia: Self-management and social contract   *155*

Part *1*

Background:
Recent trends
and issues

Introduction

Part 1 of this report reviews recent trends in a number of key areas, which have a bearing on the main theme "Incomes from work: Between equity and efficiency". Employment developments provide the main background for the later analysis of incomes from work, in both wage employment and self-employment. The remuneration of employment is basically determined by the number of hours that people work and their productivity. Part 1 discusses recent trends in hours of work in the industrialised economies. Skill levels are an important factor in the productivity of employment. In this context, the report takes up the issue of cost-effectiveness of education and training in developing countries in both the formal and informal sectors.

Labour relations have, or can have, an important impact on wages and self-employment incomes. Where wage workers are organised, they bargain with employers on wages and working conditions. And even if they are not organised themselves, they may still be covered by agreements determined by collective bargaining. On the other hand, large groups of workers, particularly casual wage workers and the self-employed, are rarely organised. The organisation of such workers could have an important impact on their incomes, enabling them to influence decisions affecting their social and economic situation.

Social security benefits replace or supplement earnings and are often financed from earnings-related contributions. Part 1 reviews recent trends in cash benefits, such as pensions, unemployment and family benefits as well as social assistance in the industrialised countries. (A review of social security trends in DCs is in the course of preparation by the ILO.)

Part 1 is divided into three chapters covering the developing countries (chapter 1), the industrialised market economies (chapter 2) and the centrally planned economies (chapter 3). All three chapters review trends in employment and labour relations. In addition, chapter 1 discusses the issue of cost-effectiveness of training, while chapters 2 and 3 review current trends in hours of work and social security.

Chapter 1

Developing countries: Employment, skills and the state of labour relations

The 1980s have seen many developing countries (DCs) caught in a difficult dilemma, obliged to adjust to unfavourable external economic circumstances in the short run, while trying to stay on the path of long-term social and economic development. As section 1 shows, the need for adjustment has dominated the national and international economic policy scene. Because adjustment policies have usually been carried out against a background of sluggish economic growth and constrained government budgets, there has been little room for structural policies to aid development and almost no progress on increasing the economic and social well-being of the population.

Productive and well-remunerated employment is one of the main conditions for improving living standards. Section 2 provides an overview of trends in employment and work incomes in the 1980s, which brings out the different experiences of sub-Saharan Africa and Latin America on the one hand and of Asia and North Africa on the other. It also distinguishes the situation of various socio-economic groups, such as the self-employed, casual and regular wage earners, both in rural and urban areas. The question of income from employment is examined in greater depth in part 2.

The improvement of skills is an important factor in increasing the productivity of employment. In a situation of stagnant or declining government resources, it is essential to use existing training systems and organisations effectively and to promote new approaches. Section 3 considers the cost-effectiveness of education and training in the formal and informal sector.

One of the obstacles to long-term social and economic development is the existence of large disparities in the degree of organisation of different parts of the workforce. Even though employers and regularly employed workers are still inadequately organised in many countries, they are effectively bargaining on wages and conditions of work and occasionally have had some voice in how adjustment policies have been carried out. But the large majority of the workforce – casual workers and the self-employed in rural and urban areas – rarely have organisations to promote their interests at work and influence the course of social and economic development. This issue is taken up in section 4.

1. The economic context

Many DCs found themselves confronting increasingly difficult domestic policy problems in the 1970s. In most sub-Saharan African countries, for example, agricultural production per capita stagnated or fell, the result, at least in part, of low investment in agriculture, often unremunerative prices for farmers and overvalued exchange rates. In some DCs high protective barriers and sometimes inefficient public enterprises reduced the competitiveness of manufacturing industry. Enterprises and governments of many DCs also borrowed extensively in international capital markets, encouraged by the negative real interest rates offered during the second half of the 1970s when the markets were awash with surplus funds from oil-producing countries.

Thus, many countries were in a highly vulnerable position when the external environment deteriorated in the 1980s.

The commodity price boom of 1977, which pushed up export prices for food, beverages and vegetable oils, was followed by a five-year decline in terms of trade (the ratio between changes in export and import prices) for non-fuel producing DCs. If a country's export prices are rising more slowly than its import prices, it is obliged to export more to maintain previous import levels. Terms of trade increased slightly in 1983 and 1984 but fell again in 1985 and 1986, and some years of continuous improvement will

Table 1.1.   Non-fuel exporting developing countries[1]: External shocks, 1978-86 (in percentages)

	1978	1979	1980	1981	1982	1983	1984	1985	1986
Change in terms of trade	−3.9	−1.7	−5.9	−4.2	−2.1	0.6	1.4	−1.1	−0.2
Real GNP growth of IMECs	4.2	3.4	1.3	1.4	−0.4	2.7	4.7	3.0	2.4
Foreign real interest rates[2]	2.7	−6.1	−1.6	16.3	19.2	15.5	11.2	15.7	5.9
Capital inflows[3]	28.4	26.0	60.6	62.9	28.3	16.2	13.6	17.8	4.0
Current account deficit[4]	−11.9	−14.2	−16.5	−20.1	−17.2	−11.1	−6.5	−5.9	−2.5

[1] Non-fuel exporting developing countries; the following countries are fuel exporters: Algeria, Bahrain, Congo, Ecuador, Gabon, Indonesia, Islamic Republic of Iran, Iraq, Kuwait, Libyan Arab Jamahiriya, Mexico, Nigeria, Oman, Qatar, Saudi Arabia, Syrian Arab Republic, Trinidad and Tobago, Tunisia, United Arab Emirates and Venezuela.   [2] Long-term rates of seven major industrial countries, adjusted for percentage changes in export prices of non-fuel exporting developing countries.   [3] "Other" net external borrowing in thousand million US dollars.   [4] As percentage of exports of goods and services.

Source: International Monetary Fund: *World Economic Outlook* (Washington, DC, 1987).

be needed in order to wipe out the losses accrued in the 1978-82 period (see table 1.1).

The growth rate in IMECs slowed sharply in 1980, partly as a result of restrictive policies (see also chapter 2). In addition, access to IMEC markets became more difficult as a result of increased protectionism. This caused problems for DCs which sell 62 per cent of their exports to IMECs, as compared to 31 per cent sold to other DCs.

Until 1980, foreign real interest rates (measured against non-fuel developing country export prices) were low or even negative. Many developing countries made ample use of readily available capital to finance terms of trade losses. But restrictive monetary policies in the industrialised nations pushed up real interest rates to record levels after 1980 making it difficult for overborrowed DCs, already struggling with low growth of export earnings, to service their debts.

The debt service problem, highlighted by the Mexican crisis, and the need to finance the increasing current account deficit of the United States, led to a sizeable reduction in capital flows to developing countries after 1982, thereby reducing their opportunity to finance their current account deficits through additional borrowing. More recently the combined IMEC current account deficit (with a large deficit for the United States and surpluses for the Federal Republic of Germany and Japan) has returned to its 1980 level. However, this has not been matched by a current account surplus for the fuel exporting countries as it was then.

Developing countries in Asia have generally been less affected by the unfavourable international economic situation than those in sub-Saharan Africa and Latin America. Countries in North Africa and in West and South Asia have benefited from remittances from and increased exports to oil-rich Middle Eastern countries (see box 1.1). Many South-East Asian countries have a strong competitive position on the international market for manufactured products. China was largely insulated from the world economy until the 1980s. Worst hit were sub-Saharan African countries whose export earnings were mainly dependent on commodities for which world prices were falling; and a number of South American countries whose manufacturing sector had been highly protected and thus was often uncompetitive.

At the beginning of the 1980s, most developing countries were forced to make rapid and drastic cuts in their current account deficits, either as part of an agreed stabilisation package or through other emergency measures. In 1983 current account deficits expressed as a percentage of exports of goods and services were back to the level of 1977 and fell further between 1984 and 1986. However, this adjustment took the form mainly of a reduction in the volume of imports (table 1.2).

A deterioration in terms of trade and the balance of payments inevitably involves a drop in real national income. Imports become more expensive. Enterprises may be forced to cut back on purchases of essential intermediate or investment goods, while consumers can afford to buy fewer imported consumption goods. Domestic production and imports thus tend to fall together. If exports are increased to reduce current account deficits the extra labour and capital must be drawn from the domestic economy. Depending on the initial economic situation and the policies pursued by governments, wages, capital and/or government revenues will bear the burden of adjustment.

1.1   Remittance inflows to labour-sending developing countries

Migrants' remittances have been widely recognised as one of the most substantial benefits of international migration for labour-sending countries. In macroeconomic terms, they constitute a major source of foreign exchange earnings in many countries. For migrant workers themselves, remittances mean that family members left behind receive relatively large amounts of additional income which can significantly boost their living standards. The table shows the most important remittance-receiving developing countries in terms of the significance of these earnings relative to exports and GDP. In the majority of these countries migrants' remittances were worth about a quarter of the value of their export earnings and about 2-5 per cent of GDP.

Remittance earnings depend heavily on economic activity in labour-receiving countries, as well as the number of migrant workers and their wage levels. Many countries linked to the Arab oil-producing countries achieved peak remittance earnings in 1983 or 1984. In Pakistan, for example, 1983 remittances were worth more than half total rice exports, the main Pakistani source of foreign exchange which peaked in the same year. Another even more remarkable example is Egypt where remittance earnings grew to an amazing US$3,981 million in 1984, more than ten times the value of its cotton exports. It is not surprising that the decline in oil prices in the mid-1980s has caused concern over the possibility of a massive return of migrant labourers from the Arab oil-producing countries. However, the evidence suggests this did not happen in 1985 and 1986, or at least not to the extent that had been antici-

pated, although remittance earnings did drop quite sharply, mainly because of falling migrant wage levels.

The table also contains information on a number of smaller but nevertheless important migration flows outside the Middle East and Mediterranean. For example, the Caribbean economies have for many years been involved in sizeable labour exchanges. In the 1980s Haiti and the Dominican Republic were the two Caribbean States to benefit most from remittances in terms of their balance of payments. In another region of the world, the drought-stricken Sahel, labour movements took place on a large scale. As a result, remittance incomes reached particularly high levels in Somalia and Sudan in 1984, while in other States the decline in merchandise exports due to the drought also had the effect of increasing the significance of migrants' earnings to these countries.

The figures in the table serve as an indicator of the relative importance of migration to different labour-sending economies. It should be noted, however, that these figures under-rate the significance of migrants' earnings. This is true not only because remittances may never be officially recorded by the banking system, but also because the figures represent net remittance earnings. In countries that are both important labour-sending and receiving countries the sensitivity of the economy to remittances is even greater than indicated by the table. For example, in 1985 the Jordanian Central Bank noted that the equivalent of US$1 left the economy in remittances for every US$4 sent home by Jordanians working abroad.

Remittance inflows to major labour-sending countries,[1] 1980-85, ranked by the ratio of remittances to exports [2]

	Ratio of remittances to exports	Ratio of remittances to GDP, 1984	Remittance inflow (millions of US dollars), 1985
1. Yemen Arab Republic	3.115	0.297	867
2. Yemen, People's Democratic Republic of	2.275	–	–
3. Pakistan	0.761	0.099	2687
4. Jordan	0.455	0.259	846
5. Egypt	0.432	0.093	3216
6. Bangladesh	0.396	0.034	395
7. Morocco	0.300	0.071	–
8. Somalia	0.295	–	19
9. Sudan	0.250	–	249
10. India	0.192	0.012	–
11. Syria	0.184	0.017	293
12. Haiti	0.179	0.024	–
13. Sri Lanka	0.160	0.046	269
14. Dominican Republic	0.145	0.019	–
15. Mali	0.128	–	24
16. Nepal	0.124	0.015	36

[1] The data presented here are for private unrequited transfers, which include workers' remittances as credits *and* debits, as well as migrants' transfers and other private transfers.
[2] Exports include merchandise goods and services and are valued as free on board (f.o.b.). The ratio is calculated for the years 1980 to 1985, or for whatever years between these dates for which data were available.

Source: Calculated using data from IMF: *International Financial Statistics Yearbook* (Washington, DC, 1986) and *International Financial Statistics*, Feb. 1987.

Table 1.2.   Export and import volumes: Developing countries, 1978-86 (annual percentage change)

	1978	1979	1980	1981	1982	1983	1984	1985	1986
Non-fuel exporting developing countries									
Exports	9.4	6.9	8.5	5.2	1.1	8.2	11.6	5.2	7.7
Imports	8.9	7.4	4.9	3.2	−5.2	1.7	5.3	4.5	3.9
Africa									
Exports	3.6	8.4	−1.2	−14.9	−5.1	3.4	5.6	7.1	2.2
Imports	3.6	−3.5	8.7	11.3	−8.1	−10.1	−0.4	−7.3	−11.0
South America									
Exports	9.6	7.6	1.2	6.0	−2.4	8.2	8.5	–	−8.8
Imports	5.5	8.3	9.7	3.5	−17.8	−22.5	2.8	2.2	−4.8

Source: As table 1.1.

In practice, adjustment was forced by external events upon DCs which were either overborrowed or unable to diversify their exports quickly. As a result it has taken the form of economic contraction and a drop in import volumes rather than increased exports and stable imports.

Adjustment to altered international circumstances cannot be brought about overnight, nor is it desirable that it should be. A rapid shift towards producing for the export market or for the import-competing domestic market is often not possible in developing economies. Such a process involves changing capital stock and shifts in labour, for which additional investment is needed. Although price structures and overvalued exchange rates in many countries have discouraged the production of tradeable goods, correcting these factors is not sufficient in itself to bring about a quick response. Domestic production capacity may not be available. Inefficiency and domestic vested interests resulting from trade protection may be additional brakes on any shift in resources.

Furthermore, sudden massive contraction through wage restraint and cuts in government spending, and important changes in price structures, can upset the social balance. This makes implementation of changes more difficult, often forcing governments to reverse earlier intended policies and so worsening the climate for further adjustment.

Thus, although the balance of payments gap for DCs has narrowed, this is not necessarily grounds for optimism. The combination of international economic changes and domestic policies has reduced employment opportunities and led to falling labour incomes in many countries. However, the nature and magnitude of these changes have been quite different in the three main developing continents.

2. Employment

The structure of employment in developing countries varies enormously. On average more than 60 per cent of the labour force in DCs work in agriculture. But the share of agricultural employment varies from over two-thirds in sub-Saharan Africa, China and southern Asia to only about 40 per cent in North Africa and western Asia, and less than 30 per cent in South America. However, these shares are still very high in comparison with the IMECs and CPECs – 7 and 17 per cent respectively in 1985.

In some DCs, such as Argentina, Chile, Jordan, Panama and Singapore, more than half of total employment is in the services sector. By contrast, services account for less than 10 per cent of employment in many sub-Saharan African countries. Similarly, the proportion of employment in industry varies from a typical 2-5 per cent in sub-Saharan Africa to over 30 per cent in some countries of South America, North Africa, West and East Asia. The lower the proportion of agricultural employment the higher the proportion of employees (those in wage employment) tends to be. Self-employed and unpaid family workers dominate agricultural employment in almost all DCs while in industry and services wage work is more widespread. The variation between DCs in employees as a proportion of total employment is documented in figure 1.1.

Figure 1.1.   Share of employees in total employment: Developing countries, 1970s and 1980s
(most recent census data, in percentages)

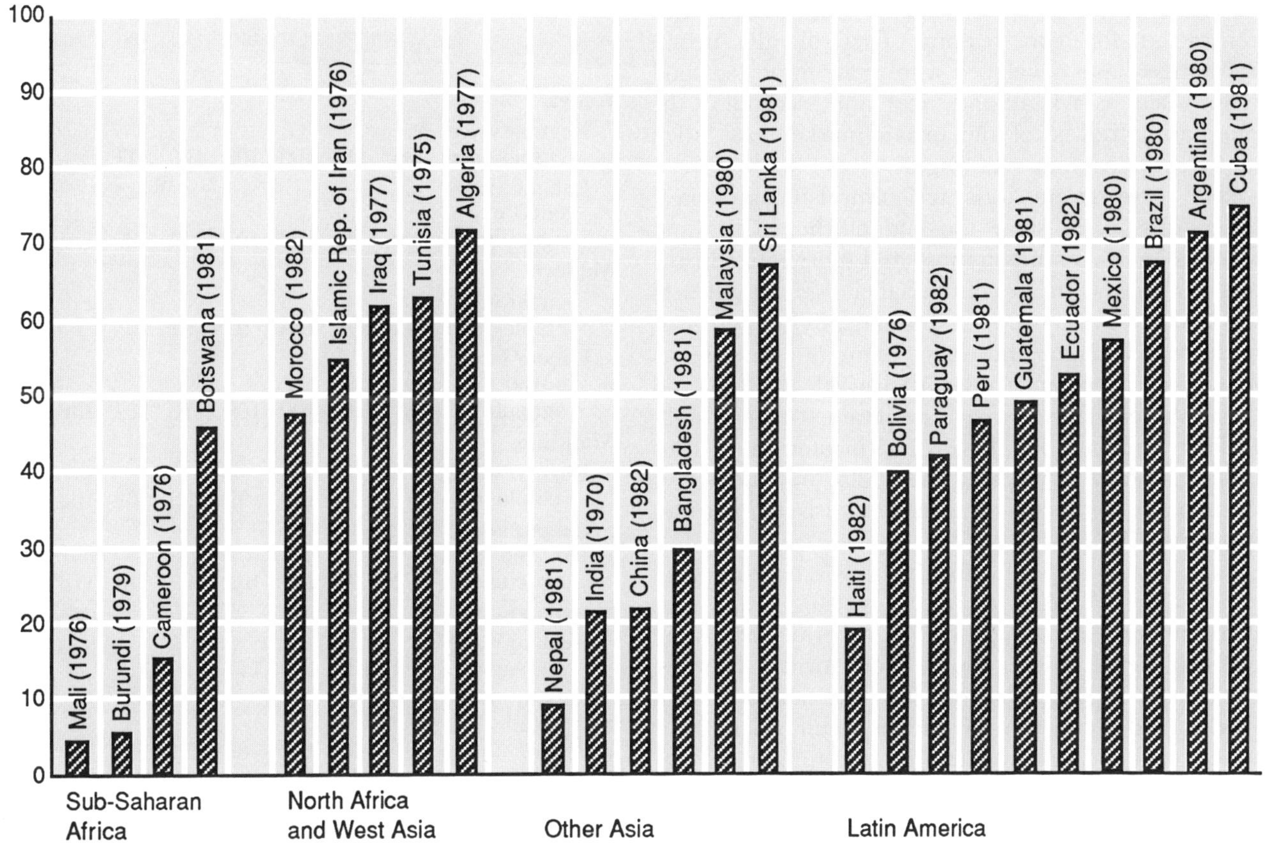

Source: ILO: *Year Book of Labour Statistics.*

Sub-Saharan Africa

Africa is a continent of great diversity, from the northern Mediterranean countries to the southern dependent economies. The northern countries have economies characterised by a relatively high degree of industrialisation and urbanisation which makes them similar to western Asian countries. The southern African countries of Botswana, Lesotho and Swaziland, though they share many characteristics with other sub-Saharan African (SSA) countries, are critically dependent on the Republic of South Africa for work and incomes.

Rural areas

More than 70 per cent of the sub-Saharan African labour force works in agriculture. Most African farmers operate on a "subsistence" basis. They assure a basic calorie-sufficiency level for their own household, but also sell their products in the market especially if prices are remunerative. They may, therefore, sell food crops in the urban domestic market and export crops in the international market. It is characteristic of sub-Saharan Africa that export and food crops are often grown together on small family-owned farms, using similar unsophisticated technologies.

Rural wage earners exist but their numbers are quite small, usually not more than 5 per cent of the total labour force on a permanent basis. Considerably greater numbers take up seasonal employment outside the family farm, sometimes on a reciprocal basis and usually with food rather than wages as the form of payment. They are mostly younger male members of a farm family rather than heads of households, reflecting the fact that there is very little landlessness in Africa.

Prices for export crops have fallen steeply over the past few years, leading to deteriorating terms of trade. Moreover, the domestic (urban) food market has contracted for two reasons. First of all, urban consumers have developed a taste for imported food crops such as wheat and rice; and, secondly, the purchasing power of the urban market has fallen along with declining real wages.

For these reasons, *cash* agricultural incomes have fallen drastically since the end of the 1970s, and farmers have withdrawn more and more into subsistence. In most countries of the Sahel, *total* agricultural incomes have also dropped dramatically because – as a result of drought and war – many families had to leave their farms and/or lost their cattle. But, by and large, African farmers have maintained their ability to feed their own families. Rural incomes have thus fallen substantially during the 1980s, but they have been better protected against the crisis than urban incomes.

The factors resposible for the crisis are a subject of continuing debate. The role of pricing policy has come under special scrutiny. In general, because of the subsistence orientation of most African farmers, the impact of prices on production decisions is limited in the food sector. In the export sector prices have much greater impact, although a crumbling infrastructure and shortage of basic agricultural inputs as well as consumer goods means that the efficacy of prices to stimulate greater output is often exaggerated. Changes in pricing policy thus have to be part of a package of measures to encourage production in the agricultural sector. Investment is needed to rebuild the marketing and distribution network. Simultaneously more consumer goods have to be made available for the rural areas so that higher prices can be translated into incentive goods.

Productivity per unit of land in Africa is low compared to that in Asia and Latin America. For example, in 1985 the yield of cereal production in Africa was about 1,100 kilograms per hectare while it was 2,500 kg and 2,100 kg in Asia and Latin America respectively. To a large extent, this is due to the weak technological and human resources base in the African agricultural sector. Technology has not advanced beyond the stage of hand tools in most African countries, and extension services are practically non-existent. Very little fertiliser is used and hence yields remain low and stagnant compared to other developing countries. An important factor

Table 1.3. Trends in regular urban wage employment and the non-agricultural labour force: Africa, 1978-85 (1980 = 100)

Country	1978	1979	1980	1981	1982	1983	1984	1985
Kenya								
Regular wage employment	86	93	100	102	105	111	–	–
Labour force outside agriculture	90	95	100	107	114	120	127	134
Malawi								
Regular wage employment	91	94	100	91	91	103	–	–
Labour force outside agriculture	81	94	100	109	118	127	136	154
Mauritius								
Regular wage employment	97	101	100	99	99	102	102	–
Labour force outside agriculture	92	96	100	105	109	114	118	123
Swaziland								
Regular wage employment	98	102	100	117	117	119	–	–
Labour force outside agriculture	91	96	100	106	111	117	122	128
United Republic of Tanzania								
Regular wage employment	88	101	100	107[1]	116	124	–	–
Labour force outside agriculture	89	94	100	108	116	123	131	139
Zambia								
Regular wage employment	97	99	100	103	96	95	–	–
Labour force outside agriculture	92	96	100	105	109	114	118	123
Zimbabwe								
Regular wage employment	95	95	100	109	114	113	–	–
Labour force outside agriculture	92	96	100	105	110	116	121	126

[1] Series complemented with national data sources.

Sources: ILO: *Year Book of Labour Statistics*; FAO: *Worldwide estimates and projections of the agricultural and non-agricultural population segments, 1950-2025* (Rome, 1986).

behind this is the lack of a generalised "green revolution" in Africa. Maize varieties have been upgraded but most other traditional African crops have not benefited from such technological progress. Returns to this kind of investment could be greater than from "getting prices right".

Urban areas

In most SSA countries, regular urban wage employment constitutes only a small percentage of total employment, typically between 5 and 10 per cent. Over the past ten years, the opportunities for regular urban employment have fallen in some countries and elsewhere they have generally not kept up with growth of the non-agricultural labour force (see table 1.3).

As a result of these trends and of drastic adjustment policies, real wages in many SSA countries have dropped very steeply since the end of the 1970s (see figure 1.2). Since 1979, real wages have often fallen by more than 50 per cent. (In this *Report* the term "wages" covers the remuneration of both wage earners and salaried employees.)

In some African countries – Uganda, Ghana, Somalia and the United Republic of Tanzania being prime examples – the drop in wages has been so severe that the urban wage can no longer support an average size family. Thus, in Uganda the minimum wage would have bought only a quarter of an average family's daily requirements of basic foodstuffs in 1984. In 1972, when the decline set in, the minimum wage would have sufficed to buy 1.7 times the basic requirement. In the United Republic of Tanzania, the minimum wage was already inadequate to support an average family in March 1984; by December 1985, with the price of the basic staple, maize meal, raised to Sh.13.75 from Sh.2.50 the previous year, the minimum wage would have bought only around 40 per cent of a family's basic foodstuffs.

The structure of African urban economies and the urban labour market in particular has undergone massive changes during the last decade. The security, if not the stability, of regular wage employment has declined. As a result, the distinction between formal and informal sector employment is becoming blurred. The gap between incomes earned in the two sectors is narrowing. With the fall in or slower growth of regular urban employment, many people have moved into self-employment or casual wage employment.

In some extreme cases, they may even return to the countryside because family ties remain strong even though individual family members may live

Figure 1.2.   Real monthly earnings of wage earners outside agriculture: Africa, 1979-85 (1979 = 100)

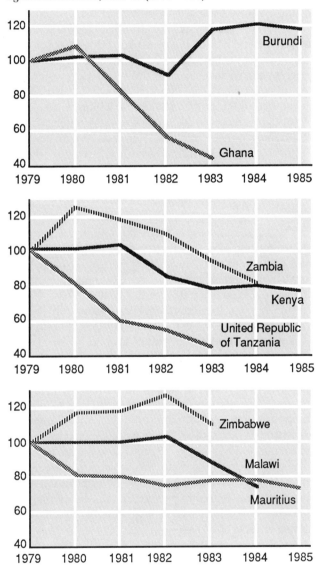

Source: ILO: *Year Book of Labour Statistics.*

very far apart. As a result open unemployment is rare in SSA urban areas.

Asia and North Africa

In 1985, almost 60 per cent of the world's population lived in Asia (excluding Japan) and North Africa. The large population and vast surface make it difficult to generalise about employment conditions. Very roughly, Asia can be divided into four main subregions, within which it is possible to identify some common threads. The two biggest subregions are China with about 38 per cent of the Asian population, directly followed by southern Asia (including Bangladesh, India, Pakistan and Sri Lanka) with 37 per cent. The South-East and East Asian countries, which account for about 17 per cent, are a more heterogeneous group, including centrally planned economies such as Viet Nam; the newly industrialised countries and territories such as Hong Kong, the Republic of Korea and Singapore; and other market economy countries, such as Indonesia, Malaysia, the Philippines and Thailand. About 8 per cent live in West Asia (the Middle East, the Islamic Republic of Iran and Turkey) and North Africa.

Rural areas

The great majority of the Asian labour force works in agriculture: 65-70 per cent in China and southern Asia and 40-50 per cent in West Asia and South-East Asia. The most spectacular development has taken place in *China* since the end of the 1970s. Grain output per capita increased from about 320 kg in 1978 to about 400 kg in 1985. The first impetus to agricultural production came around 1980, when producer prices were raised very substantially. At the same time, an extensive rural reform took place as a result of which the old commune system was broken up and the individual farmer household became the main unit of production and management. Under the agricultural production "responsibility system", each household is allocated "contract" land for its own use, ownership remaining with the collective. In return, the household has to deliver part of its production to the State, but is free to sell the remainder. Recently, households have also been given greater freedom to choose what crops to grow.

Another notable trend has been the increasing importance of non-farm employment, particularly in the coastal provinces. Since 1979, efforts have been directed not only towards stimulating the growth of township enterprises (commune and brigade rural enterprises) but also towards encouraging the development of enterprises by peasants on either an individual or a co-operative basis. The results have been quite dramatic: by the end of 1985, an estimated 18.6 per cent of the rural labour force worked in non-farming activities, compared to 9.3 per cent in 1978. Of the total labour force in non-farm activities in 1985, about 69 per cent were employed in township enterprises, 16 per cent were engaged in individual enterprises and the remaining 15 per cent in co-

operative enterprises. As a result of these developments, rural incomes have grown rapidly and rural poverty has dropped dramatically since the end of the 1970s.

Among the market economies of *South, South-East and East Asia*, there is a sharp contrast between countries where industrial employment and overall development have made substantial progress, such as the Republic of Korea and Malaysia, and those where development has lagged, such as Bangladesh. In the former, employment opportunities elsewhere in the economy have drawn the reserve of family labour into the market. In the latter, deteriorating economic conditions have forced low-income households to increase the intensity of their work on the farm.

Agricultural productivity – and hence farm incomes – depends on a number of factors. During the 1980s, agricultural productivity has increased in most South, South-East and East Asian countries (see chapter 4). Average yield of cereals has reached a level in the Republic of Korea that is comparable with Japan. Yields are also high in China and Indonesia while they are relatively low in India and Pakistan.

Rural incomes are also determined by land availability and the distribution of land. Arable land availability (excluding perennial crops) is very low in China (0.23 hectares per member of the agricultural labour force in 1984), in Sri Lanka (0.35 ha), the Republic of Korea (0.39 ha), Bangladesh (0.44 ha) and Indonesia (0.47 ha). Land availability reaches about 1 hectare per member of the agricultural labour force in India, Pakistan, the Philippines and Thailand. In most countries, there is no further scope to increase the surface of arable land (except in Thailand, Malaysia and Indonesia), with the result that increased rural incomes will have to be achieved by a better distribution of land and increased productivity.

The productivity of land and labour by farm size depends to a large extent on the capital-intensiveness of agricultural production. In countries or regions where traditional agriculture is predominant, the productivity of land is higher on small than on large farms. But labour productivity is lower because small farms tend to use more (family) labour per unit of land. However, productivity differences by farm size disappear with the application of modern technology and agricultural inputs such as irrigation, machinery and high-yielding seed varieties. Labour is then no longer the key productive factor. To afford these inputs, however, farmers need access to credit.

The greater inequality of landholdings and wider application of modern production techniques in many South and South-East Asian countries means that an increasing proportion of rural households are dependent on wage labour for their survival. This has often led to a greater *casualisation* of rural wage labour. In 1977-78, almost 30 per cent of the rural work force in India was in casual employment, and this percentage has increased since. In Sri Lanka in 1981-82, the proportion was 33 per cent.

On the basis of scattered information, it seems that, since the early 1980s, real agricultural wages have stagnated in Bangladesh, Burma, the Republic of Korea and Malaysia. In the Philippines, real wages have fallen while they have increased in some regions of India and Pakistan. These trends should be interpreted with care, because regional variations in wage trends within countries can be very large. Rural poverty remains high in most South Asian countries, and has generally not been reduced over the past decade.

Urban areas

During the 1980s, the proportion of workers employed in industry has changed little in most countries and areas. In Burma, India, Indonesia, the Philippines and Thailand, the proportion varies between 10 and 15 per cent, while it is 30 per cent or more in Hong Kong, Israel, the Republic of Korea and Singapore. In only two places for which data are available has the proportion fallen – in Hong Kong from 50 to 45 per cent between 1979 and 1985 and in the Philippines from 15.5 to 14 per cent. In the Republic of Korea, there was a temporary drop in the share of industrial employment in 1981-82 as a result of the world recession.

However, in almost all countries the percentage of workers employed in services has risen at least by 2 percentage points since the end of the 1970s. In the Republic of Korea the proportion jumped from 34.1 per cent in 1979 to 44.3 per cent in 1985. In Singapore, the share of services employment was unchanged at around 63 per cent.

There is only limited information on the proportion of regularly employed wage workers in the urban labour force. In India and Sri Lanka, for example, workers in the "organised" sector represent less than 10 per cent of the non-agricultural labour force. In western and South-East Asia, the proportion

Figure 1.3. **Real earnings of employees outside agriculture: Asia, 1979-85 (1979 = 100)**

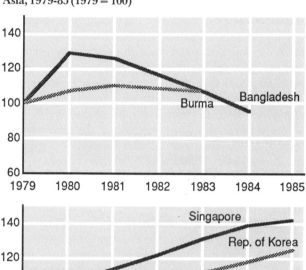

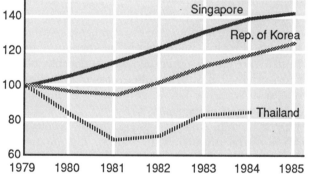

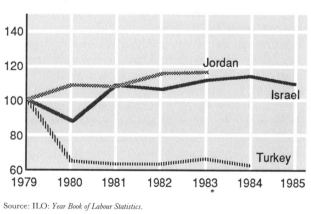

Source: ILO: *Year Book of Labour Statistics.*

varies between 30 and 60 per cent. In China, the large majority of urban workers are in regular wage employment.

Since the end of the 1970s, real wages from regular employment in Asia have followed a different pattern from those in sub-Saharan Africa and Latin America (see figure 1.3). In most South-East and West Asian countries for which statistics are available, real wages have risen, though there are some exceptions (such as Turkey, the Philippines and Thailand).

Women tend to be a highly vulnerable group in the urban labour market of many Asian countries (see chapter 6). For example, women constitute a majority of rural-urban migrants in South-East Asia, and many teenage girls enter the urban economy through low-level, low-paid and insecure forms of employment. In small-scale Asian enterprises, casual women workers have often replaced permanent male employees, because they are not covered by labour laws and minimum wage regulations. In urban Indonesia in 1980, women accounted for over one-third of all those with "informal" work statuses (self-employed, with or without family workers), while they accounted for only a quarter of those in the "formal" sector (employers and wage workers). In India, women spent twice the proportion of the time they were in the labour force in casual employment as men did. Finally, many young women in various countries are employed in the most vulnerable jobs of export-oriented industries, often drawn from distant villages to work for low wages and very long workweeks for two or three years.

Open unemployment is also gradually becoming a feature of the urban labour market. The picture of unemployment as a "luxury", which could be afforded only by well-educated youths, now belongs to the past. Most urban workers no longer have close ties with rural family members. If they cannot find casual or regular wage employment or self-employment, they will be unemployed. Unemployment in Asian countries for which statistics are available (see table 1.4) is relatively low compared with Latin America and the IMECs. But there is a trend towards higher unemployment in Israel, Jordan, the Philippines, the Syrian Arab Republic and Thailand. In other countries and areas such as Hong Kong, Singapore and the Republic of Korea, unemployment has generally not exceeded 4 per cent since the end of the 1970s, but it rises and falls with the business cycle. In China, there has been a large reduction in unemployment. After the Cultural Revolution, and in particular between 1978 and 1980, many youngsters who had been sent to the countryside were allowed to return to the cities. Between 1979 and 1981, they were absorbed not only by state-owned enterprises and organisations, but also by the urban collectives set up at all government levels (province, municipality/county, district and neighbourhood). In addition, an increasing number of young people were channelled into self-employment – a trend that continued afterwards.

Table 1.4. Unemployment rates [1]: Asia, 1979-85 (in percentages)

	1979	1980	1981	1982	1983	1984	1985
China [2]	6.0	4.9	3.8	3.2	2.3	1.9	1.8
Hong Kong	3.4	4.3	3.7	4.2	4.1	3.9	3.6
Israel	3.8	6.0	6.4	6.0	5.3	7.0	7.3
Rep. of Korea	3.8	5.2	4.5	4.4	4.1	3.8	4.0
Philippines	3.5	4.8	5.4	5.5	4.9	7.0	6.1
Singapore	3.4	3.0	2.9	2.6	3.2	2.7	4.1
Syrian Arab Republic	3.9				5.1		
Thailand		0.8	0.8	4.5			

[1] Based on labour force sample surveys. [2] Based on administrative statistics; urban areas only.

Source: ILO: *Year Book of Labour Statistics.*

Latin America

In 1986, per capita output in Latin America was nearly 8 per cent below its level in 1980 – the year before the onset of the crisis – and only slightly above that in 1978. The most disadvantaged have borne a greater part of the adjustment burden than other groups in Latin American society, especially in the urban areas where most of the population lives.

Urban areas

The economic recession of the early 1980s has had three effects on the urban labour market: regular wage employment has ceased to grow; workers have shifted towards self-employment and casual wage employment; and real wages have fallen. This is indicated clearly by table 1.5 which shows the changing composition of the non-agricultural labour force between 1980 and 1985.

Regular wage employment in large and medium-sized enterprises has suffered most during the recession. Employment in this sector may have grown by no more than 0.3 per cent per year between 1980 and 1985. On the other hand, growth of employment in the public sector, in small enterprises and in the informal sector remained well above that of the urban labour force. But unemployment increased most quickly of all; the unemployment rate rose from 6.4 to 7.5 per cent of the workforce between 1980 and 1985. Reduced opportunities for regular wage employment in the private sector obliged people to

Table 1.5. Percentage distribution and growth rates of the urban labour force: Latin America, 1980-85

	1980		1985		Annual growth-rate, 1980-85
Unemployment	6.4		7.5		6.3
Employment	93.6		92.5		2.8
of which:					
Modern sector		71.0		68.0	1.9
Large and medium enterprises		(42.0)		(37.0)	(0.3)
Public service		(23.0)		(24.0)	(4.0)
Small enterprises		(6.0)		(7.0)	(4.5)
Informal sector		29.0		32.0	4.9
Total urban labour force	100.0	100.0	100.0	100.0	3.1

Source: V. Tokman: "Adjustment and employment in Latin America: The current challenges", in *International Labour Review* (Geneva, ILO), Sep.-Oct. 1986, p. 535.

Table 1.6. Urban unemployment: Latin America, 1980-86 (average annual rates)

Country	1980	1981	1982	1983	1984	1985	1986[1]
Argentina	2.3	4.5	4.7	4.2	3.8	5.3	4.8
Bolivia	5.8	9.7	10.9	13.0	15.5	18.0	20.0
Brazil	6.3	7.9	6.3	6.7	7.1	5.3	3.8
Colombia	9.7	8.2	9.3	11.8	13.5	14.1	14.2
Costa Rica	6.0	9.1	9.9	8.6	6.6	6.7	6.7
Chile	11.8	9.0	20.0	18.9	18.5	17.2	13.4
Ecuador	5.7	6.0	6.3	6.7	10.6	10.4	12.0
Guatemala	2.2	2.7	4.7	7.6	9.7	12.9	
Honduras	8.8	9.0	9.2	9.5	10.7	11.7	
Mexico	4.5	4.2	4.1	6.7	6.0	4.8	
Nicaragua	22.4	19.0	19.9	18.9	21.1	22.3	21.7
Panama	9.8	11.8	10.3	11.5	11.0	11.8	9.0
Paraguay	2.1	4.6	9.4	15.0	12.5	8.0	8.0
Peru	10.9	10.4	10.6	9.2	10.9	11.8	10.6
Trinidad and Tobago	9.9	10.4	9.9	11.1	13.4	15.3	
Uruguay	7.4	6.7	11.9	15.5	14.0	13.1	11.0
Venezuela	6.6	6.8	7.8	10.5	14.3	14.3	11.8

[1] Preliminary figures.

Source: ECLAC: *Preliminary overview of the Latin American economy*, Santiago de Chile, 1986.

look for work in small enterprises and the informal sector, either in self-employment or as casual wage workers. Since real urban wages fell very considerably, the market for goods and services produced by small enterprises and the informal sector contracted as well. There was thus a limit to which additional labour could be absorbed in these sectors and beyond this limit open unemployment remained the only alternative.

The official figures on urban unemployment (see table 1.6) show high levels of unemployment in some countries, sometimes above those in IMECs. On average, however, there was a relatively moderate increase between 1980 and 1984, from about 6 to 8 per cent, and a decline to about 7 per cent in 1986.

Nevertheless, countries vary greatly in their experience of urban unemployment. Unemployment tends to be lower in the larger countries, such as Argentina, Brazil and Mexico, and higher in low-growth countries like Bolivia, Guatemala and Nicaragua. Cuba (not reported in the table) has a low unemployment rate and enjoyed rapid economic growth during the 1980s.

As a result of the recession, many Latin American workers had to be satisfied with low-paid, insecure and casual employment rather than a permanent job in the "formal" sector. Casual employment is,

however, by no means concentrated in small-scale "informal" enterprises. In both large-scale and small-scale enterprises, rising urban unemployment and competitive pressures have probably accelerated the trend towards the use of more temporary and unprotected workers. This has been observed in urban areas of Brazil, where the ratio of "unprotected" employees to total employees increased quite sharply in the early 1980s.

There has also been a change in the nature of urban small-scale enterprises. Subcontracting by large, often multinational enterprises, has spread in recent years, often responding to growing uncertainty and competitiveness in international trade. Studies in several Latin American cities have shown that even street vendors can be part of well-organised commercial networks controlled by large-scale modern enterprises. The majority of people employed in small enterprises produce goods or services for the domestic market. This market is shrinking because of deep cuts in real wages (see figure 1.4). At the same time increasing numbers are looking for work in this sector.

Figure 1.4.   Real earnings of wage earners in manufacturing: Latin America, 1980-86 (1980 = 100)

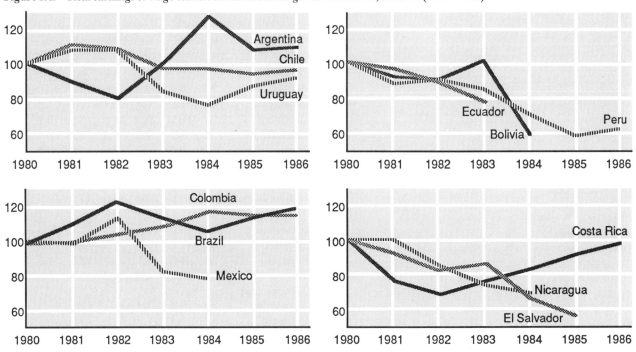

Source: ILO: *Year Book of Labour Statistics*; ECLAC: *Preliminary overview of the Latin American economy*, Santiago de Chile, 1986.

Rural areas

Since the early 1980s the long-term decline in the proportion of agricultural workers in total employment appears to have come to a halt (table 1.7) except in Chile. This is consistent with the analysis presented in chapter 4 that the surplus population accumulates in the peasant agricultural sector. In other words, falling employment opportunities in urban areas have led people to look for additional work in agriculture.

Rural and urban labour markets have become increasingly integrated in many Latin American countries. Rural employers may hire urban-based workers, while urban employers may also draw on rural-based workers. Thus, the recession which caused real wages to drop in urban areas has also affected real wages in rural areas. Many different types of workers are now competing for casual employment in rural areas. Traditionally, peasant household members who needed to supplement family income were the main group of casual wage workers. They are now in competition with rural and more especially urban-based full-time casual workers. However, where large masses of peasants remain, the

peasantry continues to provide the bulk of labour supply; and wages are subsidised by unpaid family labour on the home plot.

Over the past two decades the number of small farms has grown rapidly and average farm size has fallen. It is therefore likely that total rural household incomes have declined considerably, especially given reduced off-farm employment opportunities for peasant household members.

3. Meeting the need for skills

Partly as a result of the economic crisis, all providers and beneficiaries of training are becoming increasingly interested in assessing training priorities. Expenditure on education has already reached enormous proportions (in some countries, such as Côte d'Ivoire, as much as 40 per cent of the Government's operational budget). Since there is a constant increase in demand and no likelihood of additional resources becoming available, it is essential to assess the effectiveness of existing systems and organisations and to promote new approaches. The central question for all governments is how to ensure the timely supply of

Table 1.7. Percentage of agricultural employment in total employment: Latin America, 1980-85

	1980	1981	1982	1983	1984	1985
Panama			28.9	29.3	29.2	
Costa Rica	27.4			28.3		27.2
Chile	19.2	15.5	16.2	15.9	16.0	
Venezuela		14.8			16.0	16.1
Trinidad and Tobago	10.2	10.9	8.2	8.5		10.8
Puerto Rico	6.4	5.3	4.7	5.4	4.6	5.5

Source: ILO: *Year Book of Labour Statistics.*

appropriate skills needed for development at afford-able cost. Different patterns of demand for different skills require different forms and quantities of education and training. Allocation of resources among these forms depends in part on a country's strategies for economic and social development and in part on the efficiency and effectiveness of the education and training systems that produce needed skills.

Cost-benefit analysis is a useful tool for assessing training priorities, but it has also serious limitations. An evaluation of training modes cannot be reduced to a simple discussion of whether one mode is more cost-effective than another. First of all, there is no single criterion of cost-effectiveness and, secondly, in most countries the tremendous diversity of training provision defies easy generalisation.

Most evaluations reviewed in this section attempt to measure the difference in wages which can be attributed to training, compared to either the wage which the individual would have received throughout his career without this training, or the wage of a control group. However, there are some important conceptual problems. Higher wages may be due not simply to a worker's training but also to other factors such as personality, experience, and the influence of contacts. Furthermore, this method supposes that the labour market is in a state of perfect competition and that the higher wages correspond exactly to higher productivity, which is far from always being the case.

In more general evaluations of the effectiveness of training, recognition is given to the importance of other outcomes, such as motivation, self-esteem and job satisfaction as well as better employment prospects (Dougherty, 1987). There is usually no attempt to weigh these benefits. However, in commenting on the results of various cost-benefit studies, these aspects

will be included in the overall assessment of training priorities.

The formal sector

The State is a major provider of training, through education ministries and also through ministries responsible for labour, rural development and industry. The wide variety of public and private institutions, some of which are financed by employers' and workers' organisations, includes schools, institutes and vocational or management training centres, productivity centres, and extension services for small and medium-sized enterprises.

Institution-based training

A large part of institution-based training is provided by "vocationalised" secondary schools (those which have added vocational training to the general education programme), technical schools proper and training centres. "Vocationalisation" is expensive if only because of the cost of buildings and workshop equipment, laboratories, and so on. A recent assessment of technical secondary education in Kenya found that industrial training was twice as expensive per pupil as other kinds of training in terms of current costs. Investment costs per pupil were five to six times higher. However, costs per student depend heavily on the size of schools. A large-scale study carried out in 1,340 schools in Latin America in 1978 found that vocational schools were markedly more expensive in terms of total cost per student. But this was due less to the expense of equipment than to underuse of this equipment by an insufficient number of pupils. Furthermore, each machine may require a different instructor who is himself underused.

Is the extra cost of vocationalising secondary education justified by the benefits obtained? The answer appears to be no. In particular, graduates of vocationalised schools do not seem to find jobs more quickly and even experience slightly longer periods of unemployment – for example, in Colombia, 25 to 26 weeks before the first job against 21 to 22 weeks for graduates of general courses. Moreover, there are no significant differences in pay one year after graduation.

The introduction of vocational education in secondary schools has thus not proved a very worth-while investment. In the United Republic of Tanzania the rate of return achieved in general education courses is practically double that of speci-

Table 1.8. Rates of return in secondary education: Developing countries, 1970s and 1980s

		General education	Vocational training
Cyprus	1975	10.5	7.4
	1979	6.8	5.5
France	1970	10.1	7.6
Indonesia	1978	32.0	18.0
Liberia	1983	20.0	14.0

Source: G. Psacharopoulos: "Return to education: A further international update and implications", in *Journal of Human Resources* (Madison, Wisconsin), fall 1985.

alised training. Table 1.8 shows comparative rates of return in secondary establishments in four countries. The rate of return takes account of all training costs (for society and for individuals) and measures the return by comparing the earnings of persons trained with those of a control group which did not receive the same training.

Systems and institutions providing both initial and further training have been less frequently the subject of cost-benefit studies than those providing initial training alone. However, this gap has recently been partially filled by the World Bank, in particular by an economic assessment of the national training system in Colombia, SENA (Servicio Nacional de Aprendizaje). SENA was set up in 1957 by the Ministry of Labour. It is financially autonomous and its main resources come from a tax of 2 per cent levied on wages. Its growth has been impressive – from 1,750 persons trained in 1958 and 23,000 in 1965 to more than 300,000 a year in the 1980s. SENA began with two types of courses: an apprenticeship programme for young people and short seminars for adult workers. Today more than 1,000 courses are offered by SENA including longer adult courses. All economic sectors and skill levels are covered by the system. The programmes have just one point in common: participants have a job (including apprentices who have a contractual relationship with an employer) and the time spent in the classroom never exceeds 50 per cent of the total training time.

The World Bank study combined the direct costs of training and income foregone with estimates of income and productivity of SENA graduates, and compared these with a control group which did not receive the same training. It was able to calculate the rate of return for five types of SENA courses as well as

the comparative rates of return for short and long programmes. The main conclusions of the study are encouraging: for SENA:

– The overall financial rate of return for SENA courses is 14 per cent, which is clearly higher than the average rate obtained by investing capital and which also exceeds the rate of return to secondary education in Colombia (9 to 10 per cent).

– The rate varies according to the length of courses: it is higher for long programmes (17 per cent) and for students who have greater experience and basic school training (up to 30 per cent). SENA therefore appears to be a complement to rather than a substitute for other forms of investment in human capital.

In Africa, the World Bank has also assessed the costs and effectiveness of training systems in education, for both technical and management training. The main impression given by institutions in the region is their great fragility. This is principally due to an overdependence on the State. Few institutions have been forced to compete in the market and they have rarely adapted their programmes to the concerns of their client enterprises.

India, by contrast, has paid a good deal of attention to the cost-effectiveness of its vocational training system. A study commissioned by the Ministry of Labour on apprenticeship estimated a cost-benefit ratio for training of 3.3 (total extra earnings of trained workers during the 37 years of their working life to the total cost of their three years of training). Another study analysed five types of training: normal apprenticeship, apprenticeship for graduates, initial training of craftsmen, continuous vocational training and the training of supervisors. The rates of return for these five categories were estimated respectively at 4.2 per cent, 12.9 per cent, 14.3 per cent, 0.3 per cent and 0.9 per cent. The last two results can be explained by the high cost of training and the older age of participants (average age 26 and 39 respectively) which means that higher productivity due to training extends over fewer remaining years of working life.

When interviewed, former participants were very enthusiastic about the usefulness of their training in obtaining and carrying out their work. More than 90 per cent said it had been useful or very useful. They rated training less highly for gaining promotion, though about 80 per cent still thought it useful or very useful. Employers, for their part, were very pleased with continuous vocational training and formal apprenticeship, but less so with craftsman training. This was because they generally preferred to train people within their own enterprises.

Enterprise-based training

The initial and further training provided by State-run institutions has not always come up to the expectations of enterprises, even though in one way or another they contribute a large share of the finances. For example, Brazil obliges industrial enterprises to fund the National Industrial Training Service (SENAI) by paying a tax of 1 per cent on wages (1.2 per cent in enterprises employing more than 500 employees). It is, however, possible to deduct up to 80 per cent of the levy provided that this amount is used for training. Similarly, a 1977 law in Côte d'Ivoire imposed a training tax of 1.5 per cent on wages but this is waived for enterprises which set up their own training programmes. Twenty enterprise-based training centres have already been set up in the country.

However, a reduced training levy is not the only reason why enterprises have set up their own training programmes. They often allocate more funds to training than they are legally required to do. The principal reason is that the school or para-scholastic system is not always sufficiently geared to the world of work, and expensive training does not always lead to the acquisition of job-adapted skills.

Recommendation No. 150 of the ILO on human resources development (1975) encourages enterprises to assume the responsibility of training workers in employment. Enterprise-based training is most developed in occupations that are too specialised to be covered by schools – water and electricity services, railways, aviation, petroleum, and banks, for example.

But enterprise-based training has spread to other sectors. The rapid progress of technology and the need for structural adjustment have increasingly demanded appropriate training, retraining and conversion of skills. School and para-scholastic institutions are less well-placed than the enterprise itself to follow developments with all the flexibility and speed required to maintain an adequate stock of skills. On the other hand these institutions can make a valuable contribution, for example, by providing advice and assistance for the organisation of internal training programmes and the training of in-house instructors. The example of INDEFE (National Institute for the Promotion and Development of Enterprise-based

Vocational Training and Apprenticeship) in Algeria deserves mention in this connection.

The costs and achievements of enterprise-based training are not easy to evaluate. Even when all training takes place within the enterprise, very few budgets cover more than the wages of staff exclusively assigned to training and the cost of teaching materials and equipment. A survey of 130 enterprises carried out in the United States (Mangum, 1984) points out that none had included in its calculations the wages and reduced productivity of internal instructors assigned on an occasional basis nor the time of supervisors taken up by training activities. The same survey found, quite unexpectedly, that managers showed little interest in assessing the costs and benefits of training. It would seem that training is carried out because some highly placed member of the firm believes in it rather than on the basis of any serious economic evaluation.

From being an economic instrument in the hands of employers, enterprise-based training has increasingly become a social instrument in the hands of governments to help reduce the alarming problem of youth unemployment. Enterprises may find themselves, as in the Federal Republic of Germany, turning into open-door institutions, training more young people than they can actually recruit as workers. More and more countries are introducing legislation to provide financial incentives for enterprises which accept young people as trainees and then take them on as employees. In Togo a 1983 Act established regional vocational training and further training centres (CRFPP) to re-invigorate apprenticeship. These centres provide the complementary theoretical training for apprentices, establish with the industries concerned the duration of the alternating periods of classroom and practical training, supply teaching materials for enterprises and provide an advisory apprenticeship inspectorate.

Under a 1981 Act in Algeria, the pre-wage of apprentices is paid by the State during the first six months and is then progressively taken over by the employer. Over the same period the employer is relieved of the payment of social contributions.

It should, however, be emphasised that legislation formalising apprenticeship is often ineffective. Thus, in Côte d'Ivoire, apprentices who have signed a legally valid contract account for only 1.2 per cent of the workforce in the modern sector, whereas traditional apprentices in the informal sector are legion. In Burkina Faso, only 61 apprenticeship contracts were signed between 1978 and 1980, 86 between 1980 and 1982 and 29 in 1983-84. In Mali, 28 contracts were registered between 1975 and 1978 and 28 between 1980 and 1983.

The developments noted so far have essentially concerned large-scale enterprises in the modern sector. The establishment of an internal training centre, a specialised training service or even apprenticeship contracts which conform to the legislation in force, is rarely within the means of a small enterprise even if it is already well-structured and perhaps considered as part of the modern sector. For these small and medium-sized enterprises, most developing countries have created specialised extension services which offer integrated assistance, including training. Their effectiveness is uneven. Many of these centres are fairly bureaucratic and their staff is made up of young graduates without experience who have difficulty in establishing contact with small entrepreneurs. Mention should, however, be made of the entrepreneurship development programme of Gujarat State in India. The programme was able to train more than 6,000 candidates in setting up their own business. The failure rate amongst those who were trained was six times less than for entrepreneurs who had not been trained (3.6 per cent against 21.4 per cent). The cost of training was only US$150 per person.

The informal sector

State, formal institutions and enterprise-based centres are only the visible part of the iceberg of training activities. The invisible part – informal and out-of-school training – is the only recourse of many people excluded from the expensive system of modern education and training. In particular, traditional apprenticeship remains alive and well amongst craftsmen and micro-entrepreneurs in the informal sector and is being rediscovered and better appreciated by policy-makers.

Traditional apprenticeship

The craftsman's workshop in the informal sector is a place where many skills of a trade are acquired. Traditional apprenticeship is a training school for working life which allows young people to come into contact with the real conditions of work and the trade. The integration of training and production offers undoubted advantages as regards costs and efficiency.

Apprenticeship, in addition to being an economic necessity, also has a social function, particularly in Africa. The craftsman or entrepreneur has a great responsibility to the parents of the apprentice and must endeavour to provide, over and above the vocational training, an education for his apprentice in the widest sense of the word.

Apprenticeship is a source of training which is almost entirely free of charge, as compared with the cost of training in the technical establishments. It is generally the parents who pay the craftsman and the amount is usually less than US$150. In the best cases, the craftsman devotes some time to training, provides meals, accommodation and sometimes a little pocket money. In exchange he receives cheap labour and a certain amount of prestige.

In many cases, however, training is scanty, incomplete and unsystematic. Moreover, neither the workload nor the equipment of the workshop allow training to be very intensive. But traditional apprenticeship still remains the major source for the acquisition of skills in the informal sector. An ILO study on French-speaking Africa showed that 84 per cent of employers had received traditional apprenticeship training compared with 7 per cent who had been apprenticed in the modern sector, 2 per cent in a vocational training centre and 4 per cent in a combination of traditional apprenticeship and one of the other two forms. The same study was able to examine the relationship between management performance and the skills of the small-scale employer. The best economic performances – measured by such variables as profit and value-added – were obtained by employers who received technical school training combined with traditional apprenticeship. They were closely followed by those who completed secondary studies but who also had practical training in a workshop. It seems that a combination of the two systems gives the best results. In fact, the trend is moving in this direction as a result of industrial restructuring. Many workers who have been "eased out" of the modern sector are moving into the informal sector and will stimulate changes in its production and management methods.

Despite its shortcomings, traditional apprenticeship can be effective. In 1985 a round table was held in Abidjan attended by young jewellers trained entirely in the informal sector and their counterparts who had graduated from the Training Centre of Jewellers of Abidjan with vocational proficiency certificates (CAP). The conclusions were as follows:

– training is more complete in the workshops of the informal sector where apprenticeship covers all aspects of the trade;
– the jeweller trained in the informal sector has a greater chance of finding a job. Many young graduates are unemployed;
– the jeweller trained in the informal sector has had contact with customers. In particular, he knows how to bargain;
– the cost of training in the Centre is not commensurate with the results. In addition to the operating costs of the Centre, the groups of 12-30 students who enter each year are granted a monthly allowance of 60 dollars.

Similarly, CIADFOR (African Centre for the Development of Vocational Training) examined the case of carpenters in the Côte d'Ivoire and also concluded that traditional apprenticeship offers a particularly high benefit-cost ratio in comparison with classic training centres.

Formal training for the informal sector?

There are various ways to bridge the gap between formal training centres and craft workshops. Selected master craftsmen prepared to make the effort to take proficiency courses at centres for training in pedagogical techniques, should be allowed subsidies for the time they spend afterwards training the young. Parents would soon seek out these "approved masters" for their children and abandon routine craftsmen with no special qualifications, thereby promoting a general improvement in the level of training. For the State the cost would be minimal compared with the amounts disbursed on subsidising formal education with often dubious results.

The question of what the maximum level of these subsidies should be must be decided by the government in each case, but there seems to be ample room for manoeuvre taking into consideration the cost of training at formal centres. In Colombia, the figures published by SENA for the cost of its informal sector programmes are as follows (in 1985):

Technical training	US$89 per trainee – taking account of 22 per cent drop-outs
Management training	US$340 per trainee – taking account of 22 per cent drop-outs
Correspondence courses	US$86 per trainee – taking account of 40 per cent drop-outs

Likewise, in Venezuela the National Institute for the Coordination of Education (INCE) gives as the cost of its informal sector course US$73 per trainee, which should be corrected to allow for an apparent drop-out rate of 30 to 35 per cent, that is to say US$100 per trainee completing the course. In both cases, it should be noted that the courses in question are "light" courses, 110 hours per quarter, for example, for the Colombian programme.

For one country, Côte d'Ivoire, it is possible to compare the cost of vocational training in the formal sector and that of apprenticeship. The National Vocational Training Office (ONFP) estimated that in the Touba automobile engineering training centre, the total cost of a two-year training course for the CAP proficiency certificate in 1980 amounted to about US$11,000 per pupil. This is extremely high compared to the few-hundred dollar subsidy that the centre could provide for training an apprentice in the informal sector.

Another bridging function can be performed by non-governmental organisations (NGOs) whose strength resides in assistance work at the grass-roots level. The most underprivileged need help from people who speak their language, who share their difficult conditions of life, who encourage their participation and who are neither too well-fed nor too well-paid. Such people are often found among the volunteers of the NGOs.

There are many training programmes, in particular those for women, which are or must be organised separately outside the normal education system, or as pilot projects or tests. Their experimental nature, short duration of life and limited replicability have not yet allowed a serious study to be made of their cost-effectiveness. Moreover, the objectives of women's training programmes are multiple, mixing social and economic aims which makes evaluation very difficult. Although it is possible to assess the impact of a course on levels of pay, productivity, literacy and awareness of women's legal rights, it is hardly feasible to measure such important outputs as greater self-confidence, greater capacity to take decisions and exercise a leadership role, or the enhanced awareness of one's conditions of life and work and the capacity to influence them.

Self-instruction and the new educational technologies

This is without doubt the biggest and most difficult sphere in which to assess the cost-benefit ratio of vocational training. The ILO has made a contri-

<table>
<tr><td>

**1.2   The pitfalls of audio-visual
                     training material**

The following example comes from a management seminar organised in June 1983 in Malabo (Equatorial Guinea) by the Ministry for the Promotion of Women, with the assistance of the ILO, for women engaged in income generating activities. The trainer, who was using slides to convey his message to the least literate participants, noticed that there was considerable agitation at the back of the classroom. The slide which had just been projected concerned the presentation of goods. The message designed to be transmitted was: however modest your stall, make sure it is clean and properly arranged and place in front the goods which will earn you the most. Give them the place which they deserve. The illustration showed bottles in the front row, with boxes at the back, without stipulating the contents. The trainer was able to obtain a translation from the "fang" dialect of the cause of the agitation: "The expert was quite right, it is alcohol which earns the most" they said. Without the presence of an instructor, the distorted message would have produced unfortunate effects which were not at all intended ...

</td></tr>
</table>

A simple calculation shows that in this example 4,000 people followed a course of approximately 20 hours which cost them a modest US$11.

It is well known that images, colour and sound are powerful means to capture the attention and to improve the retention of what is taught. However, there is one great disadvantage: it is not easy to replace the human presence of the instructor. One example will illustrate this point (see box 1.2).

This example illustrates the need for caution but it should not be interpreted as a justification for conservatism in education. The presence of an instructor is important but also very expensive. With television for example, the cost of preparing a programme is high but the broadcast can subsequently reach millions of people. This is proven by literacy campaigns in French or English, for example, which in spite of possible defects and sometimes poor quality are highly cost-effective.

bution by its "Improve your business" series which helps small entrepreneurs to diagnose their own problems and learn by themselves the techniques needed to improve the running of their businesses. Since the 1960s the ILO has also used the radio serial "Double your money", which was tested in Uganda, to transmit management concepts to small entrepreneurs. As for correspondence courses, in Brazil there are ten times as many participants in such courses than pupils attending secondary technical schools. In Africa, too, NGOs such as Inades-Formation have for a number of years offered correspondence courses. A correspondence course which costs individuals between US$30 and US$50 can easily increase their remuneration by US$10 a month. The course thus pays for itself quickly.

The new educational technologies (cinema, radio, television, video, slides and so on) can be used as support material to "Do-it-yourself" teaching manuals (programmed or not) and correspondence courses.

A clearer idea of costs is now emerging. A study by CEPAC (Centro de Producción Audiovisual para la Capacitación, Peru) on the cost-benefit ratio of using video cassettes for training purposes gives the following figures (for 1979):

- programme cost per minute US$39;
- cost by course/participant US$11;
- cost by hour/participant US$0.6.

4. The state of labour relations

It is difficult to generalise about the developing countries (DCs) because they display so much variety in labour relations. Only a few characteristics appear to be common, if not to all, to at least a very large majority of these countries. One is the fact that the labour relations systems in these countries cover only workers with a regular employment contract who generally account for only a small part of the labour force, some of whom are covered by collective agreements. Another is that the governments of these countries nevertheless play a much greater role in labour relations than is the case in the IMECs, since they fear that the free play of labour relations may adversely affect the economic development of the country and even its political stability. In spite of their relative weakness, employers' and workers' organisations in a number of countries are participating in tripartite consultations on social and economic policies. Hereafter the term "social dialogue" will cover collective bargaining, workers' participation and tripartite consultations.

The large majority of the workforce in developing countries is unorganised. They mainly consist of casual wage labourers and the self-employed, such as peasants, family workers and independent workers in the informal sector. They are usually among the poorest and most deprived sections of the population.

The state of the social dialogue

Underdevelopment, inflation, underemployment and poverty have weakened the position of trade unions. The defence of employment and incomes of their members becomes inevitably more difficult, if not impossible, in a context of acute economic crisis. This is even more true when governments react to the worsening economic situation by imposing austerity plans which establish even greater control over the social partners in collective bargaining. In some cases, governments have themselves been the authors of these measures whereas in others – notably those countries of Latin America and Africa which are burdened with a heavy foreign debt – they have resulted from negotiations with the International Monetary Fund (IMF).

Of the austerity measures that are directly related to collective bargaining the most important are in the area of wage control. A detailed assessment of these measures is given in chapter 5.

In many DCs austerity measures imposed by governments have hit hardest those sectors in which the State is the employer – that is, the public service and public enterprises. Very often, these measures are intended not only to control wage movements but also to reduce employment levels. In the public service in particular, they have significantly curbed the previous trend towards an extension of collective bargaining or other devices which allow employees to participate in determining their conditions of employment.

Economic considerations have also led some governments to take measures which are likely to have more profound repercussions on labour relations than any "simple" wage control. Thus, several governments of countries in South-East Asia have recently granted the status of "pioneer industry" to new activities and created new "free zones"; in both cases trade union rights have been subject to restrictions, either in law or in practice. Mention can also be made of the recent extension of the definition of "essential services" in Singapore and Sri Lanka (which has included the banking sector since 1985) as well as the increasingly frequent use of the poorly defined concept of the "public interest" to settle certain disputes by compulsory arbitration.

The general context which has just been outlined clearly influences the development of labour relations. In those Third World countries less hard-hit by the economic crisis, the progress made in recent decades has not been fundamentally called into question. A number of collective agreements are still being negotiated, principally at enterprise level but sometimes also at industry and even the national level. This is the case in countries such as India, Malaysia, Colombia and Côte d'Ivoire. But the negotiation of collective agreements in developing countries facing the most serious economic difficulties has recently experienced a setback.

In some DCs – particularly in Asia and the Caribbean – this setback in collective bargaining seems to be stimulating a growing interest by the trade unions in other forms of worker participation in decision-making which could, in their view, partly fill the void. For the moment, this interest is limited to consultation procedures and excludes co-decision and the representation of workers on boards of companies. It is not clear at the present time whether this movement will produce concrete achievements. Nevertheless, it could produce a change in the traditionally hostile attitude of trade unions of developing countries towards participation. This is largely due to the fact that participation is generally introduced by governments which see it as a means of ensuring industrial peace. In such cases trade unions fear that participation may be used to undermine their position within the enterprise.

As for tripartite concertation at the national level, the situation is equally difficult – although the future outlook is not necessarily sombre. If concertation is taken to mean discussion between the government and the central employers' and workers' organisations on the major national social and economic policy options, there are very few developing countries in which concertation is practiced systematically. One such country is Singapore where the general wage policy has been determined to a large extent by a tripartite body for a number of years. Recently, however, the idea of concertation has been gaining ground in a number of Third World countries, particularly in Latin America. Governments and social partners are now wondering whether concertation could provide a solution to their present difficulties. In Argentina, for example, a 1985 Decree established a Social and Economic Forum presided over by the Head of State, comprising four ministers and five high-level representatives of employers and workers, to promote co-operation between employers and workers and to make suggestions concerning national, economic and social policies.

As a general rule, however, the practical application of concertation has proved very difficult. The government and some employers' and workers' organisations may lack solid and efficient structures to establish and implement a genuine form of concertation. They may lack institutions and suitable procedures as well as experience. Employers and workers are sometimes too accustomed to confrontational relations and often have little confidence in one another and in the public authorities. The authorities may then also have limited confidence in employers' and workers' organisations and end up taking the main decisions themselves. This hesitation on the part of governments to achieve concertation in practice – although it does interest them at the theoretical level – is all the more marked as economic conditions deteriorate. When, as in some parts of Africa, a country is engaged in nothing less than a struggle for survival, there is in general no concertation whatsoever.

Some less ambitious mechanisms for social dialogue have met with more success. Special mention should be made of minimum wage-fixing machinery. Employers' and trade union organisations are often represented on wage-fixing or related bodies. However, such bodies commonly have only advisory powers and where they are granted decision-making powers, government representatives normally play the major role.

In some Third World countries governments and the central employers' and workers' organisations have signed "codes of conduct" or "charters" which are designed to promote orderly and harmonious labour relations between all the parties. Documents of this kind were adopted in Malaysia in 1978, Kenya in 1980 (replacing a "charter" dating from 1962) and Thailand in 1981. In some of these countries, tripartite meetings are held periodically to supervise and improve the practical application of these codes.

The central problem for labour relations in most DCs is the design of a system which will make it possible both to ensure the economic development of these countries and respect for basic human rights, particularly as regards freedom of association. The achievement of this objective requires strong and responsible employers' and workers' organisations which have the determination and the capacity to work, together with the public authorities, towards solutions to current problems which take account not only of their respective immediate interests but also the general interest. The key to the establishment of a labour relations system along these lines must be a permanent, constructive and effective dialogue between all the parties concerned rather than the more or less erratic recourse – too often the case at present – to procedures for settling disputes.

The unorganised

Casual workers are hired usually on the basis of an oral agreement with an employer. For certain types of workers, such as tenants and share-croppers, the relationship with the landowner is not an "employment relationship" since it includes transactions involving not only labour but also production, credit or land. Family workers are not bound by a contract but accept family work as part of the cultural, social and economic obligations governing household and family life. The self-employed are independent producers with no individual employment relationship. However, these workers have a number of collective interests to defend. This is implicitly recognised in the ILO's Rural Workers' Organisations Convention, 1975 (No. 141). It calls for the establishment and growth of strong and independent organisations as an effective means of ensuring the participation of rural workers in economic and social development and in the resulting benefits.

One way of organising such workers is to extend the activities of existing trade unions. Some trade unions have tried to organise wage earners – and sometimes even self-employed people – in rural regions. They have, however, run into a number of obstacles, including legal restrictions on the right of association and resistance by landowners and other economically and politically powerful groups. Furthermore, there are many practical difficulties. Trade unions are accustomed to operating in urban and industrial environments where many workers are employed in similar jobs and thus have similar interests which encourage joint action. Peasants and casual workers, on the other hand, are much more dispersed and have much more diverse employment so that their interests must be defended, as the case may be, against employers, the public authorities, various categories of intermediaries (for example, subcontractors, including manpower subcontractors) or against other economic agents (for example, landowners and money-lenders).

Peasants and casual workers also tend to be poorer and more deprived than workers with a regular employment contract. Land ownership and economic power in rural areas is often concentrated in the hands of a chosen few, on whom peasants and casual workers may depend for their survival. Furthermore, the poverty and deprivation to which they are subject have, for many, acquired a sort of inevitability so that they resign themselves fatalistically to their state of dependence.

As a result of all these difficulties, the attempts of traditional trade unions to organise the self-employed have rarely proved successful. For this reason organisations of a new type have been established in various developing regions – often called "trade union type" organisations because, like trade unions, their objective is to protect the economic interests of their members. They include community development organisations of all kinds as well as co-operatives set up to develop agrarian reform projects, to defend the interests of their members against landowners, money-lenders, wholesale suppliers of raw materials or harvest buyers or, quite simply, to obtain effective application of existing laws.

Experience suggests that one of the conditions for success is to identify relatively small categories of individuals in similar situations. It has not been possible to improve the situation of the poorest farmers, share-croppers and rural workers by the establishment of organisations which group together all agricultural producers, including medium and large-scale landowners. In addition, efforts to organise informal sector workers may founder if steps have not been taken beforehand to make them fully aware of their situation, its causes and the possibilities open to them to improve it. Often, this is best done by non-governmental organisations.

The satisfactory organisation and protection of casual workers and many of the self-employed is one of the most important and difficult problems facing DCs at the present time. Success stories are few and far between, and there remain substantial obstacles in the search for appropriate solutions.

5. Concluding remarks

In many parts of the developing world, the employment and poverty situation has seriously deteriorated since the early 1980s, particularly in sub-Saharan Africa and Latin America. In SSA cash incomes of farmers have been cut by low export prices and sluggish growth of urban food markets. This has affected not only the plantation economy, but also small farmers who tend to grow both export and food crops. The situation has deteriorated most in urban areas, both in SSA and Latin America. With regular wage employment stagnant or contracting, an in-

creasing number of people have been forced to turn to self-employment or casual wage work. However, the market for informal sector products and services has also been affected by steep falls in real wages. In Latin America those unable to find any employment have become openly unemployed, while urban unemployment and underemployment have spilled over to the rural labour markets.

In Asia and North Africa, the picture is generally less gloomy. The most striking example here is China which, as a result of rural reforms and a change in industrial policy, has enjoyed large increases in rural incomes and a significant reduction in unemployment and poverty. Similar trends are visible in most South-East Asian countries, but with some exceptions. The proportion of people living in poverty has also probably remained at a high level in southern Asia, while unemployment may have increased somewhat in most West Asian and North African countries which – directly or indirectly – have been dependent on oil revenues.

Improving the skills of workers makes an important contribution to more productive employment. Although formal training is found to be socially and individually profitable, it seems that – at least for secondary education – rates of return for general education are higher than those for vocational training. At the same time, there has been a tendency to overestimate the need for institution-based initial training. Employers complain about the lack of general education, but they usually prefer to undertake initial training themselves or in the context of the enterprise. Apprenticeship in the informal sector is clearly a very cost-effective training instrument. Costs are very low. Apprentices receive a broader training covering all aspects of the trade and they often have a greater chance of finding a job than many young graduates. Training provided by NGOs is also effective because training volunteers often understand informal sector conditions better than trainers from the State-financed institutions. None the less, there are various possibilities to bridge the gap between formal training centres and informal sector workers.

The problem for the State is to allocate training funds most effectively. The lion's share of resources is presently allocated to the formal sector, whose needs are most clearly heard and understood in most government departments. But it may well be true for many countries that more funds for the informal sector would lead to more and better-remunerated employment and higher economic growth.

For the countries most affected by the economic crisis, collective bargaining in the private sector has come under increased pressure from governments. Many governments have directly controlled public sector wages and curbed the previous trend towards an extension of collective bargaining. The outlook for tripartite consultation at the national level may be brighter. The idea of concertation has recently been gaining ground in a number of developing countries, particularly in Latin America. However, the main labour relations issue facing the developing countries is the organisation and protection of casual workers and many of the self-employed. These workers, often representing the large majority of the workforce, have scarcely any influence on decisions affecting their interests at work and the course of social and economic development.

Chapter 2

Industrialised market economies: Jobs, collective bargaining and social security

The main issue confronting most IMECs is how to attain full employment (section 1). Unemployment increased during the 1970s, but jumped sharply at the beginning of the 1980s. While it has fallen somewhat from peak levels, it remains unacceptably high. There has been a continuing trend towards a reduction of working hours accompanied by greater working-time flexibility and more use of part-time employment. These trends may have led to greater efficiency and job creation, but at the same time they have weakened worker protection.

Collective bargaining (section 2) has been adversely affected by economic difficulties and, in a number of cases, by increased state intervention. There has also been a trend towards decentralisation of collective bargaining in almost all Western European countries. Moreover, during the 1980s employers and trade unions have increasingly been bargaining on issues such as job security, labour flexibility, new technologies and hours of work, rather than on automatic improvements in wages and working conditions.

Social security systems (section 3) have also come under pressure from changed economic circumstances. Many governments have sought new sources of finance or measures to keep costs in check, while others have undertaken radical reviews or reforms. Nevertheless, spending on social assistance financed out of general revenues has increased steadily as a growing number of people (such as the long-term unemployed and single-parent families) find themselves inadequately protected by social insurance schemes.

1. Employment and hours of work

Wage employment is the main source of employment in the IMECs – where less than 20 per cent of the world labour force live. The proportion of employees (those in wage employment) in total employment varies between 70 and 90 per cent. Between 70 and 90 per cent of the employed population works in the private sector while the remainder work in the public sector (in wage employment). This section first reviews recent trends in hours of work, employment and unemployment and then considers reasons for the steep increase in unemployment since the beginning of the 1980s.

Trends in employment, hours of work and unemployment

Unemployment began to rise significantly in the 1970s. In the wake of the first oil crisis the average IMEC rate increased from 3.5 per cent in 1973 to 5.2 per cent in 1975. It rose even more dramatically after the second oil crisis, from 4.9 per cent in 1979 to 8.5 per cent in 1983. Since then unemployment has fallen only slightly to below 8 per cent, with the result that in 1986 more than 31 million people in the IMECs were unemployed.

The rate of unemployment is lowest (between 1 and 4 per cent) and has risen least in Japan, Norway, Switzerland, Austria and Sweden. It is highest (between 13 and 20 per cent) and has risen fastest since 1979 in Ireland, Spain and the United Kingdom. Unemployment rates are fairly low in the United States (6.9 per cent in 1986) and fairly high in Belgium, the Netherlands, France and Italy (more than 10 per cent).

Unemployment is usually higher among young people, ethnic minorities, unskilled workers and, in some mainly southern European countries, also among women. It is about average for older workers, but they tend to suffer more long-term unemployment because, once out of work, they have little chance of being rehired. However, other groups too are becoming increasingly vulnerable to long-term unemployment, including youth and women, but also men in their prime age (between 25 and 45 years old). In almost all countries the proportion of the long-term unemployed in total unemployment has risen (see table 2.1). Prolonged unemployment represents a lost opportunity to build up work experience and often leads to a deterioration of skills and morale. This may in turn convey negative signals to potential employers who use duration of unemployment as a screening device when selecting new employees.

Employment and the labour force

During the first half of the 1980s the average participation rate (the labour force as a proportion of the working age population (15-64) was stable at almost 70 per cent. In the European IMECs it fell slightly from 66.7 per cent in 1979 to 65.2 per cent in 1985, while it increased modestly in North America from 72 to 74.2 per cent over the same period. In North America labour force participation among youth (students) and women is higher than in Europe and has continued to grow faster during the first half of the 1980s. Moreover, many men – particularly in Europe – have taken advantage of opportunities afforded to them to leave the labour market before reaching the age of 65, in some cases because of poor health and in others because early retirement is actively promoted. In the Federal Republic of Germany and France, for example, the participation rates of men between 55 and 64 years of age declined between 1980 and 1985 from, respectively, 66 to 58 and 69 to 50 per cent. The comparable figures for the United States and Japan were, respectively, 71 to 70 and 85 to 83 per cent over the same five years.

In all IMECs (except Japan) there was a pronounced negative shock to employment in the early 1980s. Between 1980 and 1982 growth of employment lagged a full percentage point behind labour force growth. In North America employment rose faster than the labour force between 1983 and 1985 and probably stabilised in 1986. In Japan employment kept pace with the labour force between 1980 and 1985 but may have fallen behind in 1986. In Europe the situation is not clear-cut. In some southern European countries (such as Spain, France and Italy) employment growth has continued to trail the rise in the labour force. For other European countries employment since 1984 has expanded at about the same rate as the labour force. In countries where unemployment is high, labour force growth has

Table 2.1. Percentage of the unemployed out of work for over one year: Industrialised market economies, 1981-86

	1981	1982	1983	1984	1985	1986
Australia	21.0	19.0	27.5	31.2	30.9	27.5
Austria	6.5	5.7	9.0	12.9	13.3	12.6
Belgium	52.4	59.5	62.8	68.0	68.3	–
Canada	4.2	5.3	9.8	10.1	10.3	10.9
Finland	–	22.3	22.3	22.3	21.1	–
France	32.5	42.1	42.2	42.3	46.8	47.8
Germany, Fed. Rep. of	16.2	21.2	28.5	32.7	31.0	32.0
Ireland	30.5	31.8	31.0	39.1	41.2	–
Italy	37.9	37.8	41.9	50.0	56.4	–
Japan	13.5	14.9	15.5	15.2	11.8	17.2
Netherlands	22.0	31.6	43.7	54.5	55.3	56.3
Norway	3.0	3.3	6.7	10.8	8.3	6.7
Spain	43.6	49.1	53.5	53.6	56.8	56.6
Sweden	6.0	8.4	10.3	12.4	11.4	8.0
United Kingdom	22.0	33.6	36.5	39.8	41.0	41.1
United States	6.7	7.7	13.3	12.3	9.5	8.7

Source: OECD: *Employment Outlook* (Paris, 1986).

declined since the early 1980s, reflecting the fact that many people have been discouraged from looking for work and are thus no longer counted as part of the labour force.

Hours of work

The last few years have seen a continuation of the trend towards shorter hours of work, but at a slower rate. Between 1980 and 1984, working time in 13 IMECs fell by approximately 2.2 per cent, as compared with 3.1 per cent between 1975 and 1980. In six of the ten countries for which data are available, working hours rose between 1984 and 1985.

It can be seen from table 2.2 that experience differs considerably between countries. For the period 1975-86, working time has remained essentially stable in Sweden and the United States while in Japan it has increased. The decline was relatively modest in Australia, but in all other IMECs for which data are available, hours actually worked fell by at least 5 per cent over this decade. In six of the 13 countries, the fall was approximately 8 per cent.

Table 2.3 provides comparative data on annual hours of work. These data should be interpreted with caution. They refer only to manufacturing industry, which often differs significantly from other sectors. In addition, the data are not based on survey results but are constructed from typical provisions of collective agreements. Nor do they reflect the impact of over-time, part-time work and certain other factors. None the less, they indicate the extent to which annual working time varies among workers with comparable occupations in different countries.

If paid absenteeism is taken into account, the table shows that the length of working time in Western Europe falls into a relatively narrow range, with the exception of Switzerland. Switzerland, with working time roughly 200 hours per year above the Western European average, is joined by the United States. But both are left far behind by Japan, which exceeds the Western European average by some 500 hours per year or about 30 per cent. This explains the pressure which is felt in Japan to reduce hours of work.

Table 2.3 in fact underestimates the actual working time of full-time workers, because it does not include overtime. Like absenteeism, overtime varies considerably among countries, industries and occu-pations. Recent levels of overtime in manufacturing in the countries shown in table 2.3 include 2.1 per cent of hours worked in Finland, 2.9 per cent in Sweden, 3.3 per cent in Italy, 4.1 per cent in the Federal Republic of Germany, 7 to 8 per cent in Japan, 8 per cent in the United States and 8.8 per cent in the United Kingdom.

It is worth noting that the same annual length of working time can be reached in different ways. Table 2.3 shows, for example, that relatively long annual hours in the United States are due mainly to annual leave entitlements which are nearly three weeks shorter than the European average, combined with a relatively low level of absenteeism. Switzerland has more annual leave, but it also has a work-week matched in length only by Japan.

The structure of employment

In 1985 about 9 per cent of the IMEC labour force worked in agriculture. This percentage decreased slightly between 1980 and 1985, after declining by more than 4 percentage points during the 1970s. The share of industrial employment fell by about 3.5 percentage points during the 1970s and by about 2.5 percentage points during the first half of the 1980s, to 31 per cent in 1985. On the other hand, the share of service employment rose to 60 per cent in 1985 from about 50 per cent at the beginning of the 1970s. Table 2.4 compares employment increases in indus-

Table 2.2. Average actual hours worked: Industrialised market economies, 1980-86 (1975 = 100)

Country	1980	1981	1982	1983	1984	1985	1986
Australia	98.9	98.9	97.5	97.7	98.9	97.5	–
Canada	97.1	96.0	94.6	94.2	94.7	95.1	95.9
Finland	97.0	96.7	95.7	94.8	94.2	–	–
France	96.9	96.2	93.8	93.1	92.6	92.4	–
Germany, Fed. Rep. of	97.1	96.2	96.5	96.3	95.9	94.7	94.1
Japan	102.0	101.6	101.4	101.5	102.4	101.6	–
Italy	97.2	96.9	96.5	95.8	95.0	94.3	–
Netherlands	94.5	94.7	95.1	94.6	92.2	–	–
Norway	93.3	92.1	92.1	91.6	90.8	91.4	92.8
Spain [1]	95.9	93.8	91.5	89.5	88.3	91.3	–
Sweden	97.3	96.7	97.3	97.5	98.3	99.2	–
United Kingdom	94.1	91.1	91.9	91.2	92.0	–	–
United States	98.7	98.4	97.9	97.4	96.8	99.3	–
Average	96.9	96.1	95.5	95.0	94.7	–	–

[1] 1976 = 100.

Sources: Australia, France, Japan, Spain, Sweden: ILO: *Year Book of Labour Statistics* (Geneva, 1986). Other countries: OECD: *Employment Outlook* (Paris, 1986). ILO data refer to non-agricultural employment. OECD data refer to the total economy, except for the Netherlands (private enterprise sector excluding agriculture) and the United States (employees only).

try and services since 1980. Industrial employment dropped very steeply, especially during the reces-sion of 1980-82, in the United Kingdom, France and Spain as well as in Belgium, Denmark, Luxem-bourg and the Netherlands (not shown in the table). In other countries the drop was less severe, or indus-trial employment later began to recover. But Japan and the United States are the only countries where industrial employment was higher in 1986 than in 1980.

Employment in the services sector has been much less dependent on the state of the economy. It increased by between 5 and 13 per cent during the first half of the 1980s. A significant part of this growth took the form of increased part-time employment, which is mainly concentrated among women and, in some countries, among youths (see box 2.1). On the other hand, in many countries public sector employ-ment grew less rapidly than service employment as a whole. In one country, the United Kingdom, general government employment was lower in 1986 than in 1980.

Table 2.3.　International comparison of weekly and annual hours of work in collective agreements for workers in manufacturing: Industrialised market economies, 1985

Country	Normal weekly hours (industry average) Hours	Annual leave and extra holidays Working days	Public holidays[1] Working days	Agreed annual hours[2] Hours	Absenteeism[3] Hours	Yearly hours adjusted for absenteeism Hours
Austria	40	25	10.5	1 804	152	1 652
Belgium	38	25	10	1 717	98	1 619
Denmark	40	28	9	1 792	97	1 695
Federal Republic of Germany	39	30	12	1 708	128	1 580
Finland	40	25	9	1 816	192	1 624
France	39	25	10	1 763	124	1 639
Ireland	40	24	8	1 832	201	1 631
Italy	40	30[4]	9	1 776	145	1 631
Japan	42	10	12	2 226	34	2 192
Netherlands	40	36.5[5]	7	1 740	131	1 609
Norway	40	21	10	1 840	232	1 608
Sweden	40	25	11	1 800	224	1 576
Switzerland	42	23	8	1 932	108	1 824
United Kingdom	39	27	8	1 763	116	1 647
United States	40	12	10	1 912	62	1 850

[1] Working days lost through public holidays.　[2] Normal hours of work in collective agreements from which statutory annual leave and public holidays have been deducted. Overtime and short-time working have not been considered. Basis of calculation: calendar days minus Saturdays and Sundays = 261 potential working days (Japan: 287 working days).　[3] Absenteeism due to illness, accident, cure, maternity, and other personal reasons for absence from work.　[4] 25 annual leave days plus reduction of annual working time by 100 hours on average.　[5] 24 annual leave days plus reduction of annual working time by 40 hours on average.

Source: Bundesvereinigung der Deutschen Arbeitgeberverbände and Institut der Deutschen Wirtschaft.

Since the beginning of the 1980s there have also been some changes in the distribution of employment by size of establishment. First, there seems to be a drift away from large establishments (not enterprises), especially in manufacturing. Secondly, in many countries self-employment outside agriculture has grown faster than wage employment. It is not clear whether this is the start of a long-term structural trend or a response to increased unemployment. Many workers appear to be prepared to set up their own business because they cannot find wage employment. This possibly short-term trend is comparable to that in many developing countries (see chapter 1).

Attempting to explain the trends

Most employment is generated within enterprises. The managers or owners of these enterprises have to make sure that the products or services provided are sold at a profit so that the enterprise can continue to exist. Their sales depend on the demand for their products and services in the domestic and increas-ingly also on the international market. Their profita-bility depends on the costs of labour (wages), capital (interest), investment in equipment and direct in-puts into the production process. A manager or an employer will only hire people (or provide employ-ment) if he can profitably do so. In the public sector governments work within budgets determined by parliament. Those budgets are also conditioned by the general economic situation and by the state of government finances. The government will only employ people in as far as the budget permits.

Employment trends are thus a reflection not only of changes in the labour market, but of changes in the economic environment as well as government policies.

The economic environment

Much of what happened in the 1980s had its roots in events during the 1970s. There was, first of all, the decision at the beginning of the 1970s to let exchange rates float. Then the first oil crisis of 1973-74 triggered a strong inflationary wave. There was also a profound shift in international trade flows, as a result of increased oil prices, the greater competitive power of Japan and the newly industrialising countries (NICs), and the introduction of new technologies which gave some countries or enterprises a distinct competitive advantage. As a result of growing international uncertainty, investment in capital equipment became increasingly risky. In addition, in many IMECs labour costs increased faster than labour productivity with the result that the rate of return on capital investment fell.

All these tendencies were intensified after the second oil crisis in 1979. This was partly due to changed government policies. To cope with the effects of the first oil crisis some governments adopted expansionary policies. In most countries employment in the public sector increased until the late 1970s, but so did government deficits. After 1979, governments pursued tight monetary and fiscal policies designed primarily to defeat inflation. The combination of restrictive money supply growth and high budget deficits pushed up real interest rates, depressing private consumption and investment. Moreover, increased oil prices turned the terms of trade against most IMECs, reducing national income. Under these circumstances, it is not surprising that unemployment increased massively between 1979 and 1982.

In 1982 the United States Government adopted a more expansionary fiscal and monetary policy which significantly contributed to employment creation within and outside the United States. However, with increasing Federal budget deficits fiscal restraint was again applied in 1986. Meanwhile, Japan and most European governments have maintained their restrictive policies. As a result of these policies and the debt crisis of many developing countries, real interest rates have remained high.

Between 1979 and 1983 the volume of world trade increased by only 0.6 per cent per year compared with an annual 4.4 per cent between 1973 and 1979. IMEC imports fell in 1980, 1981 and 1982 though they leapt by 12 per cent in 1984 and have continued to grow since (see table 2.5). Imports by developing countries rose in 1980 and 1981 (mainly the result of higher imports into fuel-producing countries), but have contracted since.

Roughly two-thirds of world trade takes place between the IMECs. But the DCs account for about one-quarter of world imports and there is now increasing recognition that the contraction in DC

Table 2.4. Civilian employment in industry and services: Industrialised market economies, 1981-1986 (1980 = 100)

	1981	1982	1983	1984	1985	1986
Canada						
industry	101.9	92.4	89.7	93.1	94.4	96.5
services	103.2	102.7	104.7	107.1	110.9	114.5
France						
industry	97.2	95.5	93.3	90.0	87.2	–
services	100.7	102.6	104.4	105.4	106.8	–
Federal Republic of Germany						
industry	97.7	94.2	91.1	90.2	90.1	90.9
services	100.7	100.4	100.5	101.5	103.0	104.6
Italy						
industry	99.4	97.8	95.5	91.5	89.6	88.6
services	102.9	105.5	107.8	112.7	116.5	118.9
Japan						
industry	100.7	100.5	101.9	102.7	103.5	103.2
services	101.7	104.1	106.9	108.1	109.0	111.2
Norway						
industry	98.1	97.6	93.9	95.2	95.6	97.6
services	100.9	102.9	106.7	107.7	110.7	114.5
Spain						
industry	94.9	90.9	90.2	84.4	83.3	87.4
services	100.4	102.4	104.3	102.0	106.0	112.5
Sweden						
industry	97.1	93.7	92.7	93.0	94.2	94.3
services	101.3	102.9	103.8	105.2	106.7	106.4
Switzerland						
industry	100.8	97.9	94.7	94.1	95.1	95.9
services	102.0	103.0	103.1	103.2	104.2	105.3
United Kingdom						
industry	91.3	87.0	83.2	82.8	82.7	81.3
services	98.9	99.3	99.3	102.7	105.0	107.3
United States						
industry	99.6	93.2	93.2	98.6	99.1	100.1
services	101.9	103.4	105.5	109.4	112.7	116.0

Source: OECD: *Quarterly Labour Force Statistics.*

imports has been a direct cause of unemployment in Western Europe and earlier in the United States. It has been estimated that the drastic fall in European Community exports to DCs in 1982 and 1983 may have accounted for some 14-18 per cent of the subsequent increase in EEC unemployment. For the United States this figure was about 10 per cent for 1982 and the drop in exports to DCs may have caused virtually all of the fall in manufacturing

2.1 Part-time work: Advantages and problems

The number of part-time workers in the industrialised market economy countries approximated 45 million by 1985, an increase of at least 2.5 million since 1982. The proportion of part-time workers in the labour force in 1985 was 28.6 per cent in Norway, 24.6 per cent in Sweden, 23.7 per cent in the Netherlands, 21.2 per cent in the United Kingdom, between 15 and 19 per cent in Australia, the United States and Canada and around 10 per cent in France, the Federal Republic of Germany and Japan. Part-time employment is particularly common among women, young and older workers. The proportion of women in part-time employment is 92 per cent in the Federal Republic of Germany, 90 per cent in the United Kingdom, 85 per cent in France and 84 per cent in Sweden. In Australia, Canada and the United States the part-time labour force has a greater share of young people, many of whom combine part-time employment with education.

There are several advantages associated with part-time work. It offers opportunities for those who are unable to work full time due to family obligations, education and training or other activities. It may provide a way of returning to employment for workers, especially women, who have been absent from the labour market for a substantial period. Part-time work in the form of phased retirement can be an important benefit for older workers. For employers, part-time work can be a cost-effective means of extending the time when the enterprise is operating or of overcoming specific problems of work scheduling and manning. Several governments see part-time work as a means of reducing unemployment.

On the other hand, the rapid growth of part-time work has led to the creation of a large category of workers with conditions of work and employment which are very often inferior to those enjoyed by full-time workers. One problem derives from the type of job generally assigned to part-time workers. Such workers tend to be concentrated in a small number of branches, mostly in the service sector, where they are normally employed for auxiliary or low-skilled work and in jobs traditionally filled by women. Part-time workers often have little job security, particularly when there is no written contract of employment. In addition, working hours may be irregular or the workers systematically required to work at inconvenient hours – early in the morning, late at night or at weekends – without any right to the bonuses for such schedules normally payable to full-time workers. Seniority increments, pay during absence on grounds of illness, payment for public holidays and overtime allowances may also be denied to part-time workers. In several countries participation in private or public pension schemes is not available to workers who perform less than a certain number of hours of work during a specified period or whose income is below a certain level.

Other difficulties frequently encountered by part-time workers include greater pressure of work, exclusion from enterprise-level training programmes, lack of career prospects and lack of access to full-time jobs.

These problems have led a number of countries in recent years to take action to improve the protection provided to part-time workers in law and practice.

Table 2.5. Growth of world import volumes, 1980-86 (annual percentage change)

	1980	1981	1982	1983	1984	1985	1986
IMECs	−1.6	−2.3	−0.3	4.8	12.4	5.0	8.9
DCs	7.3	7.8	−4.0	−2.4	1.8	−0.2	−3.1
All world	1.2	0.7	−2.2	2.9	8.6	3.2	4.9

Source: IMF: *International Financial Statistics.*

Table 2.6. Real interest rates: Industrialised market economies,[1] 1980-86

	1980	1981	1982	1983	1984	1985	1986
United States	2.2	3.9	6.1	7.0	8.1	7.1	5.0
Japan	4.9	5.0	6.3	6.9	5.9	5.0	3.3
Federal Republic of Germany	3.5	6.2	4.3	4.6	5.8	4.6	2.5
France	0.7	3.5	2.8	3.6	4.9	4.8	3.0
United Kingdom	−5.1	2.9	4.8	5.5	6.3	4.2	6.1

[1] Real interest rates are defined as the proportion between the long-term interest rate and the rate of increase in the GNP-deflator.

Sources: IMF: *International Financial Statistics*; and OECD: *National Accounts.*

employment in 1983. Thus, the IMECs have a clear interest in helping DCs to restore their economic growth.

Employment growth in IMECs may also be held back by high real interest rates. While real interest rates were often below zero during the 1970s they have varied between 3 and 8 per cent during the 1980s (see table 2.6). In some respects, high real interest rates are creating better conditions for employment growth, such as low inflation and lower costs for labour relative to capital. In other respects, however, the impact on employment has been nega-

tive. High real interest rates make financial transactions more attractive than business investment. This is aggravated by the fact that changes in interest rates have a destabilising effect on exchange rates which makes it very difficult for enterprises to forecast reliably their revenues from sales. For that reason, many non-financial enterprises prefer to invest in financial assets rather than in capital equipment and

Table 2.7. **Real hourly labour costs: Industrialised market economies, 1973-85 (annual growth rates)**

	1973-1979	1980	1981	1982	1983	1984	1985
United States	1.2	−0.4	1.9	0.2	−1.4	−0.2	0.2
Japan	4.5	4.1	4.6	4.0	2.0	3.3	2.3
EEC	3.2	2.7	2.3	1.3	1.2	1.5	1.9
Other IMECs	3.1	1.4	−0.2	−0.5	0.6	0.6	1.2

Note: Real labour costs are defined as the ratio of average hourly earnings, adjusted for employment taxes, to the GDP deflator, adjusted for indirect taxation.

Source: A. Newell and J. Symons: *Mid-1980s unemployment*, Working Paper No. 936 (London, Centre for Labour Economics, 1987).

Table 2.8. **Compensation of employees as a percentage of GDP: Industrialised market economies, 1973-85**

	1973	1979	1985
Larger countries			
Australia	54.2	52.7	51.7
Canada	55.0	55.3	54.1
Japan	49.0	54.2	54.7
United States	60.6	60.8	60.3
France	50.1	54.4	54.3
Federal Republic of Germany	55.5	55.8	53.6
Italy	52.4	55.1	55.1
United Kingdom	59.7	59.1	55.8
Smaller countries			
Austria	49.7	54.9	52.5
Belgium	54.1	59.2	56.5
Denmark	53.4	55.7	53.8
Finland	52.6	53.4	54.8
Greece	30.1	37.7	41.9
Iceland	51.6	56.8	54.7
Netherlands	56.8	58.8	51.8
Norway	55.7	54.2	48.2
Portugal	45.7	50.7	44.9
Spain	51.6	54.9	46.8
Sweden	58.5	64.9	57.7
Switzerland	57.5	61.2	62.2

Source: OECD: *National Accounts, 1960-85* (Paris, 1986)

productive capacity that would lead to employment creation. Finally, high interest rates increase the burden of debt repayments by the DCs and therefore reduce their ability to buy goods and services produced by IMEC-based enterprises.

Functioning of the labour market

It is in the labour market that employers and workers come together in order to bargain, collectively or individually, about wages and working conditions. While wages constitute a part of production costs for the employer, they determine the standard of living for workers and their families. Wage bargaining between employers and workers does not cover total labour costs because a large part of employers' social security contributions are determined by statutory rules.

Labour costs have risen more slowly in the United States than in other groups of IMECs (table 2.7). During the 1970s they grew more rapidly than labour productivity, particularly in Western Europe, so that the so-called labour cost gap widened for a time before narrowing again in the 1980s.

Various explanations have been advanced for these developments. During the 1970s and the early 1980s the fastest growing component of labour costs was contributions to social security and private pension funds. The other component of labour costs, real wages, was often not responsive to changes in unemployment. Newell and Symons (1987b) have observed that this responsiveness is greater in countries where trade unions and employers' organisations co-operate in a number of policy areas and where no incomes policy is imposed by the State (see also chapter 7). They argue that in countries with a laissez-faire labour market policy wages will usually

be set so high as to create involuntary unemployment. This is for insider-outsider reasons: the wage is a deal between firms and employed workers (insiders) from which the unemployed (outsiders) are mainly excluded. Insider-outsider theories usually assume that the *change* in the unemployment rate rather than the *level* influences the wage, since only the newly laid-off may be regarded as insiders in the bargaining process. In the United States slower growth of real wages reflects the fact that money wages have generally been insensitive to inflation. Real labour costs have also risen more slowly in many European countries since the end of the 1970s, where the main factors have been increased unemployment, lower wage increase demands from the workers' side and increased government intervention in wage bargaining. As documented in chapter 7, many governments have tried to reduce the impact of wage-indexation systems or have imposed wage freezes and wage guide-lines. They have also curbed the pay of their own employees to maintain fiscal restraint, to avoid increasing public service prices or to influence private sector wage movements.

Slower wages growth has led to a fall in the compensation of employees (which is almost equal to total labour costs) as a proportion of GDP in most European countries since 1979. As table 2.8 shows, in some countries the proportion in 1985 was even lower than in 1973. This is despite a higher proportion of employees in total employment in almost all IMECs, and a bigger share of employment in services where labour costs constitute a larger proportion of value added.

At the same time there has been a trend to more decentralised bargaining at the level of the workplace and greater emphasis, notably on the employers' side, on labour market flexibility. This concept covers not only the speed with which wages react to changed economic conditions, but also the speed with which employment adjusts to the wage: that is, how quickly firms hire and fire in response to business conditions. The generally sluggish rate of labour market adjustment in European countries, which some believe has contributed to higher rates of unemployment, is attributed to a combination of job protection legislation, a greater presence of workers' representatives in enterprises and personnel practices of the enterprises themselves.

2. Collective bargaining

In recent years collective bargaining has been strongly influenced by economic and technological developments. Many large enterprises have been obliged to restructure their operations and/or introduce new technologies in order to remain competitive in the international market. Other changes include a proliferation of small and medium-sized enterprises using advanced technology; rapid growth of the services sector; an increase in the number of skilled technicians; and a narrowing gap between wage earners and salaried employees. The structure of employment has altered – in particular the distribution of skill levels – and "precarious" forms of work have multiplied. This has led to a growing fragmentation of the labour market with the establishment of a privileged core of workers and peripheral groups whose fate is far less desirable.

Attitudes to work have also changed. Many people, especially women and the young, are now seeking life-styles in which work plays a less

important and less restrictive role than in the past – a situation which has helped foster the growth of "precarious" employment. Some employees are placing greater emphasis on individual effort than on collective action to ensure the development of their careers.

The result of all these changes is a much more heterogeneous workforce than in the past. This poses new problems not only for employers but also for the trade unions and public authorities. The key question is the extent to which the various categories of worker can be treated differently without creating socially intolerable situations.

Trade union organisations in most IMECs are passing through a difficult period. The economic, technological and social developments noted above have weakened their political influence and their bargaining power at the negotiating table. Anti-trade union attitudes by employers have strengthened – in particular in North America – and this has sometimes been reinforced by government measures curbing trade union activities. In the United Kingdom, for example, legislation adopted during the 1980s has introduced restrictions on the closed shop and direct action, and made secret ballots obligatory for certain trade union decisions, notably on calling strikes.

Since the beginning of the 1980s trade unions in many IMECs have suffered a decline in their membership but in others membership is stable or slightly on the increase. In large part, this is due to the effects of economic recession and structural change. Employment losses have been particularly high in industry with its traditionally high rate of unionisation, while employment in the public sector – another union stronghold – has stagnated.

Like the trade unions, employers' organisations are also confronted with changes in the character of their membership. The recent proliferation of small and medium-sized enterprises, particularly in the service and high technology sectors, has compounded the difficulty they often experience in attracting smaller companies. However, it has induced employers' organisations to start new services particularly aimed at the needs of such companies.

Role of the State

During the 1980s, a large number of IMEC governments have intervened in collective bargaining, particularly in wage fixing, when discussions between employers and workers have reached deadlock or, in their view, could produce results incompatible with the demands of economic recovery. In some countries such as Australia, Spain and Italy, governments have on several occasions participated in tripartite central agreements designed to provide an overall approach to such varied problems as unemployment, remuneration, taxation, public expenditure and the reform of labour legislation and social security.

Elsewhere, governments have taken matters into their own hands and had recourse to coercive measures to resolve outstanding problems. Sometimes, as in France, these measures have been very selective and strictly limited in time, such as a wage freeze applied for a few months. In other cases – notably in Belgium and Denmark – there has been massive and prolonged state intervention in a number of spheres traditionally regulated by collective agreement.

At the same time as these countries have strengthened the State's influence on labour relations, however, other governments have adopted the opposite approach. In the Federal Republic of Germany and Switzerland, the public authorities have traditionally avoided any kind of intervention in collective bargaining. In the United States of America and the United Kingdom such intervention has been systematically eschewed since the present governments came to power committed to free-market policies and a reduction in the role of the State. Other countries such as the Netherlands have recently endeavoured to move away from long-standing and considerable government involvement in collective bargaining.

There have also been changes in the behaviour of governments in their, increasingly significant, role as employers. In the past the public service was relatively unimportant in comparison with the private sector in most IMECs. It was, moreover, a separate entity. Civil servants generally had a different status in terms of bargaining rights, the right to strike, job security and levels and systems of remuneration. In these circumstances, collective bargaining or joint consultations in the public service – where such practices were observed – took place without much regard for the private sector.

During the last 15 to 20 years, the number of people employed in the public service has markedly increased and collective bargaining or something similar has become much more widespread, with the result that the status of civil servants is now much closer to that of workers in the private sector. This trend has recently been interrupted because a number of governments, within the framework of austerity policies, introduced measures to curb employment growth and salary rises in the civil service, often precipitating sharp conflict. The civil service comprises at present a large number of employees who are resolutely determined to protect and improve employment and incomes, and must compete with the private sector to do so. (That is because funds allocated by governments to the public service are no longer available for the private sector, for instance to subsidise job creation or finance social security benefits.) It would thus seem increasingly necessary to establish some kind of co-ordination between negotiations in the private sector and the public service. Co-ordination problems of this kind are amongst the major difficulties now affecting the climate of labour relations in Sweden. It should also be noted that an agreement concluded in 1985 in the Italian public sector, which concerned in particular the indexation of wages and the reduction of hours of work, was used – for the first time in that country – as a model for the private sector.

More decentralised bargaining in Western Europe

The role of the State in labour relations is linked to the level of negotiation between the industrial partners. There have been major developments in this area in Western Europe over the last ten years. By contrast, the situation has changed very little in North America and Japan, which remain largely attached to their traditional system of enterprise-level bargaining. However, in all IMECs there has been a trend towards more co-operative labour relations (see box 2.2).

At the beginning of the 1970s, most of the countries of Western Europe had in place well-established, relatively complex, bargaining machinery which gave priority to negotiations at industry level. In some countries centralised bargaining with two or three partners and negotiation at the level of the enterprise also played a role of varying importance.

In recent years, however, centralised bargaining has lost ground to negotiation at enterprise level. In Sweden, Norway and Denmark, the traditional bipartite central bargaining process has several times broken down and continued objections, mainly from employers but also from some workers, have cast doubt on its future. Central bargaining – both bipar-

---

2.2 More co-operative labour relations in IMECs during the 1980s

Since the beginning of the 1980s there have been some signs of a development towards less confrontational and more co-operative labour relations. However, it is difficult to say to what extent this trend is the result of a fundamental and lasting change in the attitude of the parties concerned and to what extent it is simply due to a shift – perhaps temporary – in the balance of power to the detriment of the trade unions.

In a number of IMECs greater co-operation at the bargaining table has been urged not only by employers and governments but also by some trade unions which see it as a means – and sometimes the only possible means – of resolving difficult problems of structural adjustment. The 1985 report of the AFL-CIO contains several quite surprising passages, given that American trade unions have traditionally taken a rather confrontational view of labour relations in general and collective bargaining in particular. For example, the report states that "confrontation and conflict are wasteful and that a co-operative approach to solving shared present and future problems is desirable". In practice this greater co-operation means that collective bargaining no longer leads automatically, as in the past, to consistent improvements for workers in all the areas covered by agreements. It increasingly constitutes a process in which workers, in exchange for certain benefits, give up specific acquired rights or other firmly established practices. They may renounce acquired rights by, for example, accepting a freeze or even a reduction of wages or other pecuniary benefits, or agreeing to greater flexibility in hours of work. Instances where established practices have been renounced include some agreements recently signed in the United Kingdom

with branches of Japanese firms, where the trade unions breached tradition by accepting a "peace obligation".

Finally, mention should be made of the development at plant level of new participation experiments. These cover a wide range of often very informal forms of co-operation between employers and workers designed to improve the organisation of work and increase productivity, in particular following the introduction of new technologies. Examples include participative personnel policies, quality circles or permanent consultation machinery. In some cases, however, employers have sought to exclude trade union representatives from these experiments, often by dealing exclusively with bodies of the works council type. Sometimes they have tried to bypass even the latter and deal directly with individual workers. The effect is to remove some aspects of the employer-worker relationship from the domain of collective labour relations to that of individual relations. In other words, there has been a shift away from "labour relations" (essentially bilateral) towards the "management of human resources" (essentially unilateral).

The difficulties of central bargaining, the growth of bargaining at enterprise level and the increasing importance of "the management of human resources" have important implications for employers' and trade union organisations. If these trends continue, the responsibility for bargaining will tend to shift from organisations at the top of the pyramid to those at the base, as well as to employers and invididual workers. The weight of central and branch organisations will thus be diminished unless they give greater attention to other tasks such as training and vocational retraining or management advisory services.

---

tite and tripartite – experienced alternate periods of success and failure in Italy in the 1980s, has not operated for some years in Ireland and the Netherlands, was interrupted in Belgium until 1986, has never really taken root in Portugal despite the establishment in 1984 of the Permanent Council for Concertation, and even very recently ran into trouble in Spain and Australia where tripartite agreements are currently in force. There are of course reasons for these difficulties. Employers want to avoid the extra costs which central bargaining may impose in addition to existing commitments and fear that regulations established centrally will be too rigid. In addition, budgetary restrictions often mean the public authorities can no longer offer the expected advantages to employers and workers to undertake bargaining commitments. Nevertheless, it would be rash to predict that central bargaining or concertation will disappear in the countries of Western Europe where it has been a regular feature.

There has also been a marked and growing tendency in Western European countries to complement bargaining at industry level by bargaining at the

level of the enterprise. The number of works agreements has, for example, sharply increased in the United Kingdom in recent years. Industry-wide agreements on reduced working hours concluded in 1984 in the Federal Republic of Germany stipulated that their implementation must be decided at enterprise level. In practice, application of these agreements varies considerably from enterprise to enterprise. This trend towards decentralisation in collective bargaining is no doubt due in part to the fact that some problems of structural adjustment – for example, protecting employment, boosting productivity growth and introducing new technologies – can be resolved satisfactorily only at enterprise level. In addition, many employers are convinced that greater flexibility is required in the organisation of production and that this can be achieved only by a major extension of bargaining within the enterprise.

This has given rise to some difficulties in relations between the trade unions and bodies of the works council type, which exist in a number of countries of Western Europe. The negotiation of wages and other key conditions of employment, such as hours of work, has traditionally been considered the exclusive prerogative of the trade unions. However, works councils have often assumed bargaining functions which legally belong to the trade unions. As the role of enterprise bargaining has increased, the relationship between trade unions and works councils or similar bodies has become an increasingly topical problem. In some European countries works councils are holding formal negotiations on a number of subjects without any official participation by the trade unions.

The content of collective bargaining

In the past, collective bargaining normally led to automatic improvements of wages and conditions of work. It is now increasingly used to work out pragmatic solutions that take into account the requirement for enterprises to be competitive as well as workers' basic interests. This is demonstrated by the results of collective bargaining on job security, labour flexibility, new technologies and hours of work.

Job security

The question of job security is closely linked to that of labour costs. One of the principal concerns of negotiators in recent years has been to curb the growth in labour costs so as to preserve and create jobs. Thus mechanisms linking wages to the cost of living have been restricted and even blocked in some European countries such as Belgium or the Netherlands. The resulting "savings" have been partly used to create new jobs, for example, by a reduction in working hours. Similar trade-offs resulted from concession bargaining in the United States at the end of the 1970s and beginning of the 1980s, particularly in the automobile and steel sectors. Workers gave up acquired benefits, notably on wages, in exchange for guarantees concerning job security and increased participation. More recent agreements in the United States – such as those signed at Ford and General Motors for the period 1984-87 – contain far-reaching provisions on job security in addition to accords on wage increases and other benefits. The General Motors agreement stipulates that in various contingencies (introduction of new technologies, transfer of certain forms of production to other undertakings or foreign countries, productivity increases), job security will be guaranteed to workers with at least one year's seniority. The company also committed itself to manufacturing within the United States a specific

range of new models. A fund of US$1,000 million to be used for retraining and the redeployment of workers, and another fund of US$100 million for the creation of new undertakings in which surplus manpower could be employed, will be managed by joint committees composed of management and trade union representatives. An agreement concluded in 1986 with the Saturn Corporation, a subsidiary of General Motors, also makes provision for important guarantees on job security in addition to greater worker participation. At least 80 per cent of the workers will be guaranteed "permanent job security"; that is, they may not be laid off except in the case of "unforeseen or catastrophic events or in serious economic conditions". The decision to dismiss a worker will be subject to approval by the trade union representatives.

Labour market flexibility

Employers and many governments believe that new recruitment could be increased considerably if the labour market were more flexible. In support of this view, they often quote the example of the United States and Japan which have succeeded in creating many more jobs than so-called "sclerotic" Europe. Flexibility, however, can mean many things. Sometimes it is used to refer to labour costs, for instance to the adjustment of these costs at the macro-economic level to economic fluctuations or their adaptation, at the micro-economic level, to the results of the enterprise. In other cases it is used to refer to legal provisions or regulations on employment protection, such as job security and hours of work. Or it may refer to the geographic or occupational mobility of workers, or the organisation of work.

The early debate on labour market flexibility at the beginning of the 1980s was marred by this lack of conceptual clarity. More fundamentally, however, the enthusiasm with which employers and some governments promoted flexibility was equalled only by the determination with which trade unions opposed it. They saw it essentially as an attempt to dismantle the social achievements of the last 100 years and reinforce the new balance of power to their detriment. In these circumstances the discussions generally were of a more doctrinaire than technical character. More recently the debate has made some progress. This is reflected for example, in the Dahrendorf report published by the Organisation for Economic Co-operation and Development (OECD) in 1986. A greater pragmatism has now emerged.

The advocates of flexibility no longer tend to consider it as a panacea and trade unions are beginning to admit that the labour market may sometimes contain rigidities which do not suit present needs. Both sides recognise that, rather than discuss labour market flexibility "in general", specific aspects must be examined separately, such as wages (chapter 7), hours of work (see next subsection), dismissal procedures and temporary work. It also seems to be increasingly accepted – at least in principle – that the social dimensions of more flexible employment practices need to be taken into account, and that solutions may vary on a case-by-case basis.

Shorter working hours and new technologies

Two other major areas of negotiation – which are linked to flexibility although they are much wider in scope – concern the reduction of working time and the introduction of new technology.

Relatively little of the reduction in working time in the past few years has come about through legislative action. Only two countries have recently reduced the length of the normal working week. In France, weekly hours were reduced to 39 in 1981. In Denmark, legislation has been adopted as an exceptional measure which lowers weekly hours to 39 starting in 1987. In other countries, legislation provides for a 40-hour week or longer. Several countries still have a 48-hour week in law, though of course this has long been changed in practice through collective bargaining. There has been a certain amount of pressure on governments to reduce overtime through legislation. Most countries now set maximum hours of overtime over a specified period. There has also been a modest amount of legislative action on annual holidays with pay. Austria and Finland have added a fifth week of minimum annual leave recently, joining Denmark, France, Luxembourg and Sweden.

Shorter working hours have mainly been adopted through collective bargaining. Negotiations over the reduction of working time have taken place in many Western European countries and have led in several instances to conflict. In the Federal Republic of Germany, for example, the 1984 bargaining round in the metal trades precipitated a major strike. The final industry-wide agreement on reduction of working hours to 38.5 hours a week set the pattern for many other industries.

Trade unions in most countries are continuing to push for shorter hours of work, though real wage increases have been given increasing priority lately. Most of the trade union pressure for shorter hours is specifically linked to the employment it is expected to generate. In some cases, however, particularly in the Nordic countries, the social benefits of reduced working time predominate, in particular the equalisation of working time for men and women and for manual and non-manual workers. In addition to reductions in the work-week, longer periods of *paid annual leave* are often negotiated, especially in countries where statutory provisions have not been revised recently, as in the Federal Republic of Germany and the United Kingdom. Finally, employers and trade unions have been bargaining more intensely on flexibility of working time (see box 2.3).

Trade unions have generally taken a resolutely positive approach to the introduction of new technology provided that the technology is introduced in a socially acceptable manner. Thus in a large number of countries agreements have defined some general principles to be observed. Workers' representatives must be informed in advance and consulted on measures concerning social aspects of the new technology, although the decision to introduce it remains the prerogative of the employer. When new technology is brought in, the employer and trade unions often conclude agreements which not only define measures to protect affected workers but include more wide-ranging and linked objectives, such as higher productivity, improved product quality, greater co-operation within the undertaking and an increase in job satisfaction, in particular as a result of greater autonomy for workers and better working conditions.

3. Social insurance and social assistance

The economic recession at the beginning of the 1980s and low economic growth since that time have confronted governments with a particularly difficult situation. The demand for social security benefits has been increasing for various reasons, such as the gradual ageing of the population and high unemployment. But governments have also been under pressure to reduce or slow down rising expenditures because of budgetary constraints. Thus they have had to make special efforts to contain the costs and to increase the revenues of the social insurance system,

---

2.3   **Flexibility of working time**

Working time is a very sensitive issue in many countries for both employers and workers, especially since the rearrangement of working time is often closely linked with its reduction.

Employers increasingly see flexibility in working time as a major area for initiatives. In general, they have moved from a passive stance, reacting to trade union demands on hours reduction and increases in leave, to a more active strategy aimed at optimising operating schedules and minimising costs. It is often the employers who put forward proposals on working time during negotiations and who are behind a number of experiments and innovations.

The immediate goals of employers are relatively clear. In many industries, large capital expenditures and rapid technological change have led to a need for rapid amortisation of investments. This has happened at the same time that hours of work have been falling. In addition, many enterprises have found that they can make considerable savings in operating costs if they can adjust production volume to seasonal or other variations in demand. As a result, more flexible scheduling arrangements regarding shift work, weekend work, part-time work, hours-averaging schemes and so on, have become very attractive to employers. This may extend to arrangements such as flexible working hours as well.

On the trade union side, there is a greater variety of viewpoints. One consistent theme is that flexibility should take the form of options for workers rather than for employers. Even here, however, there is concern that complete "individualisation" of working time will weaken worker solidarity and make the task of trade unions more difficult. Another development is that the strong positions taken by many trade unions on the reduction of working time have made some of them more open to negotiated arrangements for flexible scheduling.

For a number of reasons, negotiation on working time has tended recently to be increasingly concentrated at the level of the enterprise. Technical factors contribute considerably to this. A work schedule which balances the concerns of both employers and workers in, for example, a case where shift work is necessary but night and weekend work are to be minimised, is not easy to devise, much less to negotiate, except through local participation of all concerned.

Collective agreements are often a legal requirement for the application of the so-called *hours-averaging schemes*. These schemes are particularly popular in industries with seasonal or fluctuating demand. The periods of high and low activity may be established in advance or left to the employer's discretion. In the latter case, a notice period is usually required for changes in schedules. Many of these schemes are accompanied by reductions in hours of work. There may be special rules for such matters as overtime accounting at the end of the averaging period. The same wages are usually paid throughout the period.

In one specific form of hours-averaging scheme, which has taken root especially in Austria and the Federal Republic of Germany, the average work-week applies not to each worker individually but to workers in the enterprise as a whole. This means that some workers may exceed the average even over an entire year. For example, in the agreement in the metal trades in the Federal Republic of Germany, an overall average of 38.5 hours must be maintained for all employees, but individual workers may work as many as 40 hours per week or as few as 37.

There has also been an increasing tendency for employers and trade unions to negotiate *annual hours agreements* which fix hours on an annual rather than a weekly basis. Collective agreements now commonly specify a yearly total of agreed hours to be worked, which are in turn subject to a variety of provisions concerning scheduling. The flexibility may be for the employer or for the worker depending on specific contract provisions and often on direct arrangements between worker and supervisor.

Annual hours agreements frequently include a reduction in hours of work. This may be on a daily or weekly basis, but most often takes the form of "floating" holidays which may be taken at a time mutually agreed upon. In many cases, annual hours agreements have largely the same intent as the hours-averaging schemes, the major difference being a greater reliance on days off work to reduce working time rather than cutting daily or weekly hours.

---

at the same time as increasing expenditure on tax-financed welfare and social assistance schemes for the growing numbers who are not, or not sufficiently, protected by social insurance benefits.

Restoring the financial balance of social insurance

A number of countries have tried in recent years to reassess social security benefits in the light of economic and financial constraints. To restore financial balance, they have sought out new sources of finance or taken appropriate cost containment measures. Some countries have attempted to tackle their problems more radically, by undertaking in-depth reviews or reforms of social security.

Pension schemes

Expenditure on pension schemes constitutes one of the largest components of social security expenditure in many countries. This is due not only to the ageing of populations, but also to the expansion of schemes. Many programmes have not yet reached "cruising speed" and the effect of past decisions on benefit expenditure has still to be fully reflected in outlays. Another unfavourable factor is the increase in spending resulting from steps taken to ease the labour market situation (incentives to early retirement, lowering of the pensionable age and so on) which represent additional costs for pension schemes.

Many countries have adopted short-run measures to contain costs. For example, Canada (1983-84) and the Federal Republic of Germany (since 1979) have restricted the adjustment of pensions to increases in the cost of living or wages. Other countries, such as Austria, Denmark and Italy, have tightened qualifying conditions for invalidity pensions.

Other countries have considered more far-reaching revisions or reform of pension systems, among them Japan, the United Kingdom, the United States and Spain. The example of *Japan* is examined in some detail (see box 2.4).

In 1986 new legislation was adopted in the *United Kingdom*, which maintained the basic structure of the system: a universal flat-rate benefit (introduced in 1948) and a wage-related component (SERPS) built up as from 1975. However, benefits have been substantially curtailed in order to obtain, in the long run, an overall cost saving estimated at 25 per cent. New measures taken include a phased-in reduction of SERPS benefit levels, a requirement that such benefits should be related to wages received through the whole working life (and not only the best 20 years) and the reduction of entitlements for surviving spouses of insured persons.

As a counterpart to the reduction in State pensions, major incentives have been given for the establishment of personal pensions. From 1988 individuals can make their own pension arrangements, opting out of the SERPS or the employer's occupational pension scheme if they wish to do so.

In the *United States* the main pension programme, the mandatory Old-age, Survivors' and Disability scheme (OASDI), which faced short-term financial problems and longer-term threats of imbalance, was revised in 1983. The legislature decided to raise the retirement age progressively in future years and to reduce entitlements to early retirement benefits. Another important measure was to broaden the base of the programme by including in it new Federal employees together with people who will be employed in non-profit-making organisations in the future. Parallel measures were adopted to provide the programme with more resources by bringing forward planned increases in earnings-related contributions. Other changes involved mainly short-term measures, for example, a new system for indexing benefits.

In *Spain* a gradual process to reform the social security system is under way. The first stage of the reform was completed with an Act passed in July 1985 providing for the integration of a number of special pension schemes covering different groups of employees into the general scheme. The Act also

includes a series of restrictive measures: more stringent qualifying conditions for the receipt of pensions, particularly those concerning the length of the required period of paid-up contributions which has been raised from 10 to 15 years; and modifications to the base for the calculation of pensions leading to an ultimate reduction in their levels. In exchange, the decision was taken to introduce in the legislation a provision for automatic annual indexation of pensions to prices. Finally, the introduction of non-contributory pensions, based on a means test, is the first step in the process of integrating assistance and social insurance.

Family benefits

In a certain number of countries family allowances were the first category of social security benefits to be curtailed as a result of financial stringency due to economic recession. In several countries the purchasing power of benefits has fallen. Either their nominal amount has been reduced (for example, in Belgium or in the Federal Republic of Germany) or, more often, they have not been adjusted in line with increased prices. In Spain, for instance, such adjustments were blocked from 1971 with the result that, between 1974 and 1984, family allowances lost more than three-quarters of their real value. In Japan no adjustments have been made to family allowance rates since 1975, while in Denmark their adjustment has been limited to half that of the increase in the price index.

Another frequent restriction has been to reduce the number of beneficiaries by lowering age limits for the receipt of child benefits, as in the Federal Republic of Germany, Denmark, Greece and Luxembourg. Grants have also been made more selective so as to concentrate benefits on families with the lowest incomes, notably in Denmark and, for certain types of benefits, in France. Other forms of selectivity have included the adjustment of benefit levels to take into account the resources of the entire family, for example, in the Federal Republic of Germany, Belgium and Italy.

Unemployment benefits

The rise in unemployment has produced a rapid and considerable increase in the expenditure of unemployment benefit schemes.

One cost-containment measure frequently employed is to reduce the level of benefits. In the Federal Republic of Germany, for example, the level

<table>
<tr><td>

2.4

In 1985 the Japanese Government introduced a radical reform of the pension system which led to the institution of a new two-tier national pension scheme. Three main concerns inspired the reform:

- to reduce or eliminate the inequalities resulting from the co-existence of eight different pension schemes;

- to improve the situation of women, and in particular of workers' spouses, by giving them autonomous pension rights;

- to slow down the sharp rise in the cost of pensions as soon as possible in view of the rapidly ageing population.

The first tier comprises a universal basic scheme intended to provide all citizens with a relatively modest flat-rate pension *(National Pension Scheme)*. Under this scheme, women are given a pension in their own right, regardless of the age or situation of their husband, even if they have not paid contributions. Employees and self-employed workers become entitled to a basic pension to the extent that they have paid compulsory contributions during their working lives. The basic pension is financed by earnings-related contributions in the case of employees and by flat-rate contributions from self-employed workers. A state subsidy is envisaged of around one-third of the cost of basic pensions as well as a contribution from the funds of the Employees' Pension Insurance Scheme – the second "pillar" of the new system. The option of financing universal pensions through taxation was rejected

</td><td>

Reform of the Japanese pension scheme

because it would have been necessary to raise taxes sharply, a measure that was deemed inappropriate.

The retirement age stays at 65, although reduced benefits may be provided in the event of early retirement.

The second tier is earnings-related and is intended for employees in the private sector *(Employees' Pension Insurance Scheme)*. It covers all establishments and enterprises and also a number of public sector employees who are without a similar type of cover. The retirement age for men – 60 years – has not been changed by comparison with the Employees' Scheme operating before the reform but for women it will increase gradually from 55 to 60. The principle of a future general increase in the retirement age to 65 has been maintained in the reform, although its application has been postponed until a later (as yet unspecified) date. Financing is provided through employees' and employers' contributions in equal proportions.

An innovation is the adoption of a scale of benefits that in the long term appreciably reduces the earnings-related component of pensions. Contributions need to have been paid for 40 years in order to qualify for entitlement to a pension level that could have been achieved after 32 years of insurance before the reform.

The success of the reform is perhaps due to the fact that the new system incorporates both an improvement in social protection (making protection universal, abolishing unfavourable treatment for women) and economy measures through a reduction in the level of benefit that will be payable in the years to come.

</td></tr>
</table>

of insurance allowances has been cut from 68 to 63 per cent of previous earnings for unemployed persons without children. In the Netherlands, this level was lowered from 80 to 70 per cent in 1985 and is expected to be reduced further. Another way of trimming benefits has been to exclude a number of components of previous earnings when calculating benefits, as in Japan and the Federal Republic of Germany.

Other cost-containing measures have included: increasing the qualifying period before benefits can be received (Canada, Denmark and the Netherlands); making the period during which compensation is payable more strictly proportional to the qualifying period (Spain, a growing number of states in the United States, France, Japan, Portugal and Switzerland); and strengthening procedures for checking the unemployment status of benefit claimants (for instance, Belgium, Denmark, and the Federal Republic of Germany).

Increasing contribution scales

Even though some countries have searched for new sources of financing social security, most have resorted to the traditional solution of raising contri-

bution rates, in spite of the high levels already reached. For example, in 1985 pension contributions were raised in the Federal Republic of Germany, Austria, Finland and Norway. France took similar steps in 1986.

As noted earlier, the authorities in the United States have brought forward planned increases in contribution rates while, in Canada, it was decided in June 1986 to raise contribution levels which had not changed since inauguration of the pensions scheme in 1966. Many countries have also introduced large increases in unemployment insurance contributions.

In certain countries – Finland and France are cases in point – the increase has fallen principally on the insured person. This was intended to lighten the burden of social charges on enterprises, and indeed even to reduce them, as in Spain. Another measure has been the removal of the ceiling of wages subject to contributions, as in 1982 in Belgium for each branch of benefits and in France for sickness insurance in 1984. Other countries, including Austria, Spain and Greece, have considerably raised the ceiling.

Contribution rules have also been changed in order to encourage employment. The Belgian Government introduced special reductions in contributions in 1983 aimed at helping labour-intensive businesses and small enterprises. Contributions relating to low-paid workers were cut in the United Kingdom in 1985 with the explicit intention of promoting employment. In Luxembourg and Spain the Government reduces social security contributions for employers taking on young people as trainees.

"Privatisation" of social insurance?

"Privatisation" of social insurance has been widely suggested as a means to restore financial balance and to increase work incentives, personal savings and investments. Private insurance – probably meaning commercial insurance – would be used to satisfy individual needs above a basic minimum.

It is interesting to note that after a period of free and voluntary growth of occupational pensions (supplementing state benefits) several governments decided that the additional protection generated was inequitably uneven and incomplete and to some extent discriminated against those most in need. These countries (France, Japan, the Nordic countries, Switzerland, United Kingdom) have therefore made the second tier of personal protection compulsory.

Elsewhere (Australia, Belgium, Canada, the Federal Republic of Germany, Ireland, United States and others) the second tier of personal protection remains free and voluntary. Nevertheless, legislation has been passed to prevent discrimination, tax evasion, financial failures and lack of transparency in fund management. It is also clear that those who benefit most from occupational pensions are in the middle and higher income brackets, in better and more stable jobs and working for more affluent companies.

Social assistance: A change in trend

In the large majority of IMECs, particularly those in Europe, the overall development of social security over the years 1945 to 1975 resulted in a decrease in the relative importance of social assistance compared to other components of national social security programmes. This trend has been halted by the increasing incidence of poverty produced by recession and restrictions in social security programmes. Social assistance programmes have thus generally become more important. Whereas social assistance benefits were previously considered to be a last resort when other social security benefits were not available or were inadequate, they have become the sole form

of protection for increasing numbers of households. Social assistance differs from social insurance in three major respects. First, the cost of benefits is met from general government revenues, not from allocated contributions. Second, while benefits are paid as a legal right, they are payable only if the potential beneficiary can establish that he belongs to a specified category of disadvantaged or handicapped individuals or if the beneficiary is a person or member of a family with inadequate means of support. Third, the benefit, which may be in cash or in kind, depends on the needs of the beneficiary. A needs or means test which takes into account the beneficiary's income (and sometimes his assets) and his family status is normally applied. The benefit is thus determined after a degree of discretion is exercised by the administrating authority, and the objective of a cash benefit is to bring the total income of an individual and his dependants up to an acceptable minimum level.

In some countries, such as Australia and New Zealand, almost all social security benefits are subject to income or asset tests and selective with regard to need. Most other IMECs operate social assistance programmes to supplement social insurance schemes and universal benefit schemes (those which provide cash benefits from general revenue to all persons meeting age and residence qualifying conditions).

In several countries the number of people covered by social assistance has risen strongly in recent years. The number of recipients under the Canada Assistance Plan rose from 1.2 million persons (including dependants) in 1974 to 1.5 million in 1982. In the United Kingdom the average number of recipients of supplementary benefits went up from about 2.8 million in 1973 to 4.5 million in 1983. In Sweden the number of social assistance beneficiaries increased rapidly, from 343,000 in 1980 to 525,000 in 1984 (equal to 6.3 per cent of the population).

The main beneficiaries of social assistance programmes are old-age pensioners, the long-term unemployed and their families and single persons with or without children. Many single parents do not have sufficient resources and/or cannot find a job, while many long-term unemployed no longer qualify for unemployment compensation. As a result, an increasing number of people have become dependent on social assistance.

Expenditure on social assistance has increased correspondingly and now accounts for a high proportion of the total social security budget. In the United States, for example, about one-quarter of social security expenditure is devoted to social assistance while this proportion is about one-fifth in Canada. Between 1970 and 1983 annual per capita expenditure on social assistance in the Federal Republic of Germany increased twice as fast as national income per capita. In France, social assistance expenditure rose by nearly 25 per cent in real terms between 1980 and 1984.

The problem with many social assistance and welfare schemes is that they are scattered and uncoordinated so that they do not cover everyone in need of assistance. There are serious gaps in the income maintenance and support measures of many countries. Individuals and families have inadequate incomes, either because of lack of coverage, or because the level of benefits is too low compared with family responsibilities. Even the so-called "safety net" provisions are sometimes inadequate to alleviate poverty.

Some analysts have suggested that it would be simpler and more efficient to replace various welfare and social assistance programmes targeted on specific groups with a universal guaranteed minimum income, financed from general revenue. Even though such proposals would be very costly they have the virtue of making social protection more effective and of making the labour market more flexible. A first step in that direction would be a gradual modification of social assistance and, more generally, of means-tested benefits. This would aim to make benefits more coherent, effective and comprehensive, and introduce more generous minimum benefits in the various branches of social insurance (pensions, unemployment, family benefits) for those who do not fulfil the qualifying conditions. Examples of such changes can be found in various countries, such as France, Italy and Luxembourg for old-age pensions. Harmonisation of the levels of the various minimum benefits will doubtless be sought, as is already the case in the Netherlands.

4. Concluding remarks

The increase in unemployment since the beginning of the 1970s has accompanied greater instability in trade patterns, financial flows and the rates of exchange and interest. But while during the 1970s rising unemployment was largely related to rapid growth in labour costs, during the 1980s unemployment has increased mainly because of demand factors. There was a general economic contraction in the early 1980s as many governments sought to rid their economies of inflation and inflationary expectations. Restrictive monetary and budgetary policies drove up interest rates which also aggravated the financial situation of indebted developing countries. World trade shrank at the beginning of the 1980s leading to a jump in unemployment.

The deteriorating economic situation has had a profound impact on collective bargaining and social security. At the beginning of the 1980s governments increasingly intervened in collective bargaining and in many Western European countries collective bargaining has become more decentralised. In addition, the content of collective bargaining changed considerably. While during the 1970s employers and trade unions bargained on improvements in wages and conditions of work, during the 1980s they shifted their attention to job security, labour flexibility, new technologies and hours of work.

There is no doubt that the social protection provided by social insurance benefits has deteriorated in many IMECs. While pension benefits and health care coverage have generally been maintained, unemployment and family benefits have often been curtailed. These developments have been partly compensated for by increased government expenditure on social assistance. But the scant available evidence indicates that in some countries this has not been sufficient to prevent an increasing incidence of poverty.

In spite of labour cost moderation in Western Europe and the improved profitability of enterprises, unemployment has not fallen significantly. Monetary and fiscal policies followed by the Japanese and most European governments are still very restrictive and output growth is modest; real interest rates are high and exchange rates, particularly between the United States dollar and the other IMEC currencies, are very volatile. This instability makes it hazardous to invest in employment-generating capital assets and diverts an increasing share of profits into financial investments. Another consequence of labour cost moderation is that the wage share in national income has decreased in many countries, especially in western Europe. This would be acceptable only if it contributes to employment creation and the reduction of unemployment. It would therefore seem desirable to link the degree of wage moderation with the demand policies that governments follow in the future, both at the national and the international level.

Chapter *3*

Centrally planned economies: Employment, productivity and participation

During the 1980s the labour scene in the Centrally Planned Economy Countries (CPECs) has been dominated by the search for a more resource-efficient path of economic development and a new balance between central economic planning and autonomous decision-making by enterprises. The various measures which have been adopted to increase labour productivity will provide a new challenge to maintain full employment (section 1).

Another important development is the push for greater workers' participation at the workplace. All CPECs have been experimenting with work collectives and production brigades, so as to increase efficiency and productivity. This has led to important changes in legislation on labour relations (section 2).

A third development has been the decrease in labour-force growth and the gradual ageing of the population. This has led governments to sharply increase expenditure on old-age pensions and to put in place a series of social security measures to increase birth rates (section 3).

1. Employment and labour productivity

Until the mid-1970s the CPECs enjoyed rapid economic growth, achieved primarily by a steady expansion of the labour force, a high rate of accumulation, the shift of manpower from agriculture to industry, relatively cheap raw materials and energy sources, a fast-growing domestic market, and substantial improvements in productivity. Economic growth has since slowed, more so for some countries than for others, as a result of declining labour force growth and a slowdown in the rate of increase of productivity. In most CPECs labour force growth declined between 1960 and 1980 (see table 3.1), and this trend is likely to continue at least until the end of this century.

Table 3.1. **Annual labour force growth rates: Centrally planned economies, 1960-90 (in percentages)**

	1960-1970	1970-1980	1980-1985	1985-1990
Bulgaria	0.4	0.2	0.0	−0.0
Czechoslovakia	1.2	0.8	0.4	0.5
German Democratic Republic	−0.4	0.6	0.9	0.3
Hungary	1.3	−0.5	−0.0	0.2
Poland	2.0	0.7	0.8	0.5
Romania	0.6	0.0	0.7	0.7
USSR	0.6	1.6	0.9	0.5

Source: ILO: *Economically active population, estimates and projections* (Geneva, 1986).

Trends in employment and labour productivity

Labour productivity is defined as net "material" product per employee, which embraces mainly productivity in agriculture, industry, commerce, transport and communications. (For a recent discussion of some of these statistics, see Selunin and Hanin (1987), and of the need to review the collection of statistics, see Korolev (1987).) CPEC labour productivity so defined grew by 5.1 per cent a year between 1961 and 1975 but decelerated to 3.3 per cent a year between 1976 and 1980 and to an annual 2.8 per cent between 1981 and 1984. Since 1983 labour productivity growth has, however, begun to pick up once more in most CPECs (see table 3.2).

Changes in labour productivity reflect not only the productivity of labour as such, but also the efficiency with which other inputs are used and the rate of technological progress. It can be assumed that improvements in labour quality – due to higher educational and skill attainments – have continued at an unchanged pace. Other factors must therefore have played a role.

Table 3.2. Labour productivity, capital productivity and energy intensity: Centrally planned economies, 1975-86

Country	Labour productivity[1]			Capital productivity[2]		Energy intensity[3]	
	1976-1980	1980-1985	1983-1986[4]	1976-1980	1981-1985[4]	1976-1980	1981-1984
Bulgaria	6.2	3.5	3.9	−1.8	−3.1	−0.1	−2.3
Czechoslovakia	3.3	1.3	2.4	−1.9	−3.4	−0.9	−1.2
German Democratic Republic	3.6	4.3	4.7	−1.5	−0.4	−1.3	−2.8
Hungary	3.7	2.3	2.3	−3.1	−2.8	1.4	−1.5
Poland	0.9	−0.1	5.0	−5.5	−3.4	2.8	1.2
Romania	7.2	4.0	5.6	−2.9	−4.2	−2.1	−3.5
USSR	3.2	3.1	3.5	−2.9	−2.7	−0.7	−1.5

[1]Net material product per employee. [2]Net material product per fixed assets. [3]Total domestic energy consumption per net material product. [4]Estimated.

Source: Economic Commission for Europe: *Economic Survey of Europe in 1986-87* (New York, United Nations, 1987).

Since the mid-1970s capital productivity (the ratio of net material product to fixed assets) has declined in all CPECs. This stems in part from their previous "extensive" approach to economic development. In the USSR, for instance, up to 65-70 per cent of investments at the beginning of the 1980s were used for the construction of new enterprises and only 30-35 per cent for the upgrading and refitting of existing production units. Thus, the fixed assets of many enterprises were renewed only slowly, obsolete and inefficient equipment accumulated, and the new techniques and technology introduced did not offer important advantages in comparison with those already in use. However, most CPECs have been successful in reducing the energy intensity of their production since the mid-1970s, even though its level is still high in comparison with other countries at the same level of economic development.

The economic reforms that have taken place in the CPECs since the end of the 1970s have been aimed at bringing about a more "intensive" resource-efficient path of economic development. While past economic growth was achieved by increasing the *quantity* of production factors, future economic growth is to be achieved mainly by increasing their *quality* and the efficiency with which they are used.

With increasing economic development the share of agricultural workers in total employment has fallen. By 1985 less than 20 per cent of the CPEC labour force worked in agriculture. The share of industrial workers has been broadly stable over the past 15 years in Czechoslovakia, the USSR, German Democratic Republic and Poland but has sharply increased in Bulgaria and Romania, while falling in Hungary. Employment in services has become an increasingly important part of total employment in all CPECs. Table 3.3 shows that in 1984 about 20 per cent of people employed worked in the non-material sphere, including mainly public administration, education, health care, culture and science.

In 1984, the proportion of women workers in the socialist sector varied from 39 per cent to 51 per cent. Over the period 1975-84, this proportion rose fastest in Bulgaria, from 46.9 to 49.6 per cent, and in Romania, from 34.5 to 39 per cent. In the USSR, the proportion of women remained unchanged at 51 per cent of a larger workforce. Similarly, in the German Democratic Republic and in Czechoslovakia, there has been an increase in the number of women workers in the socialist sector but the proportion has remained practically the same.

The economic policy environment

CPECs are firmly committed to the maintenance of full employment. Under the plan system, enterprises and branches of the national economy are allocated labour resources according to their investment, output and labour productivity targets. Labour requirements in total are planned to equal labour availability during the plan period, taking into account the distribution of the workforce by region, sex, age and qualification. Imbalances between requirements and resources are tackled through vigorous policies for education and vocational training, and by altering the regional and technical composition of investment plans.

In principle, the plan determines for each enterprise a production target and the size of the "wage bill" which is based on planned labour requirements and average wages.

During the bargaining that takes place as part of the planning process, managers of enterprises tend to ask for more workers – and consequently for a higher wage bill – than they strictly need. This makes it easier to fulfil plan targets and protects them against the eventuality of more demanding planned targets in the future. Managers may also wish to protect themselves against unforeseen manpower needs in the short run, for example, due to irregular deliveries, high labour turnover, unavailability of workers with

Table 3.3. **Distribution of employment in the material and non-material sphere: Centrally planned economies, 1985 (in percentages)**

	Bulgaria	Czecho-slovakia	German Demo-cratic Rep.	Hun-gary	Poland	Roma-nia	USSR
Material production	82.3	78.9	79.7	80.7	81.4	87.4	76.1
of which:							
Industry and construc-tion	45.6	47.0	50.3	38.5	37.7	44.5	38.3
Agriculture and forestry	21.1	13.6	10.6	22.7	29.1	28.9	19.4
Transport and communi-cations	6.7	6.6	7.3	8.1	6.2	7.1	9.2
Commerce[1]	8.5	10.8	10.5	10.4	8.0	5.8	8.0
Other	0.4	0.9	1.0	1.0	0.4	1.1	1.2
Non-material sphere	17.7	21.1	20.3	19.3	18.3	12.6	23.9
Total em-ployment	100.0	100.0	100.0	100.0	100.0	100.0	100.0

[1] Including material supply and procurements.

Source: CMEA: *Statistical Yearbook* (Moscow, 1985), pp. 395-397.

certain skills, or absenteeism. In addition, undertakings in most CPECs (except Hungary and Poland) are responsible for retraining redundant workers and/or finding a new job for them within the undertaking. As a result, there is considerable labour slack in many CPEC enterprises, though less in manufacturing sectors such as textiles than in, for example, construction. Some commentators, such as Havasi (1984), have therefore argued that the socialist state has a duty to guarantee *full* employment, while *efficient* employment is the responsibility of enterprises. This raises the issue of the autonomy of enterprises which will be discussed in the next section.

Other factors have also contributed to inefficiency and low productivity. There is a growing tension between an increasingly qualified and educated labour force and the given structure of available jobs that often require much lower skills. Present systems of work organisation and remuneration sometimes provide few incentives for increased efficiency and productivity. In addition, relatively high labour turnover in many CPECs contributes to low productivity.

Economic measures to improve labour productivity

Since the end of the 1970s CPECs have introduced various reforms to improve their use of resources. One important strategy included in most current five-year plans is to accelerate scientific and technological progress. National programmes have been accompanied by changes in the common policy of the Council of Mutual Economic Assistance (CMEA). The CMEA Summit in 1984 was followed by adoption of the Comprehensive Programme for Scientific Progress. This provides a blueprint up to the year 2000 and selects five priority areas for co-operation between CMEA countries: computerisation; comprehensive automation; nuclear power engineering; new materials and technologies for their production and processing; and biotechnology.

The CPECs are also reviewing investment policies to give more attention to research and development and technical reconstruction. Enterprises have been granted greater autonomy and financial responsibility. In some countries reforms in the organisation of foreign trade presage their greater integration into the world market. Special attention is being paid to the speedier implementation of research and development findings in the production process.

The efficiency of modern production depends not only on investment and technology but also on skills, work organisation and incentives. Workers need to upgrade their skills to be able to work with new technologies. Work organisation needs to provide more incentives for efficient production. Thus, most CPECs have extended the use of semi-autonomous work groups or "brigades" (see also section 2) and introduced various wage incentives (see chapter 8). Measures have also been taken to strengthen labour discipline.

One example of the trend towards improved work organisation is the introduction of "certification" of workplaces, designed to boost efficiency. Certification is the joint responsibility of trade unions and management, and its content and periodicity can be regulated by collective bargaining. The workplace is evaluated against up-to-date technical, technological, organisational and social standards. For instance, the evaluation examines use of shifts, labour productivity and the amount of idle machine time. In the German Democratic Republic, 60 per cent of all workplaces in industry, construction and transport underwent this certification process between 1976 and 1985, and the system has now been introduced in the USSR. During the current five-year plan about 7 million workplaces will be certificated. This is expected to lead to the release of 600,000 to 650,000 workers, who will be re-employed elsewhere.

In most CPECs the wage bill and other enterprise funds were originally determined by central directives. They are now much more dependent on efficiency criteria. At the beginning of the 1960s the material incentive fund was introduced which inter alia determines part of the remuneration of managers. The fund's size is related to changes in labour productivity and the fulfilment of the production plan and delivery obligations. Many CPECs have now also introduced more flexible allocation of the wage bill. For example, enterprises may be authorised to increase wages if they are able to meet the production target with fewer than the planned number of workers. In other cases, the size of the wage bill itself is made dependent on production and/or profits.

The possibilities and limits of central planning have been a much debated issue in most CPECs over the past few years. There is generally no disagreement about the fact that central planning (in a modern and updated form) is a powerful instrument in promoting economic and social development. There is an increasing conviction that in order to improve productivity and efficiency more autonomous decision-making of enterprises is required concerning the use of major production factors, including labour. But views diverge on the economic context within which this increased autonomy should be achieved: a centralised model based on direct instructions from above or a decentralised model in which central policies are supported by indirect regulations through taxes and subsidies and in which enterprises independently set their production and employment targets and allocate available resources.

Working time arrangements and productivity

Working time arrangements have recently been used as part of policies designed to boost productivity and improve conditions of work and employment. Efforts have in particular been directed at encouraging potential workers to enter the labour force in order to overcome labour shortages; and at responding to the needs of workers, in particular women and pensioners, for more flexible and in some cases shorter working hours.

The pace of innovation in working time arrangements has accelerated, stimulated by plans for a larger and more responsive commerce and services sector, increased emphasis on better management of working time and diversification in the organisation of work.

Part-time employment

Part-time employment is increasingly promoted in the CPECs in order to encourage the use of untapped labour resources, in particular women with family responsibilities, pensioners, students and handicapped people, many of whom wish to work if their special needs can be taken into account. Women already have a high labour force participation rate in the CPECs and thus the question is not one of how to increase the percentage who want to work full-time but how to attract to part-time work those who are still in the home. Pensioners often wish to work (either part-time or full-time) in order to keep up social contacts, remain active and obtain additional income. Most of them have already acquired experience and skills in the jobs concerned. Students also constitute a large group of potential workers (part-time during the school year and full-time during the summer holidays). They are often eager to gain work experience and to earn extra. Finally, handicapped people are often interested in social activity and wish to make a useful contribution under suitable conditions of employment.

According to recent surveys carried out in 120 enterprises in light industry and engineering, transport, commerce and community services in different regions of the USSR, 75 per cent of working women would prefer some sort of part-time employment. Among the reasons given were care of children (62 per cent of the sample), desire to have more free time (14 per cent), housekeeping (11 per cent) and poor health (7 per cent).

Part-time work also has a number of production advantages. It may help ensure more effective use of machinery and equipment, and increase the availability of goods and services, especially in the evening hours. Absenteeism and turnover tend to be lower among part-time workers. According to estimates from a study by the All-Union Central Council of Trade Unions (AUCCTU), labour productivity of part-timers was 8 per cent higher than that of full-time workers and labour turnover 10-15 per cent lower.

Part-time employment in the centrally planned economies now concerns a significant and growing proportion of the wage-earning population. In Czechoslovakia 8 per cent of research workers are part-timers; in Hungary, more than 6 per cent of workers in education are engaged on a part-time basis; in Yugoslavia, about 10 per cent of those working in the services sector are part-timers. In the USSR, among 11 million working pensioners, 5.2 million or 47 per cent are in part-time work. In Bulgaria and Hungary, the number of students who continue their studies while doing part-time work is growing especially rapidly and has already reached 10-11 per cent. In the German Democratic Republic, more than one-third of working women are part-time.

Data for the USSR show that 33 per cent of all part-timers are pensioners (see box 3.1), 16 per cent are handicapped persons, 15 per cent are working students and 36 per cent are women (mostly housewives). Two-thirds work in commerce, communications, catering, health services, culture and education. One-third are working in light industry and the food industry.

CPECs have often taken account of the special needs of groups such as working mothers in their regulations of part-time work. For instance, a 1980 order of the State Committee for Labour and Social Affairs (USSR) and the Secretariat of the AUCCTU specifies that part-time work should be governed by an agreement between the enterprise and the worker after consultation with the trade union committee, stipulating the length of employment, daily or weekly hours of work and other relevant conditions such as further training or refresher courses. If more than four hours' work are involved in a day a meal break is granted. In addition an infant feeding break of between 30 minutes and one hour must also be granted after three hours of work. The break must be paid and counted as working time. It may be added to the meal break or taken at the end of the shift.

Most enactments in CPECs referring to part-time work give part-timers the same privileges and advantages as full-time employees, including length of basic annual leave, seniority and uninterrupted service benefits, and access to work-related welfare facilities and services.

Overtime and multiple job-holding

Overtime is generally not available as a means of overcoming labour shortages or extending the operating time of enterprises in CPECs. Overtime

---

3.1   Employment incentives for pensioners

Recently, various incentives have been introduced to encourage pensioners to take jobs. In the USSR, for example, it was permitted for pensions and wages to be paid together, partially or totally, first of all in a number of sectors or regions where there were labour shortages, and then, starting from 1980, throughout the USSR. In 1981, almost 32 per cent of pensioners were employed (or 6.5 per cent of the active population). In the Russian Socialist Federated Soviet Republic, the public authorities have recommended that up to 35 per cent of pensioners should be drawn into the production process. Other countries, such as Bulgaria, the German Democratic Republic, Poland and Czechoslovakia have introduced similar types of incentives on a relatively large scale. In Bulgaria, since 1984 pensioners accepting work in some economic sectors have been entitled to a full pension. Previously had been reduced in respect of earnings. Similarly, in Czechoslovakia, there has been no restriction since 1984 on the payment of a full pension in addition to earnings for large groups of workers. It should also be noted that in Bulgaria, the USSR and particularly in Czechoslovakia, people who delay retirement are given an increased pension (in Czechoslovakia it is increased by 7 per cent for each year of work beyond the statutory retirement age).

---

work is usually prohibited by basic labour legislation and can be undertaken only in exceptional cases and with the consent of the local trade union committee. These exceptional cases include work in the public interest, national necessity, emergencies and some seasonal processes. Even in these cases, overtime cannot be authorised for certain groups of workers (pregnant women, nursing mothers, young workers, workers attending training courses or evening school, and so on).

In addition to these restrictions, there is usually a maximum limit on overtime, which is 120 hours per year in Bulgaria, Czechoslovakia, the German Democratic Republic and the USSR. Overtime is generally rewarded by premiums which depend on the number of consecutive hours worked above normal hours. In some cases, compensatory time off is granted to the workers instead of extra payment.

However, workers are often allowed to have a second job, in the same or in a different enterprise, individually or in brigades according to a separate labour contract.

Stimulation of multiple job-holding (job-combining) is receiving special attention at the moment. Changes in the economic environment (labour shortages, the need to use human resources more effectively) and in the composition and attitudes of the workforce (a higher level of qualifications and the desire to increase living standards) have led to development of various forms of multiple job-holding. In most of the countries of Eastern Europe, this type of arrangement is widely used on an experimental basis and is also supported by recent legislation, for example in Bulgaria, Hungary and the USSR. In Bulgaria, for example, any worker or employee may accept extra work at the normal place of employment above regular duties. Another arrangement allows workers to carry out small subcontracting services for their enterprise outside normal hours of work.

Permission to work on a job-combining basis has so far been treated very cautiously and mostly concerns the replacement of workers who for various reasons are absent from work. The second job must not interfere with regular employment. For this reason, an enterprise manager may revoke authorisation to hold a second job if this leads to lower productivity or some other violation of labour discipline in the main job. People can be dismissed from their second job without the agreement of the local trade union committee and without severance pay.

Job-combining schemes have been introduced on a trial basis in the Chelyabinsk region (Urals, USSR) and several other highly industrialised regions. The majority of multiple jobholders – 63 per cent – are manual workers. Engineers and technical personnel make up 20 per cent and office workers account for 11 per cent of the total. Job-combining has given enterprises participating in the experiment a 2 per cent increase in labour resources. During nine months in Chelyabinsk district alone, about 10,000 people undertook second jobs in manufacturing, construction, transportation, commerce and food services. More than 8,000 chose second jobs within their own enterprises.

Maintaining the balance between labour requirements and resources

Full employment in the CPECs has not given rise to generalised labour shortages. However, at the national level, there has been excess demand for particular types of labour in particular jobs. In the German Democratic Republic and in Hungary, for example, there is a shortage in blue-collar unskilled jobs, especially arduous and unpleasant jobs usually done by men. Such shortages stem in part from the mismatch noted earlier between rapidly rising qualification and education levels and the nature of the jobs available. Even in these cases, "local labour markets" differ; shortage of labour in the German

Democratic Republic is mostly restricted to the industrialised South; in Hungary to the capital and to some industrial centres; and in the USSR to the mostly European centres of industry and the pioneer industrialisation settlements of the East. Other regions generally have better labour "fit", while some may have considerable labour reserves.

The path of resource-efficient economic growth will involve profound changes in the social division of labour, structure of employment and labour mobility. Under these conditions maintaining the balance between labour requirements and resources will present new challenges. Workers may be released on a large scale since productivity growth is planned to outstrip output growth in the CPECs and particularly in the USSR.

The right to work has in the past been largely associated with the right to employment in some specific permanent post. For the future, enjoyment of the right to work will inevitably entail a higher degree of labour mobility.

There is already a fairly high degree of labour mobility between enterprises within regions of CPECs, particularly in regions with labour shortages. Labour mobility increased considerably in Hungary at the beginning of the 1980s when workers wanting to change jobs no longer had to go through labour placement offices. About 1 to 1.5 million people – one-fifth of the workforce – changed jobs around this time. In the USSR 70-80 per cent of workers are now hired directly by enterprises.

How will the CPECs deal with large numbers of released workers? Part of the answer lies in improving the system of placement, retraining and material support for these workers. In all the countries under review (except Hungary and Poland) enterprises are still obliged to redeploy released manpower. However, placement offices are increasingly taking over the redeployment function, at least in most European CPECs. They are likely to encounter problems including the possible necessity for workers to change their skills, habits and maybe their homes. Scientific and technical progress requires training workers and employees for more general trades and professions, both for blue-collar and white-collar workers, and mastering adjacent professions.

The redistribution process must take into account the expected fall in the number of people employed in material production. According to some economists, far-reaching shifts will also take place with the expected reduction in manual labour. Some of these people will find a role in renovated and reconstructed workshops equipped with modern, highly productive equipment and the others should be retrained and employed in new enterprises.

With the shift towards a more resource-efficient pattern of economic growth, labour shortages may become a thing of the past. The German Democratic Republic, Hungary and Czechoslovakia have all largely overcome shortages. In the USSR, according to some calculations, 13 to 19 million people will be released from various material production jobs over a 15-year period, permitting a substantial expansion of services. For instance, hundreds of thousands of teachers are needed to make classes less crowded and to staff pre-school children's establishments.

How long does it take workers to find new jobs in CPECs? Information on new jobs can be obtained from placement offices, advertisements at special stands, and enterprises themselves. In Bulgaria, computerised information systems have reduced the period between inquiry and rehiring to an average of 4-5 days. In the USSR the figure is from 18 to 28 days. In all European CPEC countries workers are directly informed by their enterprises of any suggested reorganisation of production and redistribution of the labour force. Workers are offered at least three new jobs close to the former job in wages and skill level. If additional training is necessary this is normally provided by the recipient organisation. Pay allowances for workers who change jobs have also been introduced.

Since the beginning of the 1980s various CPECs have expanded the possibilities for work in the private and individual sector, though in most countries this accounts for no more than 5 per cent of employment. The German Democratic Republic has issued new licences for private entrepreneurs and improved the conditions under which they can operate. In Hungary legislation since 1980 (and especially since 1982) has permitted various forms of private enterprise (with up to ten employees) in addition to traditional private small-scale production and retail trade. In the past few years, production in the Hungarian private sector has grown much faster than in the State-owned sector. In Poland the private sector has been traditionally dominant in agriculture. Recent legislation has opened new possibilities for the private sector to ease problems of capital and labour shortages in the State-owned sector.

In the USSR, a Law on Individual Labour Activities was adopted in 1986 to improve the provision of services to the population and expand employment. The Law permits some individual labour activities (provided they do not involve hired labour) in areas such as services and the production of certain goods. These individuals will either pay taxes on their earnings or buy licences (permits) legalising their rights to self-employment. The Law, which came into force on 1 May 1987, lists 29 legal individual labour activities, such as taxi-driving; care of the elderly; tailoring and shoemaking; and repair of household appliances, clothes and shoes. However, this list may be enlarged by local authorities as appropriate.

2. Reforms in workers' participation

During the first half of the 1980s, new economic reforms were introduced in order to speed up the "intensive" development of the CPECs. Their essential objective is to increase further the autonomy of the enterprise vis-à-vis the central bodies of the State. The move towards greater enterprise autonomy has resulted in a series of additional measures designed to link pay with work performance and to improve workers' participation. (For a description of the scope of collective agreements and workers' participation, see box 3.2.) The emphasis has switched from expanding the participation rights of workers' representatives in the management of the enterprise towards increased participation of individual workers in the organisation of production.

The following account of changes in labour relations systems will concentrate on measures introduced in the USSR. But other CPECs have introduced similar measures, sometimes pre-dating those in the Soviet Union. For example, "brigade"-type experiments were initiated some years ago in Hungary and Czechoslovakia, and more recently in Poland and Bulgaria. These involve a contract between the management of the enterprise and a group of its workers, under which the group commits itself to carrying out a specific task in exchange for remuneration which depends upon results. The lump sum is distributed amongst the members of the group according to the contribution of each worker to the common task. In December 1982 the Council of Ministers and the Central Council of Trade Unions in Hungary granted new rights to production conferences and general assemblies of trade union members, and a further Decree in 1984 assigned a

3.2   The scope of collective agreements and workers' participation

Collective agreements must be concluded each year, in principle at the level of the undertaking. They are prepared and signed by the trade union committee and the management of the enterprise. The collective agreement must reflect the possibilities offered by economic growth and must not depend on the simple bargaining power of the parties concerned. Account must be taken of the objectives of the economic Plan, the funds allocated to the enterprise and social planning requirements.

Basic wages are fixed at the national level by the public authorities which establish minimum and maximum rates after consultation with the central trade union organisation. The State and central trade union authorities also fix the periodic adjustments to basic wages. Collective agreements determine how the regulations are to be applied at enterprise level; for example, they adapt the centrally-established remuneration schedules which are necessarily of a fairly schematic nature and contain provisions on how to distribute wage adjustments, which are not necessarily the same for everyone. Collective agreements also make provision for material incentives, in the form of bonuses and social benefits which are financed by special funds using part of the profits of the enterprise.

Collective agreements cover a number of other subjects apart from wages. These include: methods of fulfilling plan targets; ways of boosting productivity through improvement in skills; organisation of work; production standards and work discipline; and improvement of working conditions and the development of welfare services (for example, canteens, nurseries, housing, holiday and rest homes) and cultural and sporting activities. Other provisions contained in collective agreements cover such matters as the individual employment relationship (for example, recruitment, trial period, dismissal), the prevention of accidents, social insurance and medical care. Any dispute between the management and the trade union committee during the negotiation of the collective agreement is settled by the State and higher trade union authorities.

In addition to collective agreements, there are other forms of participation by workers in enterprise decisions. The trade union committee ensures application of the collective agreement, which may involve co-decision powers, usually involved in labour inspection, and acts in certain other areas such as the appointment or possible dismissal of executive staff. A number of bodies operating under the aegis of the trade union committee (for example, labour productivity councils, "creativity" bodies) also play a role in decision-making, and the direct participation of workers is further promoted by campaigns like "socialist emulation", that is, permanent competition between enterprises, workshops and workers.

In CPECs, the differences between the negotiation of collective agreements and other forms of participation are much less marked than in IMECs. This reflects the fact that in the countries of eastern Europe, trade unions play a fundamental role in all forms of participation, whereas the market economies establish a very clear conceptual distinction between collective bargaining, in which the partner on the worker side is the trade union, and other forms of participation in which the partner is the workforce as a whole, whether trade union members or not.

Trade unions in the CPECs play a key role at the central level in addition to wage fixing. The central trade unions represent the interests of workers in the formulation of national medium-term plans. They ensure that economic resources are equitably distributed between investment and consumption, participate in discussions on new remuneration systems and control the application of labour legislation. In some of these countries, the trade unions are also entrusted by the State with the responsibility of managing the part of the national budget allocated to social security.

major role to workers in the management of small and medium-sized enterprises. Similar measures have been taken in Czechoslovakia, Romania and Poland.

The USSR introduced new rules in 1983 on work collectives and in 1984 on production brigades (see box 3.3). The collective is "an association of all workers performing work in common in a state or social undertaking, institution, organisation, collective farm or other co-operative organisation". These include collectives in shops, services and subdivisions within the enterprise. Under the 1983 enactment, collectives are called upon to encourage a more rational utilisation of human and material resources, better work organisation and remuneration systems which strengthen incentives. Work collectives are also granted certain decision-making powers. They are now responsible for approving collective agreements before the trade union committee can sign them. They are also empowered to take certain decisions themselves concerning the distribution of material

incentive funds and to impose sanctions on workers who do not respect work discipline.

According to the report made by Mr. Nikolai Ryjkov, Chairman of the Council of Ministers of the USSR, to the 27th Congress of the Communist Party of the Soviet Union in March 1986, the new methods of management were at that time being applied in enterprises accounting for half the country's industrial output, in the communications system, the services industry and some transportation enterprises. It was expected to extend these methods in 1987 to all industrial and transportation enterprises and subsequently, within the shortest possible time, to the entire economy. In an earlier address to the 27th Congress, Mr. Mikhail Gorbachev, General Secretary of the Communist Party, said progress had been made in the application of the new management methods, but much still remained to be achieved. He stressed the need to approach the task by "resolutely enlarging the framework of the autonomy of associ-

3.3   Production brigades in the USSR

The brigade "associates the manual workers for the joint performance of a task in the most efficient manner on the basis of comradely mutual assistance and of a common interest in and responsibility for the results". Allocation to a brigade is subject to the consent of the worker concerned. The management of the enterprise decides whether he or she should be recruited into the brigade after taking into account the views of the existing brigade membership. The purpose of the 1984 Decree is to promote a new type of brigade, based on the principle of profitability ("economic accounting"). These brigades are remunerated according to the final results of their work and collective profits are distributed amongst the members on the basis of a work participation co-efficient. Contracts fix the mutual obligations of the management of the enterprise – for example, the provision of equipment and necessary resources for production – and the brigade – for example, the quantity and quality of the products and delivery dates. Within the framework established by the contract as well as by certain other regulations drawn up at higher levels, the brigade enjoys a large measure of autonomy in the management of production and the distribution of collective profits. The brigade has the right to propose different ways of increasing productivity. Its members must approve the proposals of the brigade leader for the fixing of individual work participation coefficients. It can establish its own fund for socio-cultural needs and decide on its use. The brigade operates according to democratic principles: thus the agreement of the general meeting of the brigade is necessary for the appointment of the brigade leader by the management of the enterprise; in the same way it is the general meeting itself which decides to what extent it will directly exercise the powers which the law confers on the brigade and which powers will be delegated to the brigade council which it elects.

ations and enterprises, increasing their responsibility for attaining the highest ultimate results". To this end it was necessary "to transfer them to genuine cost accounting, self-support and self-financing and to make the income level of collectives directly dependent on the efficiency of their work".

The USSR has recently experimented with more advanced forms of autonomy in some undertakings, with a view to revising legislation on socialist enterprises. The well-known experiment of the Byelorussian railways has now been followed in ten other railway undertakings in the country. In the Byelorussian experiment, the workforce was reduced by 12,000 people, 4,500 of whom went on retirement, with the others being retrained and placed in jobs with no loss of pay. The workers remaining in the undertaking gained wage increases as a result of increased productivity. These decisions were taken only after a referendum in which a large majority of workers expressed support for more productive work in exchange for an increase in wages. Subsequently

workers participated in the preparation of rationalisation measures within their collectives. The problem of deciding which workers to dismiss was also finally settled at the level of the work collectives, although not without difficulties since in some cases the trade union refused to approve the dismissals and in others, the workers concerned took their cases to the courts.

The experience with this and other experiments led, at the beginning of 1987, to the publication of a draft law on state enterprises, which is expected to be submitted to the USSR Supreme Soviet.

The draft law is aimed at reinforcing centralisation principles in the settlement of national economic problems; at broadening democratic principles; and at promoting the self-management of enterprises. It provides for independent use by enterprises of their self-financed income which cannot be claimed by the State. On the other hand, the State bears no liability for the obligations of individual enterprises. The enterprises use their own incomes to set up wage and social development funds as well as the fund for the development of production, science and technology.

Managers will be elected by a general meeting or a conference of the work collective for a term of five years. Shop superintendents, foremen and team-leaders are elected for a term of two to three years.

The draft law proposes that a work collective will exercise its rights and powers through a general meeting or a conference. Both a general meeting and a conference are empowered not only to elect managers but also to consider the plans for economic and social development of the enterprise, approve the collective agreement with the management, and discuss other important issues relating to the operation of the enterprise. During the period between meetings and conferences their powers are exercised by the Work Collective Council elected by them.

If the law is adopted, it is likely to lead to strengthened powers for trade unions and workers in general and, as a result, to a greater emphasis on collective bargaining and participation. But it is difficult to forecast what the probable scope of this movement will be. That will depend directly on the effective degree of freedom given to enterprises, and on what is finally considered as the "optimal compromise" between centralisation and decentralisation.

3. Social security

In the CPECs expenditure on social security is financed from the so-called social consumption funds.

The percentage of these funds in national income has gradually increased over the past 10 to 15 years, and can vary between 12 and 25 per cent, depending on the country (see also chapter 8). Roughly 70 per cent of these funds is directly financed by the state budget, while the remaining part is funded by state enterprises and organisations and by collective farms.

Social consumption funds are divided into two parts. The first part includes cash benefits which are directly paid to the population, such as pensions, scholarships and paid holidays. The second part finances public services, such as health care, education, housing and cultural activities. The share of pensions and grants in total social consumption fund expenditure has increased between 1975 and 1984 in most countries (except in the German Democratic Republic) (see table 3.4). The share of family benefits has generally remained constant (not shown in the table).

Although social security systems in CPECs follow common policies, there are differences between countries which reflect economic circumstances and national traditions. In particular, some countries have been affected more than others by world recession. Everywhere, however, demographic concerns and constraints have played an important part in recent developments in social security and have resulted in rapidly rising expenditures.

Depending on the country and the period, the increase in expenditure has been covered either by raising the budget subsidy, or by increasing contributions. This increase may be very steep. For example, in Poland, the contribution from enterprises, which was set at 25 per cent of wages up to 1982, is currently 43 per cent. In Bulgaria, the contribution rate was raised from 15 to 30 per cent in 1980. In Hungary, the contribution for state enterprises, which amounted to 24 per cent in 1979, is now 40 per cent. (One of the purposes of this heavier burden was to give employers an incentive to use their labour force more efficiently and economically.) In other countries, where contributions have remained more stable, the state subsidy has tended to rise, for example, in the USSR.

There have been some interesting recent changes in the administrative organisation of social security. With the exception of Poland, where there is a Social Insurance Institute, pension insurance is traditionally administered by the public authorities and the payment of short-term cash benefits and the provision of a whole range of social services is entrusted to the

Table 3.4. **Expenditure on pensions and grants, as a percentage of total social consumption fund outlays: Centrally planned economies, 1975-84**

Country	Pensions and grants		
	1975	1980	1984
Bulgaria	44.1	45.8	44.0
Czechoslovakia	48.3	49.7	48.9
German Democratic Republic	38.7	37.1	31.7
Hungary	56.0	58.2	58.1
Poland	39.8	44.8	42.9
Romania	51.9	51.0	55.3
USSR	37.3	37.9	40.3

Source: G. Kertesi and G. Kövári: *Real wages in Eastern Europe* (Budapest, 1986; mimeographed).

trade unions. Two countries have recently given up this format, Bulgaria and Hungary, both in 1984. In these two countries, where the administration of social insurance was carried out under the supervision of the trade unions, it has been transferred to the State.

Pension schemes

The demographic situation in the CPECs has had a fundamental influence on pension policy. In some countries, such as Bulgaria, the German Democratic Republic and Hungary, the population of working age is increasing very slowly or not at all. CPECs are also confronted with the ageing of their populations. The retirement age is set fairly low (60 for men) in most of these countries, and there is a high proportion of retired people. They accounted for 11.4 per cent of the population in the USSR in 1975 and 13 per cent in 1982. In Bulgaria, Czechoslovakia, the German Democratic Republic and Hungary, pensioners currently constitute more than 20 per cent of the population.

As a result, expenditure on pensions as a percentage of national income has increased very substantially over the past 10 to 15 years (table 3.5). Where pensions and wages could not be paid simultaneously, the growth in pension schemes resulted in a very appreciable decrease in the employment of the elderly. But recently this policy has changed, as was documented in section 1.

In 1984, average pensions as a proportion of monthly average wages ranged from about 36 per cent in the German Democratic Republic and the USSR to about 58 per cent in Hungary. Over the last few years there has been moves to counteract the deterioration in the purchasing power of pensions. This has occurred in the USSR, for example, in spite of the price stability of essential products. Moreover, because the level of pensions was fixed long ago and the earnings of the working population have been rising, a gap has opened up between workers and pensioners. The value of pensions in payment over a number of years has fallen steadily behind, hitting many of the very old and the long-term disabled. The issue of the readjustment of "older" pensions was officially raised in the 11th Plan (1981-85). Priority will be given to people currently receiving the lowest benefits.

Steps have also been taken to adjust minimum pensions. In Poland, since 1983, minimum pensions have been set as a percentage of the minimum wage (90 per cent). In other countries, where the minimum pension is a flat-rate benefit which had progressively lost value in relation to wages, the pension level has often been appreciably increased over the last few years. For example, in the German Democratic Republic the fixed amount used in the calculation of the various pensions was raised in 1985 from 110 to 140 marks. In the USSR the same year, minimum pensions for workers on collective farms were increased by 45 per cent. Starting from 1988 in Poland, pensions will be readjusted annually in line with the increase in average wages, and in the USSR "older" pensions will be adjusted every two years.

The East European countries have also taken steps to improve social security for workers in agriculture. Efforts in this direction have been motivated by the long-term goal of reducing the disparities between town and country and in some cases by the more immediate aim of improving the efficiency of agriculture (USSR, Yugoslavia, Bulgaria, Poland, Romania).

Family benefits

Demographic concerns, notably the abrupt decrease in the birth rate, explain why over the last few years particular emphasis has been placed on measures to assist the family. This is undoubtedly the most notable trend in the recent development of social security in East European countries. To encourage a higher birth rate, new cash benefits have been introduced and existing benefits have been improved.

Table 3.5. **Pensions paid as a percentage of national income: Centrally planned economies, 1975-84**

	1975	1980	1984
Bulgaria	6.7	8.1	8.8
Czechoslovakia	7.8	9.0	10.0
Hungary	6.3	9.3	10.7
Poland	4.3	7.4	8.8

Source: See table 3.4.

Two new benefits are expressly intended to help women reconcile their maternal and occupational obligations. The first of these is *leave to care for children* – or extended maternity leave – which was introduced some time ago in Hungary and has become commonplace in East European countries (with the exception of Romania, where only unpaid leave or part-time work to care for children is envisaged). This benefit enables mothers to extend their maternity leave beyond its statutory duration to care for their child in its first months, and even its first years (in Hungary, the father can benefit from this measure). It is consequently a contributory factor in improving the quality of care for young children. The allowance is either proportional to wages (in the German Democratic Republic), equivalent to the minimum wage (in Bulgaria and Poland), or a flat-rate benefit. In Poland entitlement to the allowance to care for children is conditional on the family income level. The period during which the allowance is payable varies: it is provided until the child reaches one year of age in the German Democratic Republic and the USSR, and up to the age of three in Hungary. In Poland it may be paid for up to 24 months until the child is four years old. In Hungary, this allowance is paid each year to from 5 to 6 per cent of wage earners and it is claimed mostly by workers on lower levels of wages. In some countries, the extended maternity leave may be followed by leave without pay.

The *assistance allowance* was introduced at the beginning of the 1980s and is intended for workers who have to care personally for a sick child at home. The level of the allowance is generally the same as the daily sickness benefit and its maximum duration varies widely according to the country in question: two months in Bulgaria and Poland; four to eight weeks according to the number of children in the German Democratic Republic; one month in Hungary (two months for young children); and seven days for each case of sickness in the USSR (this period will be extended to 14 days during the 12th Plan). In Czechoslovakia the parents are given 3 to 6 days paid leave for a sick child up to the age of 10; single parents are entitled to 12 days for each case of sickness.

A measure intended to encourage maternity among economically active women is the *maternity allowance* (a benefit compensating for loss of earnings during and after the birth of a child). This is quite generously set: 100 per cent of wages in Bulgaria, the German Democratic Republic, Hungary, Poland and the USSR, and 90 per cent in Czechoslovakia. The period during which the benefit is payable, which is nowhere less than sixteen weeks, has been appreciably extended in recent years in Czechoslovakia and the German Democratic Republic (26 weeks), Bulgaria (from 24 to 32 weeks) and in Hungary (24 weeks).

In addition, in the USSR since 1985 time spent bringing up children is taken into account when calculating women's pensions, while the pensionable age is only 50 for women who have brought up five children. In the German Democratic Republic women with one child receive one year of credit on their pension contribution scheme, while those with three children receive three years for each child. Under a 1984 disposition women can receive the minimum pension after 15 years of work. They usually receive the full pension only after 45 years of work.

Family allowances, another measure favouring an increase in the birth rate, generally rise with each subsequent child, though in some countries they decline after the third or fourth. They are provided for the first child, except in the USSR where they are awarded only to large families. (In view of the widely varying birth rate from nationality to nationality it is difficult to have a straightforward fertility policy in the USSR.) The level of family allowances in relation to the average wage is quite high (with the exception of the German Democratic Republic and the USSR), as shown by table 3.6.

Table 3.6.   Family allowances for two children as a percentage of the average wage: Centrally planned economies, 1980s

Country	Year	Percentage
Bulgaria	1980	22.2
Hungary	1980	24.9
Poland	1984	19.6
Romania	1980	17.0
Czechoslovakia	1980	20.0

Source: E. Borowczyk: "State social policy in favour of the family in East European countries", in *International Social Security Review* (Geneva, ISSA), No. 2, 1986, pp. 164-182.

4. Conclusions

Since the beginning of the 1980s, CPEC governments have undertaken a series of economic and social reforms that may have a long-lasting influence on the labour situation. Though full employment has been maintained, governments have been increasingly worried by the decline in productivity growth. This has encouraged them to increase the autonomy of enterprises and work collectives, introduce more flexible working time arrangements, and provide new oportunities for workers' participation in work collectives and enterprises. Social security policies have been altered to help overcome labour shortages by drawing pensioners, women and youth into the labour force and, in some countries, to boost the birth rate. At the same time, there is an increasing demand from women and other workers for part-time and more flexible work arrangements.

Thus, the CPECs are facing various challenges: to increase productivity, to meet the demand for flexible work arrangements and greater participation, and to maintain an adequate rate of employment creation. This requires a rethinking of the relations between central planning and the autonomy of enterprises (particularly in the areas of investment and employment). Another issue will be the relationship between the trade unions and the newly established work councils and work collectives.

Part 2

Incomes from work:
Between equity
and efficiency

Introduction

Those deriving their incomes from work can be separated into two main groups: the self-employed and employees. The self-employed directly receive the rewards of their labour, either by consuming what they produce (for example, in agriculture) and/or by gaining a profit from the sale of their output. Employees are engaged by a public or private employer and receive wages (in cash and/or in kind) for the work that they perform.

It is normally not possible to determine which part of self-employment income is due to the input of labour. Self-employment income is the joint result of various inputs. In agriculture, these will include land, agricultural equipment, irrigation, and seeds, while outside agriculture they may be machinery, buildings, energy and credit. Strictly speaking, it is thus not completely correct to compare wages with self-employment incomes but for lack of alternatives this comparison has to be made in practice (see box p2.1).

There are large labour income differentials between countries. The productivity of an hour's work in industrialised countries is normally much higher than that in developing countries, because industrialised countries have a better developed infrastructure, make use of more know-how and produce with more and more sophisticated capital equipment. Within countries, there may be large differentials between rural and urban areas, between wages from regular employment and other forms of labour incomes and personal incomes from capital.

The question arises whether certain labour income differentials within countries are equitable and/or efficient. Naturally, opinions about what is equitable and what is efficient diverge considerably. There is likely to be even more controversy about whether equity or efficiency considerations should predominate in particular economic, social and political circumstances. To pave the way for this debate, it is worth identifying a few main criteria against which equity and efficiency can be assessed.

As regards *equity*, a paramount concern is, of course, improvements in the overall distribution of income by reducing existing inequalities and by raising the incomes of the lowest paid or most in need as quickly as permitted by the process of economic growth. Many people in the world live in intolerable conditions. They are permanently hungry; they are sick or very likely to become so; they live in shacks or huts; and they cannot afford to send their children to school. As was shown in chapter 1, the number and even the proportion of those living in poverty has been increasing in many countries over the past few years.

But other standards of equity are frequently invoked as well, in particular regarding the determination of wages. There are the notions of "equal pay for equal work" or "work of equal value" which are included in ILO's Convention No. 100. Ideas of equity also underly the frequent reference made to the protection of purchasing power or "acquired rights". Finally, the wage determination process itself may be called equitable, if both employers and workers have ample opportunities to voice their views and to participate in decisions on terms and conditions of employment.

In the context of labour incomes, the notion of efficiency will be understood as the extent to which the structure of self-employment incomes and of wages contributes to economic growth and to other economic objectives such as low inflation, full employment and equilibrium on the balance of payments. In the case of self-employment incomes, greater efficiency means above all higher productivity. Without large increases in productivity, it will not be possible to eradicate poverty. Such increases can be achieved by private or state investments in people as well as in land, capital and tech-

---

p2.1 **Statistics on labour incomes and prices**

It is much more complicated to measure self-employment incomes than wages. Measuring self-employment incomes requires a detailed overview of all cost items as well as receipts. This is information that must be collected in enterprise and/or household surveys. Such surveys are expensive and, where they have been carried out in developing countries, this has normally been done only at long, irregular intervals. As a result, statistics on self-employment incomes over a period of time are often not available.

Statistics on wages are much more widely available and most of those used in Part II are taken from the ILO's *Year Book of Labour Statistics* and the ILO's October Inquiry. In general, they relate to *average earnings* per wage earner or, in some cases, *wage rates*.

Information on average earnings is taken from payroll data supplied by a sample of establishments. Average hourly earnings are obtained by dividing total payrolls by total person-hours worked (or paid for) during the pay period. Earnings are usually cash payments which remunerate workers for normal working hours and overtime. They also include bonuses, cost-of-living allowances and special premiums, but exclude employers' contributions to social security. Taxes and workers' contributions to social security are usually deducted from earnings and it is the resultant net earnings which provide spendable income. But statistics on net earnings are very rare, so "earnings" quoted in this report are gross.

Statistics on wage rates are mainly based on collective agreements, arbitration awards or (minimum) wage-setting decisions. They refer only to payments in cash or in kind for adults working normal hours, that is, excluding overtime payment and other supplements, but often including cost-of-living allowances.

Whenever there is a choice, we have preferred to use earnings rather than wage rates, because they give a more accurate picture of workers' purchasing power. However, earnings data may be less comparable between countries because they often cover quite different groups of the working population, such as employees, skilled or unskilled wage earners. In addition, they may refer to different time periods (per hour, day, week or month). On the other hand, wage rates cover only wage earners and are usually given by the hour. (For more details see ILO, *Statistical Sources and Methods, Volume 2: Employment, wages and hours of work (establishment surveys)* (Geneva, 1987)).

The general price index for the country as a whole has usually been used to calculate real wages and real incomes from self-employment. There are many problems involved in correctly measuring price changes over time (see the results of the 14th ILO Conference of Labour Statisticians, October 1987). In many countries, the true increase in prices is underestimated because controlled rather than market prices for food and rent have been used to calculate the price index.

---

nology and by improving their efficient utilisation. In the case of wages, efficiency considerations play a role at various levels. Wage determination can contribute to the attainment of macro-economic objectives, and also to allocative and operational efficiency. Allocative efficiency is achieved when wages provide incentives for workers to move from jobs or labour markets where a surplus exists to those where labour is in short supply. Operational efficiency is achieved when wage incentives contribute to a better use of available production factors.

1. Incomes from work in developing countries

For the large majority of households in the developing countries (DCs), labour is the main income-earning asset. For most rural households, the natural option is to engage in farming. If they do not possess land, they may rent land (as a tenant or a share-cropper), they may engage in non-agricultural self-employment and/or individual household members may look for wage employment. Urban households have a different set of options: urban wage employment (regular or casual) or self-employment in

industry and services. Each household will choose the combination of available labour income opportunities which enables the household, first and foremost, to survive and, secondly, possibly to increase its standard of living. This process of choice is a continuing activity of households and often involves looking for work far away from home. In Central America and India, for example, peasant or "unpaid family workers" may temporarily travel to far-away plantations to help with the harvesting or with construction programmes. Rural households or individual household members may migrate permanently to the cities in order to find a job in the formal or "informal" sector. In some countries, such as Brazil, groups of urban workers travel around in rural areas to help during the harvest season.

Three chapters deal with different labour income-earning opportunities for rural and urban households in DCs (see figure 2.1). Chapter 4 – on income from rural work – examines labour remuneration in agricultural self-employment and in regular or casual rural wage employment. Chapter 5 discusses wages from regular urban employment. Chapter 6 – on vulnerable workers in urban areas – describes the marginal position of an increasing number of self-employed and casual wage labourers in urban areas.

Figure 2.1.   Labour income-earning opportunities for rural and urban households

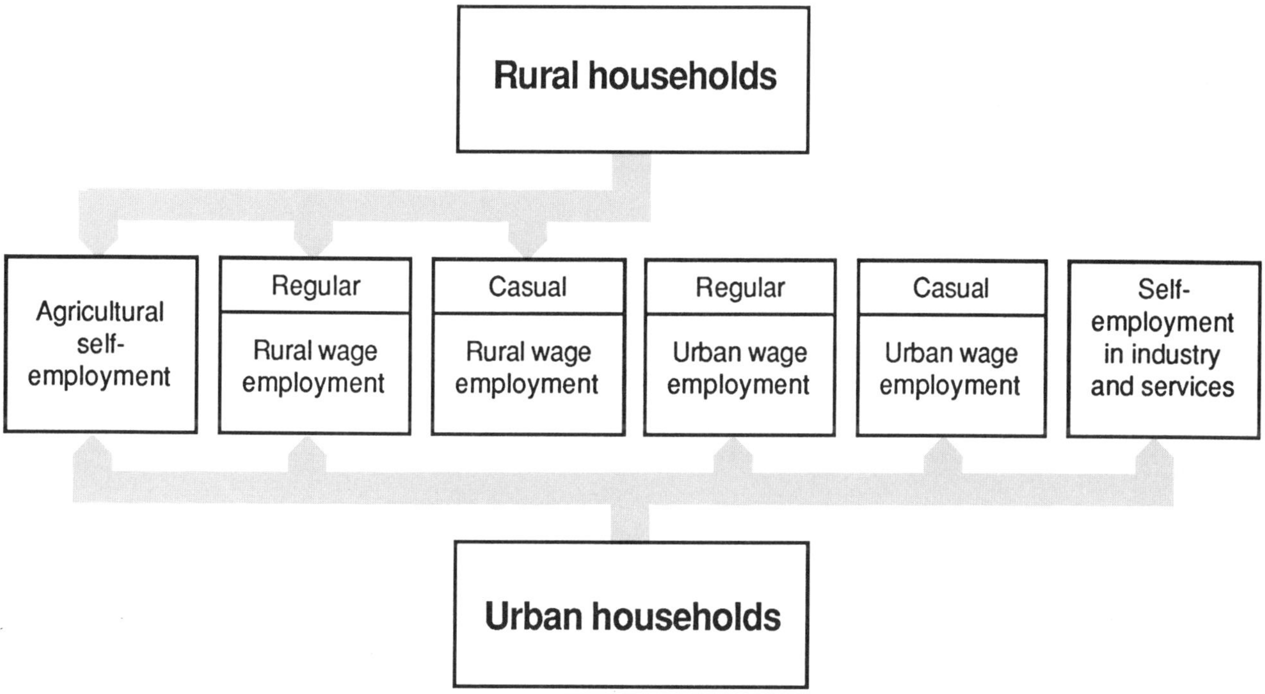

2. Wages in industrialised countries

Wage determination systems must resolve as best they can the conflict between equity and efficiency in four distinct domains.

The *first*, and in many respects the most fundamental, is the general level of wages. Chapter 7 suggests that during the 1970s relatively high wage levels in many industrialised market economy countries (IMECs) contributed to increasing unemployment. However, recent changes in real wages have been more moderate, and it was shown in chapter 2 that, within the national incomes of many IMECs, wage incomes have lost some ground to capital income during the 1980s.

The *second* domain concerns the timing and magnitude of wage adjustments in order to adapt the general level of wages to changing economic conditions (consumer prices, productivity, employment, and so on). Chapter 7 discusses the various formal and informal wage policies that governments and the social partners have conducted in IMECs. The main aim of incomes policies in the 1970s was the reduction of inflation, while equity considerations (increase in minimum wages and expansion of social security) also played an important role. This

emphasis shifted in the 1980s to the reduction of unemployment. Wage indexation, which during the 1970s was still considered an "acquired right", was called into question. In centrally planned economy countries (CPECs), too, efficiency considerations have become more important. Chapter 8 shows, for example, that wage bill and material incentive fund regulations have been changed in order to reduce labour hoarding and to increase productivity.

The *third* is the pattern or structure of wage differences amongst various groups of workers (for example, differences between similarly qualified workers in different parts of the country, types of economic activity or enterprises or between different occupational categories, or between the sexes). Wage inequality between sectors and occupations in CPECs tends to be lower than in IMECs. However, CPECs are now experimenting with larger wage differentials between occupations so as to increase the efficient utilisation of manpower. In IMECs, wage differentials between men and women have been reduced. However, the question of occupational segregation remains an important problem both in IMECs and CPECs.

The *fourth* domain concerns "wage systems" or the various procedures and rules established at the enterprise level to determine workers' remuneration. This remuneration consists of direct wages (in cash or in kind) and indirect remuneration, such as pay for time not worked, social security benefits, irregularly paid bonuses or gratuities, and welfare for employees. In both IMECs and CPECs, there has been a shift away from the traditional piece-rate systems, in the search for new performance criteria including a greater interest in group forms of remuneration. Both sets of countries have also made more use of systems linking pay to company performance – financial participation and profit sharing in IMECs and material incentive fund bonuses in CPECs.

Chapter 4

Incomes from rural work in developing countries

More than 60 per cent of the labour force in developing countries (DCs) work in agriculture. However, there are wide variations between various groups of DCs (see table 4.1). Agricultural workers account for more than two-thirds of the labour force in sub-Saharan Africa, China and southern Asia, but only about 40 per cent in North Africa and western Asia, and less than 30 per cent in Latin America. These shares are still very high in comparison with the industrialised market economy countries (IMECs) and the centrally planned economy countries (CPECs) – 7 and 17 per cent respectively in 1985. There is also a wide variation in the participation of women in the agricultural labour force, ranging from over 40 per cent in sub-Saharan Africa, China and the CPECs to about 10 per cent in Latin America. Part of these differences can be explained by the fact that women's economic activity in agriculture is often underestimated (see *World Labour Report*, Volume 2, chapter 13).

This chapter concentrates on the two main income sources of the majority of rural households: income from self-employment and family labour, and income from wage labour. To explain the levels and trends in these incomes, it is necessary to take into account the main factors that determine overall rural development, such as output growth, productivity and the terms of trade (towards both the urban and the foreign sector). Access to land, water and credit are important conditions for earning an income from self-employment. Rural wages are influenced by various characteristics such as education and skill, which condition the bargaining power and mobility of labour. The share of wage labour in agriculture is usually low (between 5 per cent in sub-Saharan Africa and 40 per cent in Latin America) and labour markets are not as developed as commodity markets. Economic factors such as wage contracts are often less important than institutional factors such as race, sex,

Table 4.1. Agricultural workers in the labour force; women in the agricultural labour force, 1970-85 (in percentages)

	Agricultural workers in the labour force		Women in agriculture	
	1970	1985	1970	1985
Developing countries				
Sub-Saharan Africa	77.6	70.4	43.9	43.6
Latin America	40.6	28.9	9.7	11.9
North Africa and West Asia	58.0	42.7	25.2	29.1
China	78.3	71.0	44.2	45.9
Southern Asia	70.9	66.0	28.9	26.1
South-East Asia	64.7	52.0	38.2	36.9
DCs	70.7	62.3	37.3	37.7
IMECs	12.3	6.8	35.3	37.5
CPECs	27.5	16.9	52.2	49.4
World	55.0	48.7	38.0	38.1

Source: FAO: *World-wide estimates and projections of the agricultural and non-agricultural population segments, 1950-2025 (a provisional report)* (Rome, 1986).

and availability of land and credit. Rural labourers, especially those with little or no land, may depend on personalised relationships which determine their ability to find work and the level of wages received. Similarly, many small cultivators are dependent on such relationships for access to land, credit and other inputs.

For most rural households labour is the main income-earning asset. Investigating the linkage between poverty and dependence on labour, Lipton (1983) argued that: "The economic circumstances of people in very poor households are largely defined by food and work. Some 70-85 per cent of outlay is needed to obtain food, and this seldom leaves much prospect of either using time or accumulating savings to acquire skills or assets. Therefore, the great bulk of poor people's household *income* derives from unskilled labour, either hired out or combined with inexpensive owned or rented assets such as small areas of unirrigated land … Thus poor households … depend for their well-being mainly on being able to transform time and strength into labour income" (p. 4).

Most rural households simply try to make ends meet and to survive. Some household members may find a permanent or casual job in agriculture or construction while others may engage in informal non-farm activities. However, rural households that own a piece of land will mainly try to intensify the labour input on the household farm. This usually results in higher output per unit of land but not necessarily per unit of labour.

This chapter is divided into three main sections, dealing separately with each of the three major developing continents – Africa, Asia and Latin America. Each section first examines the main determinants of overall rural and agricultural development, and then goes on to consider the factors that enhance or constrain employment opportunities in rural economies and the determinants of labour incomes.

1. Africa

Africa is a continent much more agriculture-oriented, much more agricultural-export-oriented, and much less commercialised than the other developing continents. It has also been in a longer and deeper economic recession. Moreover, Africa itself is a continent of great diversity, from the northern Mediterranean countries to the southern dependency economies.

Contrasts and similarities between African countries

The northern countries have economies characterised by a relatively high degree of industrialisation and urbanisation. These economies have also experienced large-scale migration flows – in particular after the oil booms in the Gulf countries. In consequence, agriculture in the northern African countries has been relegated to a minor role as a generator of income. However, agriculture still employs over two-fifths of the population and thus continues to be an important provider of livelihood for many people. Smallholdings exist, but are marginal to commercialised

agriculture and, for reasons of cultural heritage and the large scale of farming operations, women play a much smaller role in agriculture here than elsewhere in Africa.

The southern African countries of Botswana, Lesotho and Swaziland share agricultural characteristics with the core sub-Saharan African (SSA) region – small-scale farms, subsistence orientation, and reliance on mostly hand-hoe technology. However in one important respect they differ from the other SSA countries – their dependence on the Republic of South Africa. In Lesotho practically one-half of the male labour force works in South African mines and the same is true, although to a smaller extent, for Swaziland and Botswana. Wages in South Africa are much higher than incomes from domestic agriculture – which, of course, explains the "pull" of South Africa – but as a result agriculture is not an important income generator. With the men away in the mines, women play an even bigger role in agriculture here than in the core SSA region; indeed by some accounts agriculture suffers from a "labour shortage" which further explains its peripheral place in the local economies. The dependence on South Africa is also felt in the lack of leeway in setting prices for agricultural commodities.

Our concern here is with the core SSA countries for which certain important distinctions must be noted. First, the impression that African agriculture consists mostly of crop culture should be dispelled. In many countries – the Sahelian countries, Somalia, even Botswana – pastoralism is more important than cultivation, and it is a key feature of agricultural activity elsewhere, often practiced along with crop cultivation. Climate is an important determinant of the extent of pastoralism.

Climate also affects the types of crops grown, a second differentiation within SSA countries. Cereals, particularly maize, characterise the northern semi-arid areas, while root crops and tubers are more common in the humid climates of the south. The dominant cereals grown in African countries are maize, sorghum and millet and the dominant roots and tubers, cassava, sweet potatoes and plantains. Sorghum and millet are "inferior" cereals in African hierarchy; maize is the preferred domestic cereal. However in the urban areas tastes have changed significantly to wheat and rice, cereals which are not widely grown in Africa, a fact which largely explains the increasing import-dependence of most African countries.

Table 4.2.   Characteristics of agriculture in Africa and other developing regions, 1978-80

	% of economically active population in agriculture	Cultivated area per person economically active in agriculture	% of cultivated irrigated area	Tractors per 1,000 ha of cultivated area	Fertiliser consumption (kg) per ha of cultivated area	Cereal yield (kg/ha), 1975-77
Africa	69.8	1.5	1.7	1.4	8.2	850
Far East	62.8	1.0	24.8	2.0	35.1	1 700
Near East	54.0	2.5	21.4	6.6	33.0	–
Latin America	34.7	4.2	8.6	5.4	42.2	1 600

Note: The first five columns follow FAO usage: Africa includes all African countries except South Africa, and Egypt, the Libyan Arab Jamahiriya and the Sudan which are classified as Near East. In the last column the figures for Africa are for SSA only, while the figure for Far East is that reported for "Asia" in the source. These latter figures have been read approximately from a chart.

Source: FAO: *Socio-economic indicators relating to the agricultural sector and rural development* (Rome, 1984), tables 1, 3, 7, 9 and 11, except last column which is from United States Department of Agriculture: *Food problems and prospects in sub-Saharan Africa: The decade of the 1980s* (Washington, DC, 1981), figure 5.

A third basic difference is in terms of the colonial legacy. Most countries in West Africa remain closely tied to France in trade and highly dependent on French financial assistance. Their external adjustment policy options are restricted by their participation in the Franc Zone. Thus, devaluation as a remedy for external imbalances is not available to them. The rest of the countries in the region, the vast majority being former British colonies, have diversified their trading partners and have exchange rates linked to the dollar. Obvious exceptions are the former Portuguese territories which have chosen socialist economic models.

A fourth important differentiation relates to government pricing policies. There are no completely free-market economies – even in Kenya or Côte d'Ivoire, often cited as market-oriented economies, the State intervenes in important ways in setting agricultural prices. But degrees of intervention range from mild (Kenya, Côte d'Ivoire, Malawi) to significant (the United Republic of Tanzania, Uganda, Ethiopia). By and large, however, despite the differences in ideology, government pricing policies have until recently discriminated against the agricultural sector, though there are now signs of a turnaround.

A final distinction concerns "engines of growth". For most African countries agriculture is still the driving force of the economy, but there are some important exceptions, notably those economies which are mineral-driven and those which are remittance-driven.

Nigeria with its huge oil wealth is the clear case of a mineral-driven economy in Africa. Other African oil economies are Gabon and the Congo. Non-oil minerals have been important in various other countries, such as Botswana, Zaire and Zambia. Economies where the impetus to growth has come from remittances of migrant workers include the southern African countries (migration to South Africa) and the northern African countries and the Sudan and Somalia (migration to the Gulf).

Thus differences abound. But even when countries have been or have recently become dependent on non-agricultural sources of growth, they still remain basically agricultural in the sense of supporting a majority of their populations in the agricultural sector.

Main characteristics of the agrarian economy

The agricultural sector itself exhibits a number of uniform traits which have a bearing on incomes from rural work. These traits are captured in the table above (table 4.2) which at the same time provides comparative data for the other developing continents.

Small farms, poor technology and low yields sum up the situation in African agriculture. These features are of course linked. Lack of mechanised technology ensures that areas cultivated by the average farm family remain small, while the small size of farms means that modern mechanised technology cannot be economically applied. The low level of technology, especially use of fertilisers, then translates itself into low yields. These factors condition incomes from work in a rather deterministic manner.

Small farms are also characteristic of agriculture in Asia and Latin America but the technology applied in both these continents, as evinced by the use of fertilisers, tractors and irrigation, is much more advanced. Yields are higher and have increased quite appreciably in those regions, whereas in Africa they have stagnated. There has been no "green revolution" in Africa of the kind experienced in Asia and Latin America, partly because of the types of crops grown.

The small size of farms and low yields explain many other characteristics of the African agricultural sector. For the most part an average farmer's energy is taken up with providing food for his own family. Typically one or two staple crops provide the bulk of calories, with a variety of vegetables making up the rest. Specialisation within broad ecological zones is limited, constraining the possibility of exchange. Trade takes place mostly with the towns – to sell staples to the growing urban population and in the opposite direction to acquire non-staple or "town" foods, such as sugar, salt, tea, spices, and non-food needs such as cloth, soap, matches, and utensils. The limited extent of urbanisation constrains the commercialisation of food crops – the usual reckoning being that in most SSA countries only 15 to 25 per cent of food crops are marketed. Conversely, although the rural market is large numerically, its purchasing power is limited by low commercialisation and for most consumer goods the major market in African countries remains in the urban areas.

Thus, as far as food crops are concerned, most African farmers operate on a subsistence basis – that is, they are self-sufficient in basic calories. They do produce a surplus, but its extent is limited. Since own-consumption is the principal objective, price changes have little impact on this part of the farmers' output. This has important implications for understanding the performance of the food sector in Africa.

But African farmers also cultivate crops for export – mostly beverages such as coffee, cocoa, or tea, and fibres such as cotton. Domestic consumption of these crops is generally small or negligible, although after independence a greater share of cotton began to be used in local industry. Thus the return to export crops is determined largely by external markets (barring government interference in the markets, which is discussed later).

Export crops are grown under similar conditions to food crops – on small family-owned farms, using similar technologies. In fact, one of the distinguishing characteristics of African countries is that export crops and food crops are grown together by most farmers, regardless of size, often on the same farms and even on the same plot of land. Although plantations exist – called "estates" in Africa – by and large one cannot speak of "export crop farmers" or "food crop farmers" as distinct entities: everybody is both, or at least everybody who is an export-crop grower is also likely to be a food-crop farmer, and every farmer, at least in the export zone, is likely to cultivate at least some export crops.

Despite the high degree of subsistence in Africa, the economies of the region are remarkably "open". Export earnings of low-income SSA countries represent 16 per cent of gross domestic product, nearly twice the 9 per cent average for all low-income developing countries. In middle-income SSA countries exports represent 22 per cent of GDP (29 per cent if oil-rich Nigeria is excluded) compared with an average for all middle-income DCs of 25 per cent. As a proportion of cash GDP, the export ratio would be even greater. For both low and middle-income countries, however, the proportion of economic output exported has declined steeply in the past two decades as a result of deteriorating export demand and terms of trade (see next section).

The openness of African economies means that they are basically export-driven: not only do exports constitute a large part of cash incomes, they also affect directly a country's ability to import basic necessities and essential inputs for agriculture and industry. A great deal of the economic contraction in African countries can thus be attributed to the direct and indirect impact of changes in the external environment.

So far, we have been considering factors affecting returns to farmers – that is, the return to labour with land. In Africa, this is the principal form of labour in rural areas. Rural wage earners exist but their numbers are quite small – perhaps no more than 5 per cent of the total labour force on a permanent basis. Considerably greater numbers take up seasonal employment on outside farms, sometimes on a reciprocal basis and usually with food rather than wages as compensation. They mostly comprise younger male members of a farm family rather than heads of households, attesting the fact that there is as yet very little landlessness in Africa – 5-10 per cent of households perhaps being its outer limit.

Thus, the household decision to allocate its labour resources to agricultural wage employment has to be seen in relation to differential access to land, rather than landlessness. While it is often argued that there is no shortage of land in Africa, it is also the case that in Africa as elsewhere, land is scarce for the poor and abundant for the rich. In consequence, rural to rural migration in search of wage employment, frequently over long distances, is a common phenomenon in SSA countries. Some of this migration occurs across national borders – for example, the migration of labour from the Sahel countries of Burkina Faso and Niger to coffee and cocoa-growing areas in Côte d'Ivoire and of Ghanaians to the oil boom of Nigeria.

Economic contraction in Africa

One dismal characteristic shared by almost all SSA countries since the first oil price shock of 1973-74 has been deepening economic crisis. Table 4.3 documents the poor performance of the SSA countries between 1965 and 1985, which is contrasted with other developing countries.

· During just eight years of this period, 1965-73, per capita GNP increased by 17.2 per cent in SSA; in the next 12 years it declined by 8.3 per cent. SSA's 1985 GNP per capita was thus only 7.5 per cent above 1965 levels – a rate of growth of just 0.4 per cent a year. The African performance was much worse than that of all low-income DCs combined (including Africa). Asian DCs doubled their per capita income in the 20-year period under consideration. Latin America and the Caribbean fared less well, recording strong negative growth in the first three years of the 1980s, but still managed an overall increase of 56 per cent for the 20-year period. Moreover, Latin America and the Caribbean began to recover in 1984 and

Table 4.3. Rates of growth of GNP per capita: Developing countries, 1965-85

	1965-1973	1973-1980	1981	1982	1983	1984	1985
SSA	2.0	0.5	3.8	−5.0	−5.5	−4.5	−0.6
Low-income developing countries	3.0	2.7	3.0	3.2	6.1	7.4	6.1
Asia	3.3	3.0	3.5	3.7	6.9	8.3	6.6
All developing countries	4.1	3.2	1.0	−0.7	0.0	3.3	2.4
Latin America and the Caribbean	4.5	2.9	−4.2	−4.9	−4.5	1.2	2.1

Source: World Bank: *World Development Report* (Washington, DC, 1986), p. 156.

Table 4.4. Rates of growth of GNP and agriculture, and per capita food production in SSA countries, 1965-84 (% per annum and index)

Country	GNP 1965-1973	GNP 1973-1984	Agriculture 1965-1973	Agriculture 1973-1984	Index of per capita food output, 1982-84 (1974-76 = 100)
Cameroon	4.2	7.1	4.7	1.6	83
Côte d'Ivoire	7.1	3.7	3.7	3.3	110
Ethiopia	4.1	2.3	2.1	1.2	100
Ghana	3.4	−0.9	4.5	0.2	73
Kenya	7.9	4.4	6.2	3.5	82
Liberia	5.5	0.2	6.5	2.0	91
Malawi	5.7	3.3	n.a.	2.5	100
Nigeria	9.7	0.7	2.8	−0.5	96
Senegal	1.5	2.6	0.2	−0.2	66
Sierra Leone	3.7	1.8	1.5	2.0	95
United Republic of Tanzania	5.0	2.6	3.1	n.a.	100
Uganda	3.6	−1.3	3.6	−0.7	98
Zaire	3.9	−1.0	n.a.	1.4	92
Zambia	2.4	0.4	2.0	1.0	74
Zimbabwe	9.4	1.7	4.7	1.6	69
Low-income SSA [1]	3.7	2.0	2.6	1.4	92

n.a. = not available.

[1] Low-income SSA countries are those earning up to US$380 per capita. Of the above list, Cameroon, Côte d'Ivoire, Nigeria, Zambia, and Zimbabwe belong to middle-income countries (US$450-1,620 per capita).

Source: World Bank: *World Development Report* (Washington, DC, 1986).

1985, whereas Africa's plight has continued to deepen. The poor performance of the SSA region is reflected in individual country figures (table 4.4). With the exception of Cameroon and Senegal, all the countries shown experienced significant declines in their rate of growth after 1973. In fact, Cameroon, Kenya and Malawi were the only African countries to see any growth in GNP per capita in the crisis period. The story is the same for agriculture. All countries except Sierra Leone registered lower growth in 1973-84 than in 1965-73, and no country managed to achieve positive per capita growth in the agricultural sector. Finally, the table shows that only in Côte d'Ivoire was food production per capita higher in 1982-84 than in 1974-76. In Ethiopia, Malawi and the United Republic of Tanzania it held its own, while in the rest it declined, in some, such as Senegal and Zimbabwe, quite precipitously. As a result, cereal imports rose sharply. In 1969-71 imports constituted 6.2 per cent of the total supply of cereals (production and imports) of SSA; by 1980-82 the ratio had risen to 17.2 per cent, and since then it has probably reached at least 20 per cent.

The role of economic policies

Exogenous factors such as drought and tumbling world commodity prices certainly explain part of Africa's dismal economic performance. In addition, some countries have been badly afflicted by political instability and warfare. Equally, there is no doubt that much of the considerable *variation* in performance between African countries, both before and after the crisis, can be attributed to differences in policies pursued.

A recent assessment of successes and failures in African development up to 1982 (Ghai, 1987) has demonstrated the crucial importance of a sound and well-conceived policy framework. For rural development such a framework should include maintenance of real producer prices at reasonable levels, a well-functioning transport, marketing, credit and extension system, and ready access to a wide range of consumer goods and agricultural inputs.

Most of the criticism relates to policies which have discriminated against the agricultural sector. Critics point to the low level of government investment in agriculture, in relation to other sectors and by comparison with the resources extracted from agriculture in the form of export taxes. They also accuse governments of mismanaging the agricultural price determination system by keeping prices paid to farmers artificially low. But, as explained earlier, in the subsistence context prices have a very limited impact on production decisions. Farmers will continue to produce food for their own consumption regardless of the level of prices.

As far as the impact on marketed output is concerned, it is necessary to distinguish between export crops and food crops. Prices of export crops are greatly influenced by external conditions, while prices of food crops are more easily influenced by governments.

External conditions have been extremely unfavourable to African countries, much more so than in the other developing regions. From 1965 to 1978, primary product exports of SSA grew by 4.5 per cent per annum. After that, growth slowed to just over 1 per cent per annum for seven years and became negative in the first three years of the 1980s. Altogether, SSA's primary product exports have

hardly increased since 1973. Simultaneously, SSA's terms of trade deteriorated significantly. Having remained practically constant between 1965-73, they then declined by 23 per cent between 1973 and 1982. Despite some recovery in the next few years, terms of trade in 1985 remained nearly 20 percentage points below their value in 1973, meaning that African countries had to export 25 per cent more to buy the same import bundle as before.

Export performance has a great influence on total economic activity in African countries. In most they constitute the greatest part of cash incomes. Directly (export taxes) and indirectly (import duties) they determine government revenue. By affecting the ability to import, they affect production in the import-dependent industrial sector, as well as in the agricultural sector. Infrastructure is also import-intensive, so lack of foreign exchange has been a crucial cause of the deteriorating infrastructure in African countries. Thus in a very real sense the weak export market has contributed to a cumulative decline in economic activity.

Many critics have argued that over-valued currencies have been partly responsible for the poor performance of the export sector. On this view, the erosion of purchasing power of farmers' incomes due to local inflation needs to be offset by a devaluation which has the effect of raising prices of export crops in domestic currency terms.

But it is not at all certain that devaluation would generate a dramatic improvement in agricultural production. World demand for a number of commodities remains stagnant. And with the breakdown of transport, processing and marketing facilities, higher domestic prices have lost some of their power to elicit a bigger supply response. Devaluations may then simply fuel further inflation in the economy.

Government policies are also blamed for performance in the food sector. As in virtually every country of the world, African governments intervene in the food markets, in the African case with the objective of ensuring cheap food for the urban areas. But the impact of their intervention – which at first sight looks extensive – is often over-estimated. First, state intervention is heavily concentrated in two crops, rice and wheat, which are not the most common African staples. Second, in most countries, price controls affect decisions only on surplus production, not total production. Third, given the simple technology used, output is much more sensitive to exogenous influences such as climate than to prices. Indeed, there is considerable scope for dramatic increases in output (and, therefore, incomes) as a result of technical change. Fourth, transaction costs for African farmers are high, particularly transport costs. Marginal price changes for bulky products such as grains and tubers may have little impact when marketing systems are underdeveloped.

Finally, and most importantly, controls are far from effective, particularly for crops produced largely on smallholdings – millet, maize and tubers. With the emergence of "parallel markets", government-controlled prices are no longer the relevant prices in most African countries. The parallel market has emerged precisely to bypass unremunerative government prices and, far from being an aberration, it is now the dominant market in most African countries where price controls are applied. Under free market conditions, prices in the parallel market have easily matched local inflation.

If marketed output has fallen we have to look for other reasons. The breakdown of infrastructure is one of these, as has been the drop in effective demand from urban areas due to declining real incomes (see below). These points do not imply that low prices for food crops have not constrained marketed production or that higher prices are not appropriate. But it is probably a mistake in the African context to put too much weight on the output-changing impact of prices alone.

In Liberia and Zimbabwe, for example, prices received by farmers for marketed crops have substantially outstripped the prices they have had to pay for fertilisers over the past few years. In neither country did the agricultural sector perform particularly well (though Zimbabwe had an excellent 1985 harvest), nor on average did they do better than four countries - Central African Republic, Kenya, Mali and Togo – in which internal terms of trade moved against agriculture.

However, as table 4.5 shows, in some countries farmers have experienced a severe drop in the "real" prices they receive for their crops due to domestic inflation, which was not offset by currency devaluation. In Ghana and Uganda the purchasing power of farm prices fell catastrophically. In the United Republic of Tanzania, too, farmers' terms of trade fell. In absolute terms, by 1983 the fall was 15 per cent measured against 1975, or 35 per cent compared to 1978, when prices were at an all-time high because of the coffee boom. Overall, domestic terms of trade of

Table 4.5. Ratio of producer prices received to rural consumer price index: African countries, 1972-85

Country	1972	1975	1978	1980	1981	1982	1983	1984	1985
Ghana									
Cocoa		100	40	47	23	55	24	29	36
Food		100	146	–	–	–	–	–	–
Uganda									
Cotton	100	61	26	14	39	26	30	40	–
Coffee	100	84	31	18	49	34	42	52	–
Sierra Leone									
Coffee		100	–	167	131	82	–	–	–
Cocoa		100	–	188	140	96	–	–	–
Rice		100	–	84	73	71	–	–	–
United Republic of Tanzania									
All crops		100	131	103	96	87	85	–	–

Note: 1981 marks the start of currency reform in Uganda.

Sources: Hamid Tabatabai: *Economic decline: Access to food and structural adjustment in Ghana* (Geneva, ILO, 1986; mimeographed World Employment Programme research working paper); Vali Jamal: *Structural adjustment and food security in Uganda* (Geneva, ILO, 1985; mimeographed World Employment Programme research working paper); and *Poverty and inequality in Sierra Leone* (Geneva, ILO, 1984; mimeographed World Employment Programme research working paper); and ILO estimates for the United Republic of Tanzania.

export crops fell by around 40 per cent between 1976 and 1984.

However, it is a mistake to attribute changes in internal terms of trade to government policy alone. Prices paid by farmers include products with a high import content – fuels, fertilisers, pesticides, and hybrid seeds. Even the non-input purchases of farmers – mostly consumer goods produced by local industries or imported – are usually import-intensive in African countries. Thus, increases in import prices have raised the general price level facing the farmers, an effect governments can do little to counter without introducing subsidies. The United Republic of Tanzania is a prime example of how agricultural production can be undermined by changes in the external terms of trade and shortage of foreign exchange. Estimates suggest that more than 40 per cent of the unit value of coffee exports represents foreign exchange spent on inputs. Shortages of fertiliser, pesticides, and fuel for vehicles have all reduced the export capacity of agriculture.

Rural incomes

If export volumes and prices have fallen, and food production per capita has fallen, then farm incomes must obviously have declined in the SSA countries, in real terms and perhaps in nominal terms as well. However, the decline has been less catastrophic than accounts of "crisis in Africa" would suggest, as a result, first, of internal migration and, secondly, the subsistence orientation of farmers.

Migration remains at high levels in African countries – compared to pre-crisis days and to other developing countries. Thus between 1973 and 1984 the rate of growth of urban population in low-income SSA was estimated at 6.1 per cent per annum, only marginally below growth of 6.2 per cent per annum for the period 1965-73. Given that the urban population was around one-fifth of the total in 1984 and that total population was growing by 2.9 per cent per annum, it may be inferred that the agricultural population was growing at only 2 per cent per annum. Table 4.6 sets the growth of agricultural production against the expansion of the agricultural labour force to derive a crude measure of "agricultural productivity".

Given the nature of the data, only figures above 1 per cent may be taken as significant. On that basis, in only four countries – Ghana, Nigeria, Senegal and Uganda – did agricultural productivity decline. All except Senegal are special cases: in Ghana there was a drought in the early 1980s affecting food crops while cash crops were affected by pricing policy. The same applies to Uganda. In Nigeria agricultural cash crops collapsed because of the oil boom. But by the same 1 per cent criterion, only in Sierra Leone was agricultural productivity growth positive. Thus the table suggests little or no improvement in agricultural productivity in most African countries.

Incomes from family farming

The key point for the purposes of determining incomes from agriculture is that average production per member of the agricultural population at least remained constant in most African countries. As the last column of table 4.6 shows – although for a different time period – food production per member of the agricultural population held up quite well. Thus the shortfall in food production per capita noted earlier is not to feed the rural population but rather the urban population. African farmers, by and large, have maintained their ability to feed their own families ("subsistence orientation"); but their revenues from the sale of food and export crops have generally fallen.

Table 4.6. Rate of growth of agricultural production, labour productivity and food production: African countries, 1970-84 (per cent per annum)

Country	Agricultural production (1)	Economically active agricultural population (2)	Labour productivity (3)=(1)-(2)	Food production, 1970-82 (4)
Cameroon	1.6	1.1	0.5	2.1
Côte d'Ivoire	3.3	2.7	0.6	6.0
Ethiopia	1.2	1.0	0.2	1.7
Ghana	0.2	1.2	−1.0	−0.2
Kenya	3.5	2.6	2.9	2.0
Liberia	2.0	1.8	0.2	3.0
Malawi	2.5	2.0	0.5	2.9
Nigeria	−0.5	0.9	−1.4	2.5
Senegal	−0.2	1.4	−1.6	1.5
Sierra Leone	2.0	1.0	1.0	1.2
United Republic of Tanzania	n.a.	1.8	n.a.	2.1
Uganda	−0.7	1.8	−2.5	1.7
Zaire	1.4	1.4	0.0	1.3
Zambia	1.0	1.5	−0.5	1.8
Zimbabwe	1.6	1.8	−0.2	1.6

n.a. = not available.

Source: (1) From World Bank: *World Development Report* (Washington, DC, 1986); (2) and (4) based on FAO: *Production Yearbook 1982* (Rome, 1983); figures are for 1970-82; (3) from World Bank: *Towards sustained development in sub-Saharan Africa* (Washington, DC, 1984).

On the basis of this information, we can begin to arrive at some tentative conclusions about the likely magnitude of changes in incomes from rural work in Africa in recent years. As far as own-consumption is concerned, "income" remained practically unchanged, or at the most fell slightly. Marketed food output fell but prices rose; at the most, real income from crop sales fell by one-third. Export quantities as well as prices fell – perhaps depressing export income by 50 per cent. The final outcome for total income clearly depends on the contribution of each type of output to total "income". For the average farmer, as noted earlier, own-consumption represents the biggest part of his effort as well as "income". Although individual figures may be disputed, probably two-thirds of an average African farmer's income consists of self-produced food. The rest would comprise equally of food and export crops sold. That would imply a drop in "real" income of the order of 14 per cent. Even if all of a farmer's cash income were to disappear

Table 4.7. Average rural incomes in real terms for four SSA countries, 1970-83 (1970 = 100)

	1970	1973	1978	1980	1981	1983
Nigeria	100	98	87	81	78	–
Sierra Leone	100	–	–	–	120	–
Kenya	100	–	106	–	–	88
United Republic of Tanzania	100	81	–	88	–	76

Note: Per capita income of rural population, deflated by measure of rural cost of living.

Sources: Vali Jamal: *Poverty and inequality in Nigeria* (Geneva, ILO, 1986; mimeographed World Employment Programme research working paper), p. 10; idem: *Poverty and inequality in Sierra Leone* (Geneva, ILO, 1984; mimeographed World Employment Programme research working paper), p. 20; and Vali Jamal and John Weeks: *Rural-urban income trends in sub-Saharan Africa* (Geneva, ILO, 1987; mimeographed World Employment Programme research working paper).

Table 4.8. Real wages of agricultural workers in SSA countries, 1971-85 (1975 = 100)

	1971	1973	1975	1980	1981	1982	1983	1984	1985
Ghana	114	97	100	32	23	22	15	–	–
Kenya	113	104	100	116	113	93	88	87	–
United Republic of Tanzania	96	99	100	70	64	–	–	–	–
Burundi	–	117	100	–	106	91	95	83	83
Côte d'Ivoire	111	103	100	62	57	59	56	52	–
Malawi	127	120	100	97	104	126	97	86	–
Swaziland	–	92	100	146	132	143	142	–	–
Zambia	–	110	100	114	98	90	86	–	–
Zimbabwe	86	90	100	111	157	178	164	–	–

Sources: ILO: *Year Book of Labour Statistics*, collected from country sources by ILO; and Hamid Tabatabai: *Economic decline, access to food and structural adjustment in Ghana* (Geneva, ILO, 1986; mimeographed World Employment Programme research working paper).

because of price-induced cuts in marketed output, the maximum drop in income would be 33 per cent. What has actually happened in the rural sector of African countries as a result of the current crisis is that *cash* incomes have fallen drastically and farmers have withdrawn more and more into subsistence. While we should not minimise the impact of the fall in cash incomes, we should not confuse the fall in cash incomes with a fall in total income.

Information on incomes from self-employment in rural areas of Africa is rare. ILO estimations for four SSA countries are given in table 4.7. In each case, an attempt has been made to value subsistence production as well as to include cash income from crop sales. No general conclusions can be drawn from such a small sample of countries, though the four include the most populous SSA country (Nigeria) as well as two of the more populous (Kenya and the United Republic of Tanzania). In all three, average rural household income fell during the 1970s and early 1980s, but the falls were moderate. In Sierra Leone per capita income in rural areas actually increased. The information in the table is particularly revealing, since the three countries where rural incomes fell pursued quite different policy regimes. In the United Republic of Tanzania great emphasis was placed upon distributional considerations and meeting basic needs, while in Nigeria and Kenya these issues played relatively little role in policy. Yet the record on rural incomes was much the same.

Income from wage labour

Along with other incomes, those of agricultural wage workers have also fallen in Africa, though the

record is somewhat mixed. Table 4.8 provides calculations of real wages for agricultural workers for nine countries. In three, real wages fell substantially – the United Republic of Tanzania, Côte d'Ivoire, and Ghana (catastrophically in the last case). For four more, the decline was moderate (Kenya, Burundi, Malawi, and Zambia), and in two there were marked increases (Swaziland and Zimbabwe). Fragmentary evidence from other countries suggests that declines have been more common than increases (for example, Nigeria and Senegal), and from no country over the last decade are there reports of labour shortages in agriculture.

As noted earlier, wage employment in agriculture for heads of households is an exception rather than a rule. At the most, 5 per cent of the labour force work in the agricultural sector on a full-time basis. Most of these are members of a farm family, the greater part of whose income comes from the family farm. Rural workers take up wage employment, despite severely falling returns, because it represents a net addition to total family income. The opportunity cost of such employment, although much reduced, is still positive.

The extent of rural poverty

Considerably more information is available on the incidence of rural poverty in Africa, an indirect indicator of incomes from work in agriculture and of inequality. Table 4.9 shows two sets of estimates of rural poverty for seven countries, based upon ILO and FAO studies. The two estimates vary consider-

Table 4.9. Incidence of rural poverty in African countries, 1970s and 1980s (percentage of rural population)

	ILO	FAO (about 1980)
Gabon	25 (1975)	–
Kenya	38 (1976)	55
Lesotho	35 (1978)	55
Nigeria	40 (1978)	51
Sierra Leone	45 (1977)	65
Somalia	33 (1980)	70
United Republic of Tanzania	27 (1980)	60

Sources: FAO: *Development strategies for the rural poor* (Rome, 1984), p. 92; and Vali Jamal: *Rural-urban gap and income distribution: Synthesis report of seventeen African countries* (Addis Ababa, JASPA, 1984), p. 49.

Table 4.10. Rural-urban income differentials in selected SSA countries, 1970-83

Country	1969/70	1973/74	1980/81	1982/83
Nigeria				
Aver. Gap	4.6	5.5	6.6	4.6
UrbW/RurY	–	1.6	1.0	0.9
Sierra Leone				
Aver. Gap	6.0	–	4.1	3.5
UrbW/RurY	1.3	–	0.7	0.6
Kenya				
Aver. Gap	7.4	5.4	–	4.1
UrbW/RurY	3.6	2.9	–	2.3
United Republic of Tanzania				
Aver. Gap	–	–	5.9	–
UrbW/RurY	2.6	3.7	2.2	1.9

Notes: Aver. Gap – Ratio of average urban income to average rural income; UrbW/RurY – Ratio of average urban household wage income to average rural income.

Sources: Vali Jamal: *Rural-urban gap and income distribution: The case of Nigeria* (Addis Ababa, ILO/JASPA, 1982); idem: *Poverty and inequality in Nigeria* (Geneva, ILO, 1986; World Employment Programme research working paper); idem: *Rural-urban gap and income distribution: The case of Sierra Leone* (Addis Ababa, ILO/JASPA, 1982); idem: *Rural-urban income gap and income distribution: The case of Kenya* (Addis Ababa, ILO/JASPA, 1982); idem: *Rural-urban income gap and income distribution: The case of Tanzania* (Addis Ababa, ILO/JASPA, 1982).

ably, reflecting differences in method of calculation. The FAO figures are based upon estimates of calorie consumption, while the ILO estimates are derived from poverty line calculations and income distribution profiles. Care was taken to set the poverty line on the basis of the most frugal consumption basket. Thus the ILO estimates attempt to capture rock-bottom poverty. The fact that we still get figures in the range of 30-40 per cent implies a high degree of basic poverty – in the subsistence context, implying an inability of households to produce a minimum needs diet. All of the estimates refer to the late 1970s or 1980. Since agricultural wages and self-employment rural income have fallen during the 1980s, the incidence of rural poverty must have increased.

Rural-urban interactions

The economic crisis of the last decade has not only brought great human suffering to Africa, but has also profoundly changed the relationship between rural and urban labour incomes. The accepted view of African countries during the 1960s and 1970s was of societies sharply divided between a relatively privileged urban sector and an impoverished rural sector. In particular, urban wage earners were judged to be an "aristocracy of labour", enjoying extravagant advantages over rural dwellers in terms of both money incomes and public services. It is no longer possible to make such a generalisation, for urban incomes have fallen considerably more than rural incomes in most countries over the last ten years. This dramatic change, documented in a series of ILO studies, is a consequence of the different sensitivities of rural and urban incomes to conditions of falling aggregate demand and contracting output due to import constraints.

The gap between average urban and rural incomes remains wide but it has narrowed considerably since at least the mid-1970s in most countries. Table 4.10 gives estimates for four countries for the period 1970 to 1983. The apparent widening of the gap in Nigeria up to the early 1980s was a consequence of the oil boom, disguising a decreasing differential between other (non-oil) urban and rural incomes.

The trend in the other three countries is similar – a decline in urban labour incomes relative to rural labour incomes. Somewhat ironically, the unfavourable world market conditions for primary products have hurt urban wage earners more than rural producers, since balance of payments pressure has a direct impact upon both government employment (via export and import revenues) and private sector employment (via import restrictions on productive inputs). While wages have fallen drastically in urban areas, often below the purchasing power needed to acquire a basic food basket, farmers have at least managed to provide food for themselves.

The fall in urban labour incomes and employment

opportunities is relevant to rural living standards for two reasons. First, rural households in Africa have followed a quite complex income-earning strategy in the past, allocating their labour resources to urban as well as rural areas, and within urban areas to both formal and informal sector employment. Thus, falling urban wage incomes in the last decade are likely to have cut remittances to rural areas. In fact, in many African countries – Uganda, Ghana, Somalia and the United Republic of Tanzania are prime examples – it is the urban areas which are now the beneficiaries of remittances from rural areas in the form of food.

Secondly, falling urban wages have directly reduced the incomes of rural producers, because of declining urban demand for foodstuffs. The decline in urban economic activity has also indirectly reduced the income options available to rural households, since it has lessened the probability of obtaining formal sector employment and put downward pressure on incomes in the urban informal sector.

However, the acute need for money incomes has sustained demand for formal sector employment and urban informal employment, despite the contraction in both types of activities. It is perhaps for this reason that one finds no strong evidence of an abating of rural-to-urban migration despite narrowing differentials between urban and rural labour incomes.

The experience of the last ten years in Africa has demonstrated an important characteristic of labour markets, both rural and urban. In the past it was conventional wisdom that formal sector labour markets in Africa, including employment in large-scale agriculture, were characterised by real-wage rigidity. This was attributed to government minimum wages and trade union influence. The more judgementally inclined took these rigid real wages to be the cause of unemployment and a host of other "distortions", such as excessive capital-intensity. If such judgements were once valid they are no longer so. Real wages, both in urban and rural areas, have proved extraordinarily downward-flexible, to a degree unheard of in developed market economies. At the same time, this wage flexibility has not been associated with increases in employment, rather the contrary. All available evidence indicates that both urban and rural employment has either fallen or stagnated. What one sees in Africa over the last decade is the working out of a familiar relationship in which employment is primarily output (demand) determined, so that employment, real wages, and output have declined together.

Conclusion

The countries of Africa have been subject to a number of severe and debilitating exogenous shocks in the last 15 years. The international economic environment has been particularly unfavourable – two sudden increases in petroleum prices (1973-74 and 1979), high real interest rates, detrimental shifts in the external terms of trade even when petroleum is excluded, and a weak demand for the region's primary products. In rural areas, monetary labour incomes have declined substantially. Fortunately for most of the region, the incomplete integration of rural households into the cash economy has cushioned the fall in living standards.

The exogenous economic shocks have resulted in a severe shortage of foreign exchange. Petroleum prices declined sharply in the mid-1980s, but with other primary product prices weak, cheaper oil has merely served to throw the petroleum-producing countries, too, into the ranks of the economically distressed countries, without bringing significant relief to the oil-importing countries.

In addition to economic shocks, Africa has suffered from drought and the scourge of famine. These associated phenomena are not purely the work of nature. Population growth in the context of a relatively unchanged agricultural technology in part laid the basis for famine by generating ecologically unwise use of land. The foreign exchange crisis, by reducing the capacity of governments to provide services to the agricultural sector, also has been a contributing factor. But perhaps the most obvious and disquieting contributors to starvation have been social factors – the distribution of land and other agricultural wealth. The better-off in rural areas of Africa have protected themselves by selling assets (such as livestock), hoarding, or taking advantage of less drought-sensitive technologies. These survival strategies are closed to the poor.

The recent shift in emphasis to macro-economic adjustment policies and away from programme and project funding has put the stress on achieving static allocative efficiency. Along with this, considerations of distributional equity have lost some of the prominence they held in the 1970s. For Africa, this change has come at a particularly inopportune time. The burden of economic contraction and stagnation has fallen upon groups at the lower end of the income distribution – unskilled urban workers, agricultural wage earners, and rural households on smallholdings.

Table 4.11.　Composition of employment in agriculture by employment status: Asia, 1972-85 (in percentages)

Country	Data source	Year	Self-employed	Employees	Unpaid family employed workers	Year	Self-employed	Employees	Unpaid family employed workers
Bangladesh	lfss					1983-84	38.7	39.3	22.0
Republic of Korea	lfss	1972	39.9	14.5	45.6	1985	50.5	11.7	37.7
Malaysia	cens					1980	45.8	31.8	22.4
Pakistan	lfss	1972	51.2	7.7	41.1	1985	44.2	11.1	44.7
Philippines	hs	1974	45.0	13.3	41.7	1985	49.9	22.4	27.8
Thailand	lfss	1973	34.3	6.3	59.5	1982	31.5	9.7	58.8
Sri Lanka	cens	1971	40.1	51.0	8.9	1981	48.0	47.0	5.0

Notes: cens = census; hs = household survey; lfss = labour force sample survey.
Source: ILO: *Year Book of Labour Statistics*.

The earlier emphasis on distributional considerations was prompted by a judgement that the gains from growth should be shared throughout a country's population. Now the argument for distributional equity is even stronger – that the losses be shared out and not made the burden of the poor.

2. Asia

Rural incomes from work depend on a number of economic and demographic factors. Population pressure is high in Asia. In most countries, particularly those of the south and south-east, households own tiny plots of land (if anything at all) and they have to sustain many dependants. Rural labour incomes also depend on the availability of employment opportunities in both agricultural and non-agricultural sectors. Among the Asian market economies there is a sharp contrast between countries where industrial employment and overall development have progressed quickly, such as the Republic of Korea and Malaysia, and those where development has been sluggish, such as Bangladesh. In the former, employment opportunities elsewhere in the economy have drawn the reserve of family labour into the market. In the latter, the general deterioration of economic conditions has forced low-income households to increase the intensity of their work on the land.

Population and employment trends

About three-quarters of the world's agricultural population live in Asia. During the 1960s the Asian agricultural population rose by 1.6 per cent per year, but growth slowed to 1.3 per cent during the 1970s and to 0.8 per cent during the first half of the 1980s. The population is projected to stabilise at the beginning of the next century. This growth pattern is repeated for the agricultural labour force but with a lag of about 15 years. As a result, the increase in the agricultural labour force has been highest between 1970 and 1985.

Dependency ratios – that is, agricultural population divided by the agricultural labour force – have thus been declining over the past 15 years, from 2.19 in 1970 to 2.08 in 1985. These ratios are lower than in Africa (respectively 2.34 and 2.48) and in Latin America (respectively 3.12 and 2.89).

However, there is a great variation in dependency ratios within the Asian region. In Bangladesh and Pakistan one member of the labour force has to support on average 3.5 people (including him or herself), while in China and Thailand it is less than two people. In several more economically developed countries, such as the Republic of Korea and Malaysia, the dependency ratio has declined very substantially as an increasing part of the population has been drawn into the labour force. The opposite happened in, for example, Bangladesh and India where the dependency ratio has risen.

Employment structure

Between 1970 and 1985, the share of the Asian labour force in agriculture dropped from 70 to almost 60 per cent. The reduction was most pronounced in industrialising countries such as Indonesia, the Republic of Korea, Malaysia and Thailand. The share of agriculture is still about 70 per cent in Bangladesh, India and China, while it has fallen to

---

4.1   China's policy of encouraging peasants "to leave the land but not the village"

Since the consolidation of the commune system in rural areas, rural-to-urban migration of labour has been strictly controlled in China. Even so, the proportion of the rural labour force in the total labour force declined from 82.5 per cent in 1962 to 76.1 per cent in 1978 and further to 74.3 per cent in 1984. However, much of this decline (particularly during 1962-78) is explained by two factors: a substantial increase in the participation rate in urban areas and its virtual constancy in rural areas; and the occasional extensions of the boundaries of cities.

The policies pursued in the 1960s also had the effect of concentrating the rural labour force in farming. Private non-farm activities were discouraged and commune and brigade enterprises (now called township enterprises) began to be developed only in the early 1970s. In 1974, only 3.4 per cent of the rural labour force was employed in commune and brigade enterprises. Employment in these enterprises, however, grew rapidly; they employed 9.3 per cent of the rural labour force by 1978, an average annual rate of growth of employment of nearly 30 per cent. Nevertheless, this proved quite inadequate to prevent the emergence of significant surplus labour in farming, particularly in crop production.

One of the major objectives of the rural reforms implemented since 1979 has been to speed up the process of transfer of labour from farming to non-farm activities within the rural sector. Efforts have been directed not only to stimulating the growth of township enterprises but also to encouraging the development of enterprises by peasants on either an individual or co-operative basis (also called village enterprises). The results have been quite dramatic; by the end of 1985, an estimated 18.6 per cent of the rural labour force was engaged in non-farm activities. Of the total labour force engaged in non-farm activities in 1985, about 69 per cent were employed in township enterprises, 16 per cent were engaged in individual enterprises and the remaining 15 per cent worked in co-operative (or village) enterprises. Employment in township enterprises grew from 28 million in 1978 to 30 million in 1980 and further to around 46 million in 1985. Employment in co-operative and individual enterprises was negligible in 1978, 3.6 million in 1980 and about 21 million in 1985. Between 1980 and 1985, the average annual rate of growth of employment in township enterprises was 9.0 per cent while that in co-operative and individual enterprises was 42.5 per cent.

Two aspects of this process are worth noting. Firstly, the relative rates of growth between 1980 and 1985 suggest that the expansion of co-operative and individual enterprises may be inhibiting growth of township enterprises. Secondly, the rural non-farm sector accounted for 18.6 per cent of the rural labour force but 42.3 per cent of the value of rural output in 1985. This suggests much higher labour productivity and incomes in the non-farm sector than in the farm sector. Thus, it is possible that the non-farm sector is drawing away the more able and skilled workers from the farm sector.

---

less than 40 per cent in the Republic of Korea and Malaysia. In most South and South-East Asian countries the self-employed are the dominant group in agriculture (table 4.11), followed by unpaid family workers, most of whom are women. Over the past 15 years, however, the share of wage earners in agricultural employment has risen in most of these countries including Bangladesh, India, Pakistan, the Philippines and Thailand. In many countries this has also led to a greater *casualisation* of rural wage labour – a trend that will also be documented for urban wage labour (see chapter 6). In 1977-78 almost 30 per cent of the rural workforce in India was in casual employment. In Sri Lanka this percentage was 33 per cent in 1981-82. Krishnamurti (1984) observed for India that "demographic and economic factors including reduced access to land are likely to have led to a rising proportion of casual workers dependent on wage employment often of an intermittent kind". In China, the employment status of many agricultural workers has changed over the past ten years. Instead of being commune members, most are now engaged in family farming (even though families do not own the land). Chinese rural policy is now encouraging peasants to leave agriculture and to engage in industrial and service activities (see box 4.1).

Table 4.12.   Land availability: Asian countries, 1969-84 (in hectares per member of the agricultural labour force)

Country	1969-71	1979-81	1984
Bangladesh	0.53	0.47	0.44
China	0.30	0.24	0.23
India	1.00	0.89	0.84
Indonesia	0.42	0.44	0.47
Republic of Korea	0.38	0.38	0.39
Pakistan	1.68	1.44	1.31
Philippines	0.95	0.84	0.82
Sri Lanka	0.37	0.35	0.35
Thailand	0.86	0.98	1.00

Note: Land under perennial crops is not included. For Indonesia, the Philippines and Sri Lanka it is quite significant.

Sources: FAO: *Production Year Book*; FAO: *World-wide estimates and projections of the agricultural and non-agricultural population segments, 1950-2025* (Rome, 1986).

Landownership

The ownership of land is the main determinant of rural labour incomes. This section therefore reviews trends in the availability, productivity and distribution of land.

Figure 4.1. Yields in cereal production: Asia, 1974-85 (1,000 kg/ha)

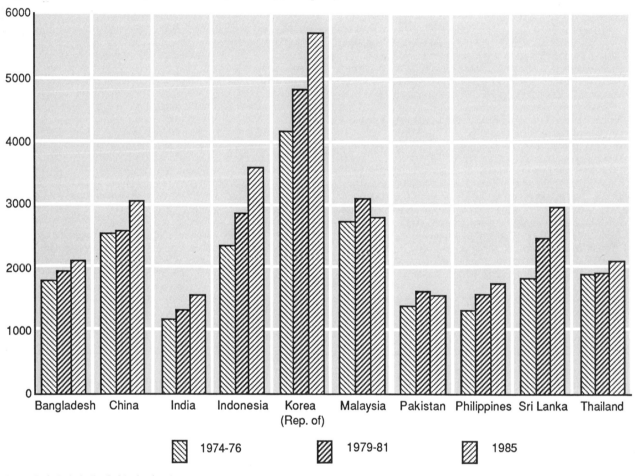

Source: FAO: *Production Year Book* (various issues).

Thailand and Indonesia seem to be the only countries where the availability of land has significantly increased (see table 4.12). For some countries the land/worker ratio in agriculture has fallen substantially, notably in China and Bangladesh. There has also been a significant decrease in the ratio for Pakistan, from 1.68 hectares in 1970 to 1.31 hectares in 1984. Available figures on Indonesia and Sri Lanka are more difficult to interpret because both countries are major producers of perennial crops, which are excluded from the figures. Considering only annual crops, however, land availability appears to have been broadly stable. This is also the case with the Philippines.

It is in general unhelpful to make cross-country comparisons of land productivity because different mixes of crops are produced in different countries. Figure 4.1, however, refers to physical yields on cereals only, which should be more comparable. In general, yields have been rising in all the countries shown, but since the beginning of the 1970s the most spectacular increases have occurred in Indonesia. Yields there increased from 2.34 metric tons per hectare during the period 1974-76 to 3.56 metric tons per hectare in 1985. Very substantial yield increases have also occurred in China, India, the Republic of Korea and Sri Lanka. However, by far the highest absolute yields are found in the Republic of Korea, which approach Japanese levels.

The distribution of landholding, which can be used as a proxy for total asset holding, is remarkably unequal in various countries of South and South-East Asia. Dramatic changes have occurred in, for example, Bangladesh. Between 1967-68 and 1977 the richest 10 per cent of farmers increased their share in total landownership from about 35 per cent to more than 50 per cent. In the meantime, landlessness also rose sharply in rural Bangladesh. Between the same two dates, the proportion of landless cultivators increased from 19.8 per cent to 36.8 per cent, and the absolute number of landless labourers rose from 3.40 to 7.75 million. Perhaps 1.35 of the increase of 4.35 million can be attributed to the increase in population. Thus even if we make the conservative assumption that only landless households increase the ranks of the economically active population in agriculture over time, the discrepancy of 3 million with the total increase must be due to the dispossession or fragmentation of land. The fragmentation of landholding may also substantially lower the average farm size. For instance, between 1960 and 1977, the average farm size in Bangladesh decreased by a third, from about 3 acres per farm to about 2 acres.

A similar pattern of very unequal landholding distribution is found in other countries for which data is available, with the notable exception of the Republic of Korea (see box 4.2). And the average size of landholding is small in almost all countries of South and South-East Asia. The amount of land owned is usually highly correlated with the amount of land farmed, except among very small, and very large landowners without mechanised farming. Small farmers tend to lease *in* land, while the near-landless and large farmers lease *out* land. In the case of the near-landless, this is not necessarily because of the economic size of operational holding; these farmers often do not have the wherewithal to pay for the expenses they have to incur before they reap their harvest. Thus for instance, in West Java, where 23 per cent of households own no land, 25 per cent operate none. Whereas 19 per cent of households own up to 0.1 hectare, only 15 per cent operate landholdings of this size. These observations are also applicable to rural India.

Farm household decisions on production and labour

Households that are fortunate enough to have access to a plot of land have to make decisions about the use of various production factors. Land is scarce and so are liquid assets with which various agricultural inputs can be bought such as high-yielding seeds, animal and/or mechanical power, irrigation and fertiliser. Family labour is abundantly available and can be used either to increase the productivity of scarce production factors, or to obtain wage employ-

ment elsewhere in the rural economy. However, women and children often have limited "marketability" for outside employment and they may be needed during harvesting or other times of the season when much work needs to be done (such as planting or weeding). Male members of the family may not wish to work elsewhere if that means a loss of output on the family farm.

The problem of finding employment for "non-marketable" family labour is an important incentive for the small farmer to operate his own land rather than lease it out for others to farm. Instead, he will try to maximise the return from family resources, including labour, by leasing *in* land if he can and acquiring other production factors as well, such as draught animals. Underemployed family labour, especially in non-peak seasons, can be used to graze cattle, thus saving on animal feed costs. This is widely practised in rural South and South-East Asia. Even in peak seasons, grazing can be done by a child who is otherwise unable to contribute significantly to strenuous agricultural operations such as harvesting. Similarly, cattle can be fed with straw from the farm. By using complementary production factors in this way, farmers gain maximum benefit from their ownership of land and family labour.

Farming: A risky operation

Farming, especially with small unirrigated plots of land, is extremely risky. Every farmer basically wishes to remain a farmer for good economic reasons, given income prospects for landless workers in poor rural societies. Each yearly cycle of production and consumption is dependent on survival in the preceding year. Thus, meeting the minimum necessary expenses in the current year becomes the farmer's first priority. If he owns assets (which in rural Asia is highly correlated with landownership) and if farm income in the current year is inadequate to meet his current expenses, he could consider borrowing against his future prospective income. However, the smaller the farm the more difficult it becomes to borrow. Expected future incomes from a small farm are relatively low and the interest rates charged by moneylenders are high. Below a critical level of asset-holding, it is no longer wise for the farmer to borrow.

However, some small farmers, the very small in particular, cannot choose to be cautious. A farmer with no source of income other than that from an acre plot of land may discover that he is unable to meet essential expenses to support the family. But in this

---

4.2   **Distribution of land and rural development in the Republic of Korea**

The most significant change in the Korean rural landscape has been the successful implementation of land reform measures. At the end of the Second World War, 51.6 per cent of all farm households owned no land at all. In 1947 only 16.5 per cent of farm households cultivated fully owned land yet in 1964 that proportion had soared to 71.6 per cent. In addition, at the latter date, 14.8 per cent of households who owned most of the land they farmed had leased in small fractions of their operational holding. The success was remarkable by all international comparisons; it was brought about by a combination of historical and economic factors peculiar to the country. Immediately after the end of the Second World War, land belonging to the Japanese landlords was distributed to Korean cultivators, and after 1950 very large areas of land belonging to Korean landlords were distributed among tenants. The fervour for confiscation of land belonging to Korean landlords was heightened since the majority of them had collaborated with the Japanese. But additionally, nearly as much land was sold directly by the landlords to the tenants as was taken from them. In 1949 the Korean Government set selling prices at only 1.5 times the average annual product of the land, payable over five years. For redistributed land, a tenant might be paying up to 30 per cent of his harvest to the Government. Under such circumstances, both landlords and tenants had a powerful incentive to make private deals outside the land reform legislation.

Such far-reaching land reforms unleashed unprecedented growth of labour productivity, as contractual relations changed in land and credit markets. The majority of former tenants became landowning cultivators, and the institution of professional money-lending almost disappeared. This led to some disruption in the credit market because substitute institutions were slow to develop. When available, however, loans cost between 8 and 15 per cent per annum from government-organised institutions as against 50 to 60 per cent from money-lenders. These two developments associated with land reform produced the desired results. The use of machinery and fertilisers and high yielding seed varieties, already on the increase, grew at phenomenal rates, and despite small farm sizes Korean agriculture achieved extremely high yields. By the mid-1970s, Korean farmers' yields and input use compared very favourably with those of Japanese farmers. Even though all available land had long been in cultivation, the intensive use of material inputs continued to produce increased farm income, and since the rentier class had virtually disappeared increased returns were secured by mostly family labour.

One of the interesting features of Korean agriculture has been the insignificant use of hired labour. In 1970, only 2.9 per cent of households were classified as farm labour households (including households cultivating on "burnt fields"). This is partly because of the migration of non-cultivating rural labour into cities, and because there was no land dispossession of small farmers. The legal limit on farm size is approximately 3 hectares. This limit, combined with booming investment opportunities in non-agricultural sectors, has inhibited the growth of a land sales market, and therefore prevented any significant increase in inequality in the distribution of rural assets. The land that cannot be cultivated with family labour and sophisticated farm equipment is leased out to tenants, who may themselves be owners of land.

---

situation he would not be able to borrow from any commercial source. He would then be forced to increase his exposure to risk. He might choose to allocate more land to production of a crop with a high gross revenue which is, however, unacceptably risky to a more substantial farmer. The smallest farmers in Bangladesh, for instance, are found to allocate the highest proportions of their land to a risk-prone jute crop, and these proportions are much higher than for large farmers. This observation clearly contradicts the conventional wisdom that only the wealthy are prepared to take risks.

Patterns of labour use

The decision to hire or to sell labour will mainly depend on whether a household owns land and on farm size. Table 4.13 demonstrates this clearly for some clusters of villages in the Dinajpur district of Bangladesh.

The landless rural households depend very largely on selling their labour, nearly one-half as casual labour but a substantial portion also as "permanent" labour. The small farmer hires in some labour, mostly on an exchange basis with other small farmers; the

rest of their hired labour – presumably during busy agricultural seasons – is on casual contract. Small farmers also sell a large part of their labour time to other farmers; some do so in exchange for labour bought, others on casual and permanent bases. Medium farmers, although they sell a significant amount of their labour time, on exchange and casual bases, are high net hirers of labour time from small farmers and landless labourers. These purchases are mostly on a casual basis, followed by exchange, permanent and contract labour. The large farmers, surprisingly, are also sellers of labour – though mostly in exchange for other labour – but this is insignificant in comparison with the amount of labour time they hire in. These farmers are the biggest buyers of labour time on a permanent basis among all categories of farmers. As a rule, in South and South-East Asian countries, small farms cultivate their land more labour-intensively and use more family labour as a proportion of total labour input than large farms (tables 4.14 and 4.15).

In Bangladesh, for example, a village-level study carried out for three different regions found that work-days put in per acre were consistently highest in

Table 4.13.   Percentage distribution of labour hired and sold, by type of contract and farm size; Dinajpur villages, Bangladesh, 1982/83

Type of household	Landless		Small farm (up to 2.5 acres)		Medium farm (2.5-7.5 acres)		Large farm (more than 7.5 acres)	
	Hired	Sold	Hired	Sold	Hired	Sold	Hired	Sold
Type of contract								
Casual		46.1	24.6	25.9	46.2	43.4	40.1	29.0
Contract		11.5	–	8.0	10.2	–	10.2	–
Seasonal		4.6	–	4.4	–	–	5.0	–
Permanent		37.8	–	39.1	21.7	–	42.2	–
Exchange		–	75.4	22.6	21.9	56.6	2.5	71.0
Total		100.0	100.0	100.0	100.0	100.0	100.0	100.0
Total days		4445	301	1020	2529	986	4870	262

Source: R. Islam and A. Rahman: *Agrarian change, labour contracts and inter-linked transactions in labour, land and credit in rural Bangladesh: A study with micro-level data* (Bangkok, ARTEP, 1985).

small farms (up to 2.5 acres) and least in large farms (above 7.5 acres). The same was true for family labour used per acre and the proportion of family labour in total labour used. A similar pattern applies to Indonesia, where on small farms each hectare is cultivated by not less than seven household workers. In Malaysia, where agriculture is much more developed, much less family labour is used per hectare on all sizes of farm, but small farms still make more intensive use of family labour than large ones.

Table 4.14.   Work done by family labour as a percentage of total labour input: Asian countries, 1970s and 1980s

Country	Bangladesh (1982/83)			Indonesia (1975)	Malaysia (1975)
Region	Region 1	Region 2	Region 3		
Farm size					
Small	78.5	78.7	67.3	63.4	67.5
Medium	73.4	69.4	62.5	52.3	66.7
Large	45.7	48.9	44.8	47.6	61.0

Notes: Bangladesh: Farm size: small, 0.11-2.5 acres; medium, 2.51-7.50 acres; large, more than 7.50 acres.
Region: Region 1 – low agricultural growth; region 2 – high agricultural growth; region 3 – near industrial centre.
Indonesia: The data refer to paddy cultivators in the Aceh region.
Farm size: small, less than 0.5 ha; medium, 0.51-1.00 ha; large, more than 1.00 ha.
Malaysia: The data refer to paddy cultivators in the West Malaysian region.
Farm size: small, less than 2.0 ha; medium, 2.01-3.00 ha; large, more than 3.0 ha.
Sources: Bangladesh: M. Muqtada and M.M. Alam: "Hired labour and rural labour market in Bangladesh", in S. Hirashima and M. Mugtada (eds.): *Hired labour and rural labour markets in Asia* (New Delhi, ARTEP, 1986). Indonesia and Malaysia: D.S. Gibbons et al.: *Agricultural modernization, poverty and inequality* (Farnborough, Saxon House, 1980).

Productivity and farm size

Since small farms use more family labour per unit of land, they can be expected to produce more per unit of land than large farms. This is borne out by the data on Bangladesh (see table 4.16). However, this does not mean that labour productivity (output per unit of labour) is higher. In the example of Bangladesh, labour productivity is about the same for all three farm-size categories. A similar pattern of land and labour productivity is found for Indonesia, but not for India and Malaysia (see table 4.17), where the introduction of high-yielding seed varieties has been more widespread.

In India studies have found that before the introduction of high-yielding seed varieties, crop yields do not exhibit any uniform relationship to farm size, while small farms often achieve a larger output per

Table 4.15.   Labour intensity per unit of land: Asian countries, 1970s and 1980s

Country	Bangladesh (1982-83)			Indonesia (1975)	Malaysia (1975)
Labour intensity	Work-days per acre			Number of household workers per hectare	
Region	Region 1	Region 2	Region 3		
Farm size					
Small	82.5	78.8	71.9	6.9	1.6
Medium	73.6	69.3	68.8	2.6	0.7
Large	65.6	67.8	61.2	1.4	0.5

Note: See table 4.14.

Table 4.16. Productivity of land and labour in Bangladesh, 1982/83

Farm size	Gross output per acre (1,000 taka)			Gross output per labour day (in taka)		
	Small	Medium	Large	Small	Medium	Large
Region 1	5.56	4.75	4.34	67.4	62.8	66.2
Region 2	5.80	5.27	5.33	73.6	76.0	78.5
Region 3	4.97	4.69	4.01	69.1	68.2	65.5

Note: See table 4.14.

Table 4.17. Productivity of land and labour incomes in Indonesia and Malaysia, 1975

Farm size	Net return per hectare (in US$)			Net per capita income (in US$)		
	Small	Medium	Large	Small	Medium	Large
Indonesia	1056.1	666.6	575.4	103.3	125.1	181.3
Malaysia	1150.4	1163.0	1058.0	347.9	662.4	882.9

Note: See table 4.14.

hectare with a higher cropping intensity and labour input. Immediately after high-yielding varieties are introduced, yields on large farms for that crop go up sharply; small farms still put in a larger labour input per hectare, but without a corresponding achievement in larger output per hectare. When the substitution of high-yielding for older varieties is complete, yields become more uniform across farm size.

The impact of the Green Revolution in Malaysia has been quite widespread. The major emphasis in developing the agricultural sector, apart from the extension of the land frontier, was laid on the public provision of infrastructural facilities. These included the supply of electricity, irrigation, fertiliser, insecticides, pesticides, tractors, roads and agricultural extension services. Public provision of these essential factor inputs, particularly control of water supply, was so successful that while in 1951 less than 1 per cent of the total acreage devoted to paddy cultivation in West Malaysia was cropped twice a year, by 1976 double cropping covered over 60 per cent of the area – a phenomenal increase. The Malaysian paddy farmer has turned from subsistence to producing for the market. Thus, while the large Aceh farmer of Indonesia produced a surplus of only 7 quintals per year, the small farmer of the Malaysian region produced a surplus of 17 quintals per year; the average farmer produced a surplus of 58.3 quintals. The normal inverse relationship between farm size and land productivity was "corrected" through public provision of essential inputs to all groups of farmers. Also, the average Malaysian farmer is considerably larger than in Bangladesh or Indonesia. Returns to family labour, however, rise with farm size as much in the labour surplus conditions of Indonesia as in market-oriented Malaysia. This is so in Malaysia because, while there is no systematic relationship between farm size and productivity, there is an inverse relationship between farm size and family labour endowment. In the case of Indonesia, the inverse relation between farm size and family labour endowment is considerably stronger than that between farm size and the productivity of land.

Trends in wage earnings

Real agricultural wages in South and South-East Asian countries seem to have fared better than in other developing continents (see figure 4.2). In Bangladesh real wages for skilled wage earners declined during the 1970s, but remained at about the same level during the 1980s. In the Republic of Korea, on the other hand, agricultural workers have enjoyed impressive real wage increases. Between 1971 and 1979, real wages increased by 139 per cent for male workers and by 162 per cent for female workers. This stemmed from the very rapid agricultural development described in box 4.2. At the beginning of the 1980s, however, real agricultural wages dropped, a result of the recession which also reduced industrial wages (see chapter 5). They have picked up once more but at a much slower pace than during the 1970s.

Trends in real wages of plantation workers in peninsular Malaysia are not clear-cut. Rubber tappers seem to have made some real wage gains until the beginning of the 1980s, but have since lost considerable ground. This may be due to the particular circumstances of rubber plantations because such a severe drop was not observed for oil-palm harvesters. In the Philippines real wages in rice and corn agriculture fell by about 30 per cent between 1978 and 1985.

The above data relate to national wage trends for various countries. Wage rates, however, vary considerably from region to region, even from village to village, and over seasons. Comprehensive surveys of such variations in wage rates for these countries are

Figure 4.2. **Real daily wage rates in agriculture: Asia, 1971-85 (wage earners)**

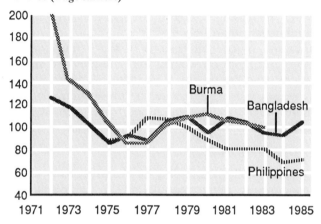

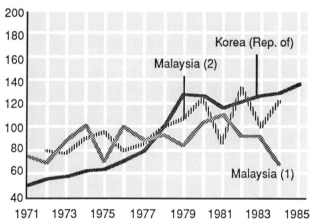

Bangladesh: male skilled wage earners. Burma: monthly earnings per male employee. Republic of Korea: monthly. Malaysia: (1) monthly wage rates of rubber tappers; (2) monthly wage rates of oil-palm harvesters. Philippines: wage earners (rice and corn).

Source: ILO: *Year Book of Labour Statistics.*

Conclusion

There is very little scope for extending the arable land frontier in most Asian countries so demographic pressures are intense. In some countries, such as Bangladesh, there is an active process of dispossession of land mainly from the poorest farmers. In general, the size of the population dependent on agriculture is very high, even in successful countries like the Republic of Korea; and in many countries farm size has considerably declined. Clearly, employment opportunities outside the rural sector would relieve the pressure on agriculture – as has happened in the Republic of Korea, Taiwan, China, and Malaysia. In the absence of such possibilities, one option is to increase the intensity of cultivation – that is, increase the factor inputs to land in order to raise its productivity. In the Republic of Korea and Malaysia, higher productivity has been obtained by considerable increases in the application of material inputs. In the Republic of Korea, there is in fact a general shortage of farm labour which has drawn women into agricultural work as a substitute for male labour. In various other countries, greater productivity of land is achieved by the increased expenditure of labour. This seems to have taken its most acute form in Bangladesh. There are some indications that a similar process may have occurred in the densely populated small-farm agriculture of Indonesia.

Small farmers can intensify their effort by drawing on the reserve of female labour in the workforce, and increasing the length of the day and the number of days in the year worked. They may adopt more labour-intensive techniques of production and cultivate crops that utilise more intensively the available labour in the family.

However, this process of intensification does not significantly increase labour productivity, which is the basis of any increase in living standards. That can be brought about by land reform and the provision of complementary inputs such as irrigation, credit, improved seeds and equipment. A successful example of such a policy has been provided by the Republic of Korea.

3. Latin America

Population and employment trends

In all Latin American countries, there has been a continuous rapid decline in both the share of rural population in total population and the share of agricultural workers in the total labour force. For Latin

not available, but what evidence there is on significant wage differentials for similar work even between neighbouring villages suggests important limitations to geographical mobility.

An ILO study of several villages in West Bengal, India, shows that while wage differentials exist for different kinds of work and labour contracts in agriculture, wages do not vary for different levels of skills for the same work in the same village for casual labourers of the same sex. The main reason advanced by both labourers and employers is that labourers will not accept different wages. Significant proportions of both groups also suggest that at busy periods it is not possible to select from among labourers; during less busy periods the importance of long-term labour contracts is greater and less-skilled workers are usually screened out.

America as a whole (19 countries), these shares declined respectively from 50 per cent to 34 per cent and from 49 per cent to 32 per cent between 1960 and 1980. Thus, no longer does agriculture employ the majority of Latin Americans. However, higher per capita income countries have markedly lower shares of total gross domestic product (GDP) originating in agriculture and lower shares of rural population and of the agricultural labour force. The observed rapid decline in these two shares can thus be expected to continue as economic growth progresses.

The share of rural population has, in general, declined only slightly more slowly than the share of the agricultural labour force, with a 1 per cent drop in the latter associated with a 0.73 per cent decline in the former. This indicates a generally weak ability on the part of the Latin American economies, with their current highly concentrated patterns of urban-industrial development, to generate non-agricultural employment opportunities in their rural sectors and thus to retain a larger proportion of their labour force in the rural areas. This ability to generate non-agricultural employment in the rural sector is, however, greater in the higher per capita income countries, which suggests it may improve with economic development.

Rural-urban migration rates have generally been exceptionally high by international standards during the last 30 years. Migration rates are linked with overall economic expansion and with growth of non-agricultural activities, so are likely to accelerate as economies grow and industrialise. Migration rates also increase with growth in agricultural GDP per capita, underlining the labour-saving and land-concentrating nature of agricultural development in Latin America.

In addition to high levels of rural-urban migration, there is an increasing incidence of rural-rural migration in the form of seasonal labour markets, a phenomenon that is well documented in Mexico. These seasonal labour markets are based on regional disparities and the development of areas of advanced commercialised agriculture which, because of crop specialisation and partial mechanisation of the labour process, require large numbers of casual workers for short periods of time. The development of one such migrant labour market in the northern states of Sinaloa and Sonora complements the more traditional migrant labour market of the southern coffee and sugar-cane regions.

These migrant labour markets draw on the large pool of landless labourers and those *ejidatarios* and

minifundistas who can afford to be away from their plots for long periods of time. Local labour markets, which increasingly offer more sporadic and casual employment than before as specialisation and mechanisation invade all regions of the country, draw more and more on women and children and smallholders who live nearby. This off-farm employment is a necessary complement to the production of many smallholders who cannot support a household from their plots.

Employment in the traditional sectors

Table 4.18 gives figures for the proportion of the economically active population in the traditional sectors. Traditional activities in both agricultural and urban areas are defined as including own-account workers and non-paid family members. In the urban areas, paid domestic services are also included in the traditional sector. The modern agricultural sector includes agricultural workers, employers, professionals and technicians. Because the population censuses tend to underestimate the importance of women in the agricultural labour force, the data on the number of unpaid family members and agricultural workers have been "corrected" on the basis of comparisons with the agricultural censuses.

The table shows that between 1970 and 1980 the share of traditional activities increased in both the agricultural and the urban sectors except in a few countries such as Cuba (see box 4.3).

In spite of a rapidly falling share of agriculture in the total labour force, the size of the peasant sector (small farmers) has increased in most countries both in absolute numbers and as a proportion of the agricultural labour force. In general, growth in the modern agricultural sector has created little new employment, and the overall size of the proletarian workforce in Latin American agriculture has remained relatively constant over the last 30 years. Since the number of peasants has increased and their dependency on wage income also seems to have increased, total proletarianisation (full and semi-proletarianisation) will also have increased.

Employment by farm size

Large and medium-sized farms are often overly mechanised because various fiscal incentives and government credit programmes tend to favour the more substantial farmers. As a result, these farms create relatively little employment. The main losers from such policies are the marginal farmers and the

Table 4.18. Percentage of the traditional sector in the labour force: Latin America, 1970 and 1980

	Agriculture		Urban areas	
	1970	1980	1970	1980
Argentina	37.4	41.7	15.6	19.4
Bolivia	86.6	90.7	19.6	23.2
Brazil	72.8	73.8	14.9	16.9
Chile	34.2	38.6	16.7	20.1
Colombia	52.2	54.2	17.7	22.3
Costa Rica	43.6	43.0	12.9	12.4
Dominican Republic	67.4	59.6	15.5	16.0
Ecuador	70.1	73.4	23.7	25.4
El Salvador	48.4	57.4	16.6	18.9
Guatemala	61.6	59.7	17.3	17.8
Honduras	62.9	57.1	13.8	17.2
Mexico	53.2	48.9	18.2	22.0
Nicaragua	50.1	56.9	20.7	28.3
Panama	78.9	73.0	15.8	20.9
Peru	78.5	80.0	20.7	23.8
Uruguay	36.7	45.7	16.8	19.0
Venezuela	73.4	77.4	22.4	16.4
Latin America (17 countries)	63.7	65.1	16.9	19.3

Note: Traditional sector in agriculture includes own-account workers and non-paid family members, excluding professionals and technicians. The urban traditional sector includes domestic servants, own-account workers and unpaid family members in non-agricultural activities, excluding professionals and technicians.

Source: PREALC: *Mercado de Trabajo en Cifras, 1970-80* (Geneva, ILO, 1982).

landless who depend for their living mainly on agricultural wage employment.

Landlessness is generally not measurable through census data since a large number of those who appear as hired workers in the agricultural labour force also have plots of land which are not sufficient to support their households. Thus, the extent of landlessness must be estimated through household surveys or by other means which often lead to widely varying results.

On the basis of very incomplete data, two facts stand out: the high levels of landlessness; and the relatively higher levels of landlessness in countries, such as Brazil, Chile and Costa Rica, with low shares of agricultural GDP in total GDP compared to agrarian countries, such as Guatemala, Honduras and Nicaragua. It can thus be expected that landlessness will further increase in Latin America as its pattern of development reduces agriculture's share in economic output.

As noted earlier, the number of peasants has risen over time. Of the 17 countries for which there are data, 15 have an increasing number of small farms (the exceptions being Panama and Venezuela). The number of small farms in Latin America as a whole grew by an estimated 92 per cent between 1950 and 1980, or 2.2 per cent a year.

The size of small farms has also been shrinking. Taking 16 countries for which there is information, peasant farm size declined in 11 while it increased in only three, the other two showing no significant change. Overall, for the 14 countries on which there is recent information, the average size of peasant farms declined from 2.4 to 2.1 hectares between 1950 and 1980, a contraction of --0.4 per cent a year.

Moreover, peasant farms, as a proportion of the total number of farms and the land they occupy, have increased in most Latin American countries.

All these observations confirm the picture of the peasantry as a cornered sector of the population, increasingly dependent on non-farm sources of income but unable to find sufficient employment opportunities either to migrate and abandon the agricultural sector or to depend fully on wage earnings for subsistence. Thus, while the peasantry has grown in numbers, it has changed character, no longer being pure farm producers but having an increasing involvement in the labour market. This is clearly demonstrated by the example of Brazil, where the peasantry increased in periods of depressed economic conditions and declined in periods of rapid economic growth. In other words, marginal labour tends to accumulate in the peasant sector (box 4.4).

Agricultural and non-agricultural employment in rural areas

The similarity in trends over time of the rural population and of the agricultural labour force could erroneously be interpreted as indicating a stable commitment of the rural population to agriculture. This is not the case. Fundamental changes have occurred over the last 20 years which have led to an increasing integration of the agricultural and urban labour markets. The agricultural labour force has become more and more urbanised (mainly town-based) and the rural labour force increasingly works in non-agricultural activities (table 4.19).

The share of the urban-based agricultural labour force has risen everywhere in the region, the biggest increases being in Puerto Rico and Brazil. At the same time, the proportion of the non-agricultural

---

4.3   **Cuba: A declining proportion of peasants in the agricultural labour force**

Prior to the Revolution in 1959 wage earners made up the bulk of Cuba's rural labour force. Some 70 per cent of rural workers were wage employed in 1957; only Uruguay had a higher incidence of rural wage work at the time. This reflected the dominance of plantations and other large holdings in the agrarian structure: farms of over 67 hectares controlled more than three-quarters of agricultural land just before the Revolution. Since then, however, wage work in rural areas has become even more important. Data for 1981 show that while the level of rural proletarianisation declined in the rest of Latin America, it rose in Cuba. An estimated 80 per cent of the rural workforce was employed outside the private small-farm sector, either on state or collective farms, and this percentage is reported to have continued to increase in recent years.

What are the reasons for this rise? Although Cuban policy sought to socialise the economy, it did not implement any specifically designed strategy to do away with private small-scale farming. Credit to the small-farm sector, for example, increased substantially after the Revolution. The real reasons must be found in the very profound transformation of the economy as a whole.

First, private farmers voluntarily joined the state farms, in particular those that could expect to increase their standard of living. But there was another even more important reason why farmers gave up their private plots. Rural areas faced an increasing labour shortage as seasonal wage workers were given permanent work on the state farms and as rural educational enrolment rose to unprecedented levels. Private farmers not only found it increasingly difficult to secure labour, they also had problems in handing their farms on to their children in order to retire. Children raised on small-scale farms were able to obtain better employment elsewhere because their education had considerably improved. Cuba's policy of "urbanising the countryside" had also led to rapid growth of non-agricultural employment in rural areas. As a result of these factors, the private farm sector gradually "withered away", dissolving itself.

Secondly, in 1977 a policy was introduced enabling private farmers to organise themselves in producer co-operatives, or collective farms, pooling their land and other resources. To motivate farmers, considerable resources were made available to these new farms. This measure was primarily intended for those farmers in areas without state farms. By 1985 some 60 per cent of the economically active rural population outside the state farms were *socios* of the collective farms. Private farmers are now joining the collective farms at a faster rate than they are joining the state farms, and it is expected that private small-scale farming will involve only 5 to 10 per cent of the agricultural work force by 1990.

---

rural labour force increased in every country except Peru, most markedly in Mexico and Brazil. Mexico's non-agricultural share of the rural labour force jumped dramatically from 23 per cent in 1970 to 42 per cent in 1980.

It is important to note that census data tend to overestimate non-agricultural employment in rural areas. This is due to the fact that peripheral urban areas are often still classified as rural areas, and their residents as rural workers. The overestimation is particularly high in those countries where migration to the urban periphery has been extensive.

The origin of the urbanisation of the agricultural labour force can, in many cases, be traced to the introduction of new agricultural labour laws (Chile and Brazil) which led to the expulsion of resident workers from the large farms, their relocation in urban towns, and the generalisation of the practice of hiring non-resident workers on a temporary basis (in Brazil, in particular), often through the mediation of labour contractors. In Chile, labour legislation forced employers in 1970 to substitute payment in kind by 100 per cent payment of minimum wages in cash, inducing landlords to replace permanent workers *(inquilinos)* by temporary workers. In 1979, labour laws restricted union activity to farms with more than 15 permanent workers, further inducing landlords to

reduce their staff of permanent workers and to shift to temporary farmhands. Land concentration and the resulting increase in landlessness also accelerated rural out-migration in most countries.

This labour force of landless workers had a tendency to concentrate in the neighbourhoods of small rural towns, especially in the areas of temporary employment in agriculture, where they can be easily mobilised by labour contractors. Where this has happened, the town-based rural labour force increasingly displaces the traditional peasantry from employment opportunities. Town-based workers are easier to recruit on a temporary basis and there is no conflict with the labour needs of their own farms, which often affects peasants in the critical weeks of harvest. The traditional peasantry then becomes increasingly disconnected from the labour market and is forced to migrate to the towns if it cannot subsist on its small plots of land.

In Chile, between 1970 and 1982, the rural population increased at an annual average rate of 0.2 per cent and the population of the large cities by 2.8 per cent, while that of small towns rose by 3.6 per cent. Workers living in urban areas and working in agriculture, principally on temporary contracts, also participate in the urban labour market and have contributed to the greater integration of the two

4.4 — The accumulation of marginal labour in the peasant sector: The case of Brazil

In the 1960s, Brazil saw a 50 per cent increase of family labour together with a substantial decline in the number of wage earners. This phenomenon can be explained by changing labour laws. In 1963 regulations and minimum wages were introduced for wage earners. As a consequence, resident workers were expelled from the *fazendas* as their costs rose to non-competitive levels for employers. At the same time, unfavourable economic conditions meant a lack of employment opportunities in the urban areas for these workers and, hence, the reconstitution of a semi-subsistence peasantry outside the *fazendas*.

In the 1970s, the economic situation was much brighter, with rapid growth in both the agricultural and non-agricultural sectors. Wage-earner employment rose, in particular on large farms and –

for all farm sizes – with a greater increase in numbers of temporary workers than permanent (see table). As a result, the employment of family labour grew only slowly, so that the importance of the small peasantry declined. This transformation can be explained by economic conditions outside the peasant sector itself. The booming industrial economy provided opportunities for small peasants in the urban areas. At the same time, agricultural growth and technological change raised land prices, affecting purchase prices even more than rents. Small farmers and landless workers were thus strongly motivated to look for employment elsewhere. As a result, migration sharply increased in the 1970s. Small farmers often used their capital to migrate to the frontier where they acquired larger plots, while the landless migrated to the cities.

Structure of agricultural employment by farm size: Brazil, 1960-80 (in percentages)

Farm size	Up to 10 ha			10-100 ha			Over 100 ha		
	1960	1970	1980	1960	1970	1980	1960	1970	1980
Family labour	81.4	93.2	90.7	64.5	79.7	73.9	27.0	39.0	31.7
Permanent workers	2.2	1.2	1.6	6.6	4.8	7.3	23.8	26.5	33.6
Temporary workers	12.4	4.4	7.0	20.1	9.9	15.3	32.8	22.0	29.3
Share-croppers	4.0	1.2	0.7	8.8	5.6	3.5	16.3	12.4	5.4
Total	100.0	100.0	100.0	100.0	100.0	100.0	100.0	100.0	100.0

Source: Agricultural censuses.

markets. For Chile, in 1982, Rivera and Cruz (1984) show that household income from work for residents of small rural towns was made up as follows:

	Per cent
Agricultural temporary labour	33
Agricultural permanent labour	10
Urban temporary labour	11
Urban permanent labour	7
Public minimum employment programmes	6
Self-employment	3

In Brazil there has been a decline in the qualification of temporary workers in agriculture due to the greater integration of markets. Jobs in agriculture usually have less desirable attributes, such as instability, interruptions, lack of social security rights and weak enforcement of labour legislation, compared to employment on the urban labour market. Because of this, agriculture does not attract the more able workers. There has been growing participation of unskilled workers, the handicapped, women, old men,

and children in this urban-based agricultural labour force. Thus, the market for temporary agricultural labour has increasingly acquired the characteristics of a secondary labour market.

Competition between this new urban-based labour force and the peasantry for complementary temporary work can, indeed, in many circumstances turn against the peasantry. Urban-based workers (once they are plentifully available due to sufficient dispossession of the peasantry through changing labour laws and reduced access to land) are more flexibly accessible, and the concentration of urban dwellings facilitates and cheapens access to workers by labour contractors. While the traditional peasantry remains the main wage labour reserve for the modern agricultural sector in most countries, this role has been undermined in some countries by the emergence of a landless town-based labour force that gravitates with great fluidity among temporary employers in agriculture and among agricultural and urban employment opportunities.

Table 4.19. Structure of employment in agricultural and rural sectors: Latin America, 1960-80

Country	Year	Share of agricultural workers of urban origin (in %)	Share of rural workers in non-agriculture (in %)
Brazil	1970	12.3	15.2
	1980	17.7	23.4
Pernambuco	1970	13.1	n.a.
	1980	16.3	n.a.
São Paulo	1970	26.6	n.a.
	1980	38.0	n.a.
Costa Rica	1963	5.4	29.1
	1973	6.2	41.2
Ecuador	1962	6.5	19.3
	1974	6.8	26.4
Mexico	1970	23.8	23.1
	1980	26.0	42.4
Nicaragua	1963	11.0	12.8
	1971	11.7	20.0
Peru	1961	18.3	20.1
	1972	23.7	18.8
Puerto Rico	1960	6.5	56.1
	1970	11.8	80.8

n.a. = not available.

Note: Census definition of urban is as follows: Brazil – unspecified; Costa Rica – administrative centres of cantons; Ecuador – capitals of provinces and cantons; Mexico – centre of population with at least 2,500 inhabitants; Nicaragua – administrative centres of departments and *municipios*; Peru – populated centres with 100 or more occupied dwellings; Puerto Rico – centre of population with at least 2,500 inhabitants and employed persons only.

Sources: For Mexico, *Censo General de Poblacion y Vivienda*, 1970 and 1980. For Brazil, Demographic Censuses, 1970 and 1980. For other countries, United Nations, Department of International Economic and Social Affairs: *Patterns of urban and rural growth*, Population Studies No. 68 (New York, 1980).

Rural labour incomes

Trends in agricultural and non-agricultural wages

Table 4.20 shows trends in real agricultural and non-agricultural wages for permanent unskilled workers since the mid-1960s. For most countries, only a minimum wage is available for agricultural workers and, when this is the case, it is compared with the minimum urban wage. When an average wage is reported it is compared with the average wage of construction workers (when available) and, otherwise, with that of manufacturing workers.

In quite a few countries the real agricultural wage (either minimum or average) was substantially higher in 1979-80 than in 1965-66. These countries were Mexico (where it was 60 per cent higher); Ecuador (52 per cent higher than in 1968); Colombia (47 per cent); Brazil, Chile, and Costa Rica (40 per cent);

and Panama (30 per cent). In some other countries, real wages in 1980 were either at the same level as 15 years earlier or substantially lower, the most extreme case being that of Argentina where the real average wage fell by more than 40 per cent.

During these 15 years, GDP per capita increased significantly in most countries. An exception was Mexico where it was only 10 per cent higher. Thus, during this favourable growth period agricultural wages rose less rapidly than average incomes generally in all countries except Chile and Mexico.

This phenomenon of relative impoverishment in the rural areas of a majority of Latin American countries has become absolute impoverishment in the 1980s. Real agricultural wages have fallen drastically in almost all countries, the only exceptions being Colombia and Panama. In Mexico, for example, where wages rose enormously between 1965 and 1980, the dramatic fall in wages in the early 1980s has brought the agricultural wage back to its 1965 level. In Brazil, wages in 1984 were only 11 per cent higher than in 1965; in Chile, 17 per cent.

For some wage earners, falling real wages may have been compensated by greater access to land. As noted earlier, the number of small farms increased by 92 per cent between 1950 and 1980 while the agricultural labour force increased by 67 per cent. But we do not know whether the growing number of small farms is due to greater access to land for the landless or to the increasing subdivision of medium farms. While land reform programmes have given access to land to landless workers, in Peru, for instance, the aggregate effect of these reforms has been small and the subdivision process has probably dominated in the creation of small farms.

This overall evaluation of wages trends during the last 20 years overlooks very contrasted periods in each country. Most countries have had highly unstable growth of GDP per capita with, in the majority of cases, either a change in economic regime or a short recession in the mid-1970s. Noticeable exceptions are Colombia, Costa Rica, and Ecuador which have had moderate but sustained growth, at least until 1980. Wages trends are observed to be strongly influenced by macro-economic changes. It is interesting to note that agricultural wages do not seem to be influenced by the growth of the agricultural sector itself but more by overall economic growth.

Comparisons across countries in periods of economic growth show great diversity in trends of real

Table 4.20. Trends in real agricultural and non-agricultural wages: Latin America, 1965-84 (annual percentage increases)

	Type of wage	Period (mid-1960s to mid-1970s)	Non-agriculture	Agriculture	Period (end of 1970s)	Non-agriculture	Agriculture	Period (early 1980s)	Non-agriculture	Agriculture
Argentina	aver.	1965-74	0.1	3.6	1976-80	−16.8	−21.9			
Brazil	aver.	1967-74	−0.5[1]	3.3	1974-80	1.6[5]	1.8	1980-83	−9.3	−4.5
Chile	min.	1965-70	−1.8	2.7	1975-81	7.0	4.7	1981-84	−12.4	−12.2
Colombia	aver.	1965-73	0.9	0.5[2]	1973-80	2.3	4.5[6]	1980-84	5.0	−1.2
Costa Rica	aver.	1970-74	−2.2	−4.2[3]	1974-79	8.8	11.7	1979-83	−7.9	−4.5
Ecuador	min.	1965-73	−1.8	−7.2	1973-79	1.7	2.3	1980-84	−14.5	−12.1
Guatemala	min.	1965-77	−11.2	−11.7	1977-80	0.3	−3.4	1980-82	3.7	3.1
Mexico	min.	1965-77	3.2	3.7	1977-81	−4.3	1.0	1981-84	−15.0	−15.0
Panama	min.	1965-73	0.1	3.6	1977-81	−0.6	1.3	1980-84	−3.3	−3.3
Paraguay	min.	1965-76	−1.2	−1.1[4]	1976-80	−7.6	3.0	1982-84	−3.8	−3.8
Uruguay	aver.	1965-74	1.5	1.9	1974-80	−9.5	−2.3	1980-84	−3.1	−6.3

[1]1969-74. [2]1965-70. [3]1971-74. [4]1966-76. [5]1974-78. [6]1976-80.

Note: Abbreviation: aver. = average; min. = minimum.

Source: Calculated from A. de Janvry et al.: *Rural labour in Latin America* (Geneva, ILO, 1986; mimeographed World Employment Programme research working paper).

wages but more similarity in changes in the ratio of agricultural to non-agricultural wages. From the mid-1960s to the mid-1970s, characterised by subperiods of annual GDP per capita growth rates of 2 to 4.5 per cent and by fairly low rates of inflation (below 15 per cent for most countries), the ratio of the agricultural to non-agricultural wage in most cases remained fairly constant. In the late 1970s, characterised by subperiods of higher growth rates (3.5 to 7 per cent) and higher rates of inflation (over 20 per cent in most countries), the ratio of agricultural to non-agricultural wages increased. This narrowing of the wage gap can be attributed, in some countries, to the increasing integration noted earlier of the agricultural and non-agricultural labour markets, particularly in periods of rapid economic growth.

Periods of stagnation and recession, by contrast, exhibit less uniformity in relative wage trends. Absolute levels of real wages remain strongly affected by overall economic performance and by the rate of inflation. Thus, during periods of economic stagnation in the late 1970s and in all periods of recession in the 1960s, real wages declined everywhere (with the exception of Colombia). However, the magnitude of the decline seems to be related chiefly to the rate of inflation rather than to the depth of recession.

Real wages paid to permanent and temporary workers

In Brazil and Chile temporary workers' wages are higher than those of permanent workers to compensate for flexibility on the employer's side and irregularity of work on the worker's side. The case of Brazil shows important differences in wage levels between the rich south and the poor north-east, although wages in the north-east have partially caught up with those in the south during the last 20 years. This reflects greater integration of the region induced by the very rapid growth of the economy.

Trends over time show a similar pattern to that in table 4.20, with 1975 and 1981 as turning points. Growth rates in permanent workers' wages were, respectively, 5.1, 0.2, and −9 per cent during the three periods shown. Temporary wages were more volatile, with growth rates of 7.1, −0.9, and −10.6 per cent. While in the last three years permanent workers' wages have fallen at about the same rate as the minimum urban wage, temporary workers' incomes have deteriorated much faster. Temporary workers are in a more precarious situation than permanent workers when facing adverse economic circumstances since both their employment and their wages fluctuate more widely in response to changes in the labour market environment.

Implicit remuneration of family labour

In Brazil, the number of active family members per farm increased slightly between 1970 and 1980 (table 4.21), while the average size of farms smaller than 10 hectares declined. These two forces combined to increase the population pressure on the land for

Table 4.21.   Implicit remuneration of family labour: Brazil and Chile, 1970-80

Brazil

Farm size hectares	Number of active family members				Income per active family member [1]				
	1970	1980	1970	1980	1970	1980	Annual growth rate	As a proportion of average wage of permenent workers	
	Per farm		Per cent of total		1970 cruzeiros		(%)	1970 (%)	1980 (%)
0-5	2.09	2.13	33.0	32.8	417	719	5.6	27.7	31.1
5-10	2.34	2.41	14.7	14.0	718	1 436	7.2	47.7	62.1
10+	2.48	2.53	52.2	53.3	1 783	3 986	8.4	118.4	172.5
Total	2.32	2.38	100.0	100.0	1 163	2 487	7.9	77.2	107.6

Chile (Region IV, 1976)

Farm size hectares	Proportion of farm households (%)	Income per active family members [2]		Proportion of minimum wage	
		On-farm income (US$, 1976)	Total income (US$, 1976)	On-farm income (%)	Total income (%)
0-2	59	92	224	17	42
2-5	25	385	511	72	95
5-10	11	830	967	156	181
10+	4	1 899	2 270	356	424

[1] Income calculated as difference between gross value of sales and expenses.   [2] Income from all sources and there are 3.8 active family members per household.

Sources: For Brazil, agricultural census (various years); for Chile, A. Monardes: *El Empleo en la Pequeña Agricultura: Un Estudio del Valle Central de Chile* (University of Chile, 1979).

small farms. In spite of this, income per family worker increased substantially in real terms because of rising product prices, probably induced by high economic growth (see box 4.4). The result is that, on the average for all active family members in Brazilian agriculture, the level of implicit income caught up with and surpassed the average wage of permanent workers between 1970 and 1980. However, for small farmers – on farms less than 5 hectares, which represent 37 per cent of all farms and employ one-third of family labour – income from home production is only 31 per cent of the wage of permanent workers. This percentage barely increased during the 1970s. On large farms, by contrast, implicit income increased from 118 per cent of wages to 173 per cent. Even though the absolute income of the poorest rose at an annual rate of 5.6 per cent, inequality in family farm incomes has increased substantially over the decade. There has thus been a reduction in absolute poverty and an increase in relative poverty, an observation consistent with similar changes at the national level.

The implicit remuneration of family labour from home production on small farms can be used as a measure of surplus labour on those farms if the wage of permanent workers is taken to indicate their potential full-time income. We thus see that there is a considerable degree of surplus labour for one-third of farm family members (0 to 5 hectares), reaching 69 per cent in 1980, and that this surplus has not fallen appreciably over the last decade. On farms of 5 to 10 hectares, with 14 per cent of family labour, surplus labour was still 38 per cent in 1980, though it declined by 28 per cent during the last decade. Absorption of surplus labour thus appears to have benefited medium farms more than smaller farms.

In Chile (Region IV), as in Brazil, on-farm income for family members increases rapidly with farm size indicating how important land is as the limiting factor on income levels. Using, again, the minimum wage of permanent workers as a measure of full-time income, we see that the small farms (0 to 2 hectares), with 59 per cent of farm households, have as much as

83 per cent surplus labour; farms of 2 to 5 hectares, with another 25 per cent of farm households, still have 28 per cent surplus labour. Off-farm income sources, principally wage income, nearly erase surplus labour for this farm category. For the smallest farms, however, there is still 58 per cent surplus labour after taking into account both on- and off-farm incomes.

Conclusion

The general picture that emerges is one of a rapidly declining share of agriculture in the total labour force, of weak capacity for generating non-agricultural employment in rural areas, and of extremely rapid rural-urban migration. With little employment creation in the modern agricultural sector, insufficient access to land, and limited urban and rural non-agricultural employment opportunities, the peasantry persists not as a superior form of agricultural production but principally as a refuge sector for surplus population. Over time, the number of small farms has grown rapidly; but average farm size has been falling and landlessness has probably risen as well. Peasants are thus forced to rely increasingly on off-farm income opportunities – principally employment on larger farms.

Unpaid family labour remains the principal source of work in agriculture. The bulk of wage labour still appears to be supplied by peasant household members, not by full-time wage workers. It is for this reason that an analysis of rural labour markets in Latin America needs to incorporate a study of not only the landless population but also of peasant households.

An increasing integration of the rural and urban labour markets in some countries has induced a partial catching-up of rural with urban wages. But a rapid decline in permanent relative to temporary employment together with land consolidation has relocated a considerable number of agricultural workers in rural towns. These urban-based farm workers compete with peasant household members for access to scarce temporary employment opportunities in agriculture. Because they are easier to recruit on a short-term basis, these town-based workers may well outcompete peasants on the temporary agricultural labour market. The net effect on peasant living standards is, however, not clear from the existing data.

Between 1965 and 1980 real wages in agriculture rose or stagnated in most countries but have generally fallen since 1980; land availability per peasant household has declined; but temporary employment has grown as well as access to non-agricultural employment. In all, rural poverty remains extensive in Latin America and it has probably increased since the beginning of the 1980s.

Chapter 5

Wages from regular urban employment in developing countries

The more than 100 developing countries (hereafter DCs) display enormous differences not only in their economic circumstances but also in the sophistication of their wage determination institutions and in basic approaches to wages policy. In some DCs the parties involved in wage determination are well-organised, experienced and continuously involved in resolving problems, whereas elsewhere decision-making on wages is taken on an ad hoc, uncoordinated basis in response to immediate pressures. In some the prime responsibility for decision-making rests with employers, workers and their organisations, as in the industrialised market economy countries (IMECs), while in a few the main decisions are taken by the State on a centralised basis, as in the centrally planned economy countries (CPECs) of Eastern Europe. In view of these and many other differences, it is difficult to identify common wage problems and policy responses that in some sense "typify" DCs in general or even certain well defined categories amongst them. Indeed, it is argued below that the tendency to think in terms of stereotyped wage problems of DCs has often been carried too far, sometimes leading to questionable policy advice. The present chapter therefore seeks simply to identify some broad trends that appear relevant for at least certain DCs, some of the more frequently discussed wage issues raised by these trends and how policy-makers have or have not sought to deal with them.

While DCs vary considerably amongst themselves and have been subject to many of the same sorts of economic pressures as the more developed countries, their wage determination problems have been characterised by some common distinctive features of their own. Whereas in IMECs the predominant concern has been the resolution of the wage-price spiral in a stagflationary context subject to repeated external shocks, for a number of DCs in Asia and Africa and certain parts of Latin America a key concern has been the adaptation of poorly developed wage determination institutions to unprecedently high rates of inflation. While labour cost pressures are commonly regarded as a potentially dangerous direct source of inflationary pressures in more developed economies, this is much less plausible in DCs where a large proportion of the labour force is self-employed, and where wages often account for a much smaller proportion of total unit costs in the private sector. However, inflation in DCs is more apt to be generated within the public sector which often provides most of the regular wage employment. Since labour costs are a high proportion of government expenditures, wage increases may exert considerable pressure on government budgets. To the extent that consequent deficits must be financed through credit expansion rather than domestic or foreign savings, there is a risk of generalised inflationary pressures.

Moreover, in many DCs, wages and incomes policies have often been concerned with rectifying major structural imbalances in the economy (notably between rural and urban areas). These imbalances are often associated with apparently large differences in incomes and job opportunities that have few parallels in more developed economies.

Another basic difference is that, in many DCs, the government has been obliged by circumstances to play a much more important role in wage determination than has generally been the case in IMECs. Even where governments have not sought to pursue a centralised wage policy patterned after the CPECs of Eastern Europe or where the public sector has not been the main provider of regular wage employment, their influence in wage decisions has still generally been comparatively strong. Both employers and workers are usually not well organised and workers in particular have needed government support in labour markets characterised by chronic labour surplus conditions.

Finally, it should be noted that whereas both developed and developing countries have experienced major external shocks and pressures for basic structural adjustments to their economies, the relative impact on many DCs, especially in Africa and Latin America, has been much greater. Over the last 10 to 15 years they have been obliged to accommodate falls in real income, shifts in resource allocation and financial and balance of payment constraints that have been far more severe than those experienced elsewhere or previously. And governments' predominant position in wage determination, either as employers or labour market regulators, has put extreme pressure on their wage policies. It is against this economic background that wage determination and wage policies have to be understood.

1. Wage levels

In many respects, the key wage policy question confronting DCs is whether wages paid to regularly employed wage earners are appropriate as compared with other categories of income earners. Indeed, for many years this question has been at the heart of debates over the dynamics of the development process, the causes of various types of urban unemployment or underemployment and the inevitability of large income inequalities. Thinking on this issue has had an important bearing not only on wage policies but also on the general orientation of labour and development policies.

Some development theories and wage determination

One of the most prominent development theories has been the labour surplus model, according to which the "traditional" or "non-capitalist" sector has surplus labour in the sense that workers may be transferred to the "capitalist" sector with little or no loss of output. Despite their low marginal product, workers in the "traditional" sector receive a share of the total output of their sector determined by subsistence requirements. Competitive pressure from surplus labour is expected to keep wages for unskilled labour in the capitalist sector to this institutionally determined level, due allowance being made for differences in the cost of living and other characteristics in the two sectors. The key to the process of economic development is the use of the capitalist

surplus which it is hoped will be reinvested to create new jobs. As development proceeds, labour is withdrawn from the low productivity non-capitalist sector at the fixed wage rate, while employment and accumulation continue to expand in the high productivity capitalist sector. Growth accelerates through reinvestment until such time as the labour surplus is fully absorbed and real wages finally begin to rise. The implication is that the initial stages of economic development will (or should) be characterised by relatively modest real wage improvements (hence greater income inequalities) in order to foster capital accumulation and employment growth in the high productivity sectors of the economy.

In retrospect, it is evident that at least some of the more successful economies in terms of economic growth (for example, Japan, the Republic of Korea and Singapore) did pass through a "labour surplus" phase during which wage increases were moderate. Afterwards, once the labour surplus had been absorbed, the advances in real wages have been truly remarkable. However, for many DCs neither formal sector wages nor the process of economic development have followed the course anticipated by the labour surplus models.

Several inconsistencies have been identified. To begin with, the expansion of industrial employment has often lagged behind the growth in industrial output, that of the urban population and, even more seriously, that of the rate of national population growth. Second, evidence of growing urban unemployment and underemployment suggests that the rapidly expanding urban centres of the Third World have been attracting more workers than they can effectively absorb. Third, in many DCs, wages from regular urban employment have tended to rise faster than incomes in agriculture. They have also often exceeded wages earned by workers with comparable qualifications in other sectors, by margins that appear well in excess of what might be justified by cost of living or other economic differences. The reasons for these trends have been commonly, and rather casually, attributed to misguided government wage policies (statutory minimum wages and public sector pay) or the exercise of trade union power through collective bargaining and political action.

All these considerations have led to the widely held and stereotyped view that urban earnings are fixed at artificially high levels that reduce employment growth by hampering capital accumulation while encouraging capital intensive production techniques.

At the same time, high urban earnings induce excessive rural-urban migration which is only kept in check by the rise of open urban unemployment or low earnings in the informal sector. This view underlies the well-known Harris-Todaro models of internal migration. The driving force in these models is high real urban incomes that make "expected" urban incomes greater than real agricultural incomes at the margin despite rising urban unemployment. The relevance of this aspect of the model is argued by Todaro in the following terms: "One of the most striking features of urban labour markets and wage determination in almost all developing countries has been the tendency for these wages to rise substantially over time, both in absolute terms and relative to average rural incomes, even in the presence of rising levels of unemployment" (Todaro, 1976, p. 25).

While there seems to be much evidence from the past that urban incomes have often risen to levels substantially in excess of those earned elsewhere in the country, there has been a growing doubt about the extent to which this image of substantial and growing labour market distortion remains relevant. To begin with, much of the evidence on high urban/rural income differentials is derived from the experience of a limited number of African countries in the decade or so following their independence. During this period a series of special conditions prevailed: the process of "Africanisation" through which many Africans came to occupy high-paying urban jobs formerly held by Europeans; the influence exercised by urban-based trade unions which had played a critical role in the independence struggle; and the launching of ambitious development programmes that had their main effects on urban areas. Thus the great income differences passed down as a colonial legacy changed their appearance from an European/African to an urban/rural gap. However, it is much less evident to what extent these pressures for raising formal sector wages exist or existed in other parts of the developing world. Certainly there are a number of DCs in Africa (for example, Egypt) and elsewhere (for example, Indonesia) which never experienced this pattern of escalating formal sector wages and marked duality in development. Moreover, there is substantial evidence suggesting that income differences have, in general, been far larger in Africa than in other parts of the Third World. Thus in a compilation of comparisons made between agriculture and non-agriculture incomes for 12 developing countries for various years, mainly around 1970, it was found that for the seven non-African countries the disparity varied between 203 and 252 per cent, whereas it ranged from 394 to 885 per cent for the five African countries.

Comparing formal sector wages with other labour incomes

Large differences in GNP per capita or average incomes between urban and rural areas do not necessarily mean that similar large differences exist for labour incomes for comparably qualified workers in the formal sector and in agriculture. Profits, rents and other non-labour incomes often comprise a much more significant part of urban than rural household incomes. Moreover, the average level of skills and the scarcity premium that they may command are generally higher in urban areas. In the earliest stages of economic development, many of the skills required by formal sector urban activities are in quite short supply, and the returns to human capital correspondingly large. In part, greater non-labour incomes and skill intensities in urban areas may reflect the urban bias of past development programmes, but this is a different matter from wage level distortions. On the other hand, a much higher proportion of rural incomes represents income from work, even though it is difficult to measure its exact level because a considerable proportion of agricultural production is used for own consumption.

There is also evidence that wages for similarly qualified workers may vary considerably more within the formal sector than do labour incomes in other parts of the economy. Indeed, in accounting for overall income distribution inequalities, variations within the urban and rural sectors are often more decisive than variations between them. In assessing the appropriateness of the formal sector general wage level, it is therefore much more relevant to compare the lower income levels in the two sectors where the labour markets are linked through migratory movements.

For example, a study in Thailand found that rural household incomes ranged from 30 per cent of urban incomes in the north-east to 70 per cent in Bangkok-Thanburi and that average labour productivity in agriculture in 1970 was only 12 per cent of that in non-agriculture and only 10 per cent of that in manufacturing. Yet for a relatively homogeneous category of unskilled labour (construction workers) the wages paid in the Northeast were only 15 to 20 per cent below those paid in the Central Plain. Similarly, a compilation of intersectoral wage differentials for low-skill labour, covering the period from the mid-1960s to the early 1970s, found that in only eight out of the 23 developing countries covered did the differential of manufacturing over agriculture exceed 50 per cent. For construction compared with agriculture, the differential exceeded 50 per cent in just six cases. The interpretation of these comparisons is difficult because the agricultural wages used may be biased in some cases by the inclusion of high-paying plantations and the exclusion of payments in kind, whereas the reported manufacturing wages may exclude various fringe benefits. None the less, they are sufficient to illustrate that wage comparisons often yield inequalities that are much lower than average income differences. It needs also to be kept in mind that the ratio between unskilled urban and agricultural wages in seven developed economies during the 19th century ranged from 1.2 in Japan to 2.0 in Australia, with an unweighted mean of 1.6.

Even when the income comparisons are confined to urban areas the results are not always as once imagined. It has become customary to view the urban labour markets of DCs as being divided into formal and informal sectors, which are uniformly characterised by high and low wages respectively. Because of their attractiveness, access to the high-paying jobs in the formal sector must be strictly rationed and the informal sector serves as a staging area where recent migrants wait their turn to get good jobs, even though their incomes may be temporarily below those that might be earned in agriculture. However, even within the formal sector there may be a large difference between wages earned by workers in regular and in casual employment (see chapter 6). Moreover, earnings of small entrepreneurs are often higher than wages earned by regularly employed wage earners. Many workers are found to have improved their earnings by migration from rural to urban areas and the informal sector provides more than simply a transitional source of employment.

Thus a study in Peru found that nearly 60 per cent of incomes in the urban informal sector (defined as units employing four or fewer workers) were in the top two urban quartiles. A series of other studies have shown that many craftsmen and other workers in the informal sector have earnings that compare quite favourably to the modern sector, even though there are, of course, also very low incomes in the informal sector (see chapter 6).

Wage comparisons amongst similarly qualified workers do not always reveal the true differences in standards of living. On the one hand, the position of workers in regular employment is often better than suggested by the usual wage information owing to greater employment security, more extensive fringe benefits provided by their employers and more ready access to public services which are often concentrated in urban areas. On the other hand, the position of rural workers and to some extent informal sector workers may be better than initially presumed because many (but not all) of the prices and necessary expenditures they face may be lower (for instance, food, housing, travel and fuel) and they may have more ready access to secondary income-earning opportunities for all household members. The usual assumption has been that these considerations, along with higher effort levels expected of formal sector workers, would warrant some wage differential in their favour. But its exact magnitude is a matter of considerable debate.

Particularly during the earliest stages of development the level of wages in the formal sector is sometimes influenced by the fact that these employers may draw upon different sources of labour supply than do other segments of the urban labour market. The bottom of the urban wage ladder will in many cases be determined by the alternative income in agriculture of rural-urban migrants. But the alternative incomes and costs of temporary and permanent migrants may be quite different. Temporary migrants may be absent from their rural activities for only short periods and may leave their families behind. They may lose much less income than permanent migrants because they are mainly available during the slack season and their loss of income may be offset by increased activities by other family members. On the other hand, for permanent migrants the cost of supporting a family in town has to be taken into account. This may be substantially higher than in rural areas because it may be more difficult for other family members to supplement household incomes. Moreover, permanent migrants are obliged to find alternatives to the security against old age, ill health, unemployment and other misfortunes provided through customary practices in rural areas. Formal sector employers, at least for their permanent staff, must set wages high enough to attract permanent migrants, whereas elsewhere in the urban labour market the lower supply price of temporary migrants may be more relevant.

The level of wages
from regular employment

Even if wages paid to regularly employed workers are above what employers need pay to attract sufficient workers of the required quality and qualifications, they are still not necessarily "too high". If high wages were imposed upon reluctant employers by government wage policy measures, such as high statutory minimum wages or public sector wages, or by trade union pressures, then some wage restraint might appear justified in order to improve labour market allocative efficiency and to reduce income inequalities. However, higher wages are often voluntarily paid by employers, because they perceive a positive relationship between the wages they pay and the operational effectiveness of their enterprises. Advantages include more selective recruitment of capable and trainable workers, improved worker nutrition, health, commitment and motivation, more effective work discipline, reduced industrial conflict (overt or implicit) and lower labour turnover (and hence lower training and recruitment costs and risks of production disruption).

A number of reasons have been suggested why large employers in developing countries might specially be willing to pay high wages to establish internal labour markets, with their characteristic emphasis on internal promotions, training and long job tenures. The weakness of education, especially technical education, obliges firms to do most of their own training, and hence to offer attractive wages and stable employment in order to keep those who have received extensive training. Also, since typically there may be few alternative job opportunities in individual industries, the training that workers receive will be largely firm specific, also favouring attachments to individual enterprises. Moreover, employers may be reluctant to hire "outsiders" because they have less information on new candidates than in developed economies, owing to the absence or weakness of trade-skill accreditation, apprenticeship schemes and labour exchange services.

There exists much research on wage determination in developing countries that suggests that recruitment and "efficiency-wage" considerations play a significant role in determining wage levels of regularly employed workers. Thus, for instance, in Indonesia, where by general consensus it is agreed that institutional factors have played only a very limited role in wage determination, urban wages are still typically higher than rural wages, with segmentation within the urban sector being more pronounced than in rural areas. Even where there is extensive trade union and government intervention in wage determination, the wages actually paid by employers often exceed significantly levels established statutorily or through collective agreements. Furthermore, historical studies of labour markets suggest that regular workers in large-scale modern industry were comparatively well-paid long before the influence of trade unions and labour legislation became significant.

This is not to suggest, however, that wages from regular employment are generally established at appropriate levels and that this has always been the case. The point being made is that the extent to which economic dualism has been the product of inappropriate wage levels generated by misguided public or private sector wage policies may be greatly exaggerated by various forms of global income and wage comparisons. Assessing whether wages from regular employment are appropriate on economic grounds is a more complex problem than often assumed and generalisations on this point are difficult, if not meaningless. Moreover, from the equity perspective as well, the full implications of high wages may be far from straightforward. For instance, studies have shown that flows of remittances from urban to rural areas are significant in some countries, thus mitigating the extent of inequality in consumption associated with given differences in income levels between city and countryside. Moreover, the alternative to lower wages may not necessarily be higher incomes for the poor but rather increased profits and foreign transfers that cannot be effectively taxed for the benefit of the community at large. Also it cannot be assumed that the process of reducing income inequalities would necessarily be costless. Whether the costs would be worth it is a question not easily answered in most countries. It is therefore not surprising that various analysts looking at more or less similar empirical evidence on wage and income patterns have frequently reached quite different policy conclusions.

Trends in real wages

While past research has not been terribly successful in quantifying in meaningful ways the extent of wage level distortions, and even less successful in assessing their economic implications, nevertheless it is clear that during the last 10 to 15 years many governments in DCs became convinced that wages from regular employment were too high and that consequently wage restraint was essential. In a few instances (such as China, Botswana and Malawi) the elimination of rural-urban income gaps has been established as an explicit wage policy objective. However, even where this is not a stated policy goal, it still appears to have been an important consideration underlying wage decisions in the 1970s and 1980s.

This is borne out by the real wage trends shown in figures 5.1, 5.2 and 5.3 (Africa, Asia and Latin America) and table 5.1. For most countries, earnings statistics are available covering all non-agricultural sectors. Otherwise earnings in manufacturing have been taken. In as far as possible the statistics cover the period between 1971 and 1985. Figures 5.1, 5.2 and 5.3 are based on index numbers taking the average of the years between 1976 and 1980 as a base. This makes it possible to compare the trends between different countries and also to examine for each individual country to what extent real wage trends have changed between the second half of the 1970s and the first half of the 1980s. Table 5.1 attempts to make this comparison between the 1970s and the 1980s in greater detail. It compares the annual growth rates of real wages with those of GDP per capita for the periods 1971-79 and 1979-85. The year 1979 has been selected as a turning-point because it marked the start of the second world-wide recession of the 1970s.

Figure 5.1. Real earnings of employees outside agriculture: African countries, 1971-85 (1976-80 = 100)

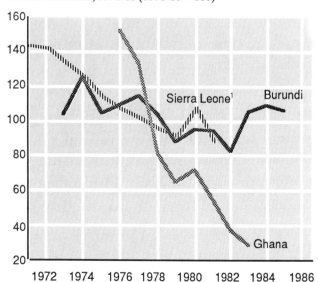

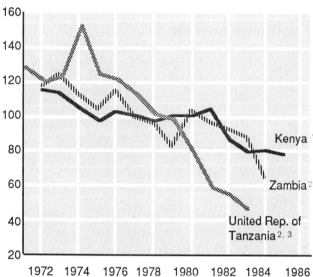

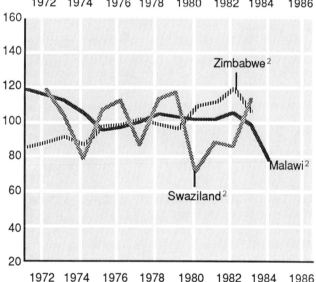

[1]Manufacturing. [2]Wage earners. [3]Mining, manufacturing, public utilities and construction.

Source: ILO: *Year Book of Labour Statistics.*

At the outset, it must be recognised that there are important limitations to the data presented here. They omit many of the smaller developing countries, particularly in the Caribbean, Africa and the Middle East, which do not publish wage trend statistics. The wage data generally only cover larger industrial establishments and may therefore not be representative of wage developments in all parts of the formal sector, for example, smaller enterprises, the public service and casual wage workers. And real wages have been estimated in a rather crude fashion, by deflating a broad-based statistic of average earnings

Figure 5.2.   **Real earnings of employees outside agriculture: Asian and North African countries, 1971-85 (1976-80 = 100)**

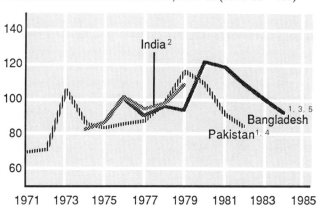

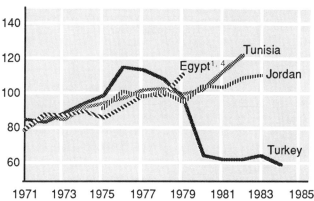

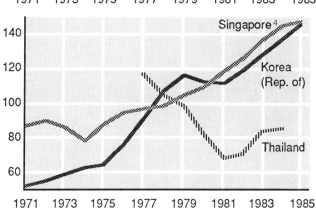

[1] Manufacturing. [2] Mining, manufacturing, public utilities and construction. [3] Wage rates. [4] Wage earners. [5] Skilled wage earners.

Source: ILO: *Year Book of Labour Statistics*.

by the official consumer price index. No attempt has been made to take into account disposable as opposed to gross wages or changes in indirect forms of remuneration. Nor has it been possible to make corrections for technical weaknesses in the wage and price statistics used, to allow for changes in consumer spending patterns under inflationary conditions or for

shifts in the sectoral or occupational distribution of the labour force.

Nevertheless, the data reveal substantial variation amongst DCs in real wage trends. From figures 5.1, 5.2 and 5.3 it would appear that there have been substantial real wage improvements (roughly 50 per cent or more since 1971) for at least a few countries and areas (Brazil, the Republic of Korea, Malaysia, Singapore and Tunisia). In a number of others, such as Costa Rica, Colombia, China, Ecuador, Egypt, Fiji, Israel, Hong Kong, Pakistan and Zimbabwe, real wages have grown between 20 and 50 per cent since 1971. What is perhaps more remarkable is the large number of countries where real wages have scarcely been maintained or have suffered significant declines. In quite a few countries the drop has been 30 per cent or even much more (Ethiopia, Ghana, Kenya, Malawi, Sierra Leone, United Republic of Tanzania, Zaire, Zambia, Burma, Bolivia, Dominican Republic, El Salvador, Nicaragua, Peru, Uruguay).

Generally speaking, real wages in Asian and North African countries have risen since the beginning of the 1970s, while they have fallen in sub-Saharan African countries. In Latin America the situation is mixed: in some countries such as Brazil, Costa Rica, Colombia, Ecuador and Venezuela real wages have increased significantly, but in most they have declined.

Table 5.1 provides a more detailed comparison of trends. It compares annual growth rates of real wages and GDP per capita, for three time periods – the 1970s, the 1980s and the period between 1971 and 1985. If real wages grow more slowly than real GDP per capita, then other incomes (both from capital and/or from self-employment) must have grown faster. This comparison may therefore give some indirect indication whether wages from regular urban employment have been "moderated". Moreover, it can show us whether wage trends have significantly changed since the world economic downturn began in 1979.

Since the beginning of the 1970s, real wages have fallen in more countries than they have risen. Of the 41 countries included in table 5.1, 20 show real wage declines of more than 1 per cent per year, while only 14 experienced an increase of more than 1 per cent per year. For many of the smaller DCs not covered by the table, the available fragmentary evidence suggests that real wages have generally fallen, often dramatically. The table bears out the picture revealed in figures 5.1 and 5.2 – that real wage drops have mainly occurred in sub-Saharan Africa and in quite a few Latin American countries.

Figure 5.3. Real wages of wage earners in manufacturing: Latin American countries, 1971-86 (1976-80 = 100)

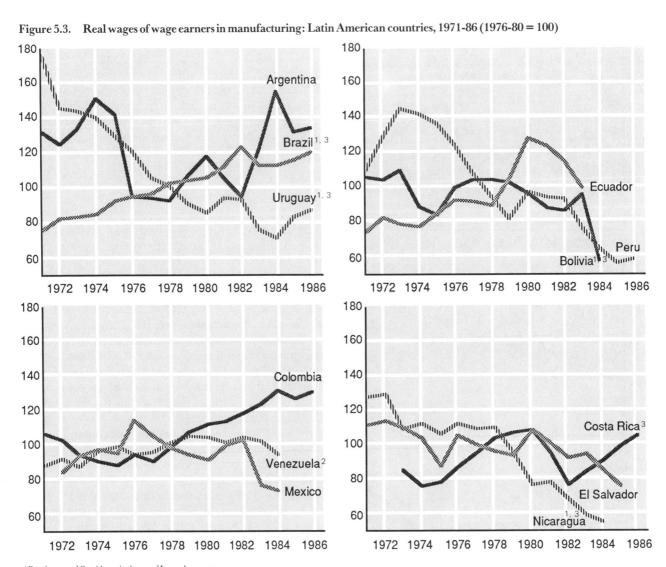

[1] Employees.   [2] Outside agriculture.   [3] Insured persons.

Source: ILO: *Year Book of Labour Statistics* and PREALC.

It also confirms that countries with high rates of growth have generally seen greater real wage increases and vice versa. In other words, there is a rough positive correlation between the rate of economic growth and real wage improvement. (While this may not seem so surprising, it does conflict with the predictions of the labour surplus development models and is not in line with earlier comparisons that generally found little correlation.)

Changes in real wages nevertheless appear to have fallen well behind the rate of economic growth in most DCs, as column (9) of table 5.1 shows. Real wages rose faster than GDP per capita in only nine of the 41 countries over the period. In some of these

countries the difference in growth rates is quite small and may be spurious or clearly attributable to special circumstances, such as the tight labour markets occasioned by exceptionally fast growth in the Republic of Korea or the impact of oil in Venezuela and Ecuador or simply the highly irregular movement of wages. On the other hand, in many countries where the comparisons show real wages lagging behind, the differences have been substantial suggesting that other incomes have been rising much more rapidly than wages. It seems that the degree of real wage "moderation" was more pronounced during the 1970s than in the 1980s. The gap between real wages and GDP per capita growth rates

Table 5.1.　Average annual growth rates of real wages and GDP per capita: Developing countries, 1971-85

Country	Period (1970s)	Real wage (1)	GDP per capita (2)	Difference (1)-(2) =(3)	Period (1980s)	Real wage (4)	GDP per capita (5)	Difference (4)-(5) =(6)	Period (1970s-1980s)	Real wage (7)	GDP per capita (8)	Difference (7)-(8) =(9)
Africa												
Burundi	1973-79	−2.4	+2.5	−4.9	1979-84	+3.9	+0.5	+3.4	1973-84	+0.4	+1.1	−0.7
Egypt	1971-79	+4.2	+4.5	−0.3								
Ethiopia	1974-79	−9.0	−5.3	−3.7	1979-81	1.0	+3.4	−2.4	1974-81	−6.3	−2.9	−3.4
Ghana	1971-79	−13.4	−2.3	−11.1	1979-83	−18.6	−5.2	−13.4	1971-83	−15.2	−3.3	−11.9
Kenya	1972-79	−1.9	+1.2	−3.1	1979-83	−5.5	−1.6	−3.9	1972-83	−3.3	−0.0	−3.3
Malawi	1971-79	−1.9	+1.3	−3.2	1979-84	−5.5	−2.3	−3.2	1971-84	−3.3	−0.1	−3.2
Mauritius	1971-79	+5.3	+6.7	−1.4	1979-81	−9.9	−3.9	−6.0	1971-81	+2.1	+4.5	−2.4
Nigeria	1973-78	−4.0	−0.4	−3.6	1978-80	+5.6	−0.1	+5.7	1973-80	−1.4	−0.3	−1.1
Sierra Leone	1971-79	−5.3	−0.2	−5.1	1979-81	−1.9	+2.9	−4.8	1971-81	−4.6	+0.4	−5.0
United Republic of Tanzania	1971-79	−3.4	+2.3	−5.7	1979-83	−17.3	−3.0	−14.3	1971-83	−8.3	+0.5	−8.8
Tunisia	1971-79	+2.9	+4.5	−1.6	1979-82	+7.0	+0.7	6.3	1971-82	+4.0	+3.4	+0.6
Zaire	1977-79	−28.2	−5.6	−22.6	1979-83	+4.2	−1.6	+5.8	1977-83	−8.0	−2.9	−5.1
Zambia	1972-79	−4.7	−3.1	−1.6	1979-84	−4.6	−2.1	−2.5	1972-84	−4.7	−2.6	−2.1
Zimbabwe	1971-79	+1.5	−2.3	+3.8	1979-83	+2.4	+4.9	−2.5	1971-83	1.8	+0.0	+1.8
Asia												
Bangladesh	1976-79	−2.5	+1.7	−4.2	1979-84	−0.5	+1.1	−1.6	1976-84	−1.2	+1.3	−2.5
Burma	1971-79	−7.8	+1.8	−9.6	1979-83	+1.1	+3.3	−2.2	1971-83	4.9	+2.3	−7.2
China	1971-79	+2.7	+3.3	1.2	1979-85	+8.7			1971-85	+4.9		
Fiji	1971-79	+4.8	+2.1	+2.7	1979-84	−1.8	−0.6	−1.2	1971-84	+2.2	+1.0	+1.2
India	1971-79	+1.2	+0.8	+0.4								
Israel	1971-79	+2.9	+1.6	+1.3	1979-84	+2.7	+0.3	+2.4	1971-84	+2.9	+1.1	+1.8
Jordan	1975-79	+1.3	+10.1	−8.8	1979-83	+3.6	+5.4	−1.8	1975-83	+2.4	+7.7	−5.3
Korea, Rep. of	1971-79	+10.6	+7.8	+2.8	1979-84	+3.3	+3.7	−0.4	1971-84	+7.8	+6.2	+1.6
Pakistan	1971-79	+5.5	+9.6	−4.1	1979-81	−11.7	+5.6	−17.3	1971-81	+1.8	+8.8	−7.0
Singapore	1971-79	+2.2	+6.9	−4.7	1979-84	+6.8	+7.3	−0.5	1971-84	+4.0	+7.1	−3.1
Thailand	1971-79	−8.4	+5.6	−14.0	1979-84	−2.9	+3.8	−6.7	1977-84	−4.5	+4.3	−8.8
Turkey	1971-79	+1.8	+2.9	−1.1	1979-83	−9.5	+0.6	−10.1	1971-83	−2.2	+2.1	−4.3
Latin America												
Argentina	1971-79	−2.7	+0.6	−3.3	1979-84	+7.9	−2.5	+10.4	1971-84	+1.3	−0.6	+1.9
Brazil	1971-79	+4.2	+5.7	−1.5	1979-84	+1.5	−1.2	+2.7	1971-84	+3.2	+3.0	+0.2
Bolivia	1971-79	−0.5	+2.8	−3.3	1979-83	−1.5	−6.9	+5.4	1971-83	−0.9	−0.5	−0.4
Colombia	1971-79	+0.0	+3.2	−3.2	1979-84	+4.0	+0.4	+3.6	1971-84	+1.6	+2.1	−0.5
Costa Rica	1973-79	+3.8	+2.9	+0.9	1979-84	−3.3	−2.8	−0.5	1973-84	+0.5	+0.3	+0.2
Dominican Republic	1971-79	−1.1	+3.5	−4.6	1979-84	−4.6	+0.3	−4.9	1971-84	−2.5	+2.3	−4.8
Ecuador	1971-79	+4.2	+6.4	−2.2	1979-83	−0.9	−1.1	+0.2	1971-83	+2.5	+3.8	−1.3
El Salvador	1971-79	−2.2	+1.7	−3.9	1979-84	−1.7	−6.6	+4.9	1971-84	−2.0	−1.1	−0.9
Guatemala	1971-79	−5.5	+3.1	−8.6	1979-83	+9.1	−3.2	+12.3	1971-83	−0.8	+0.9	−1.7
Mexico	1972-79	+1.5	+3.2	−1.7	1979-84	−5.0	0.0	−5.0	1972-84	−1.3	+1.9	−3.2
Nicaragua	1971-79	−3.7	−4.5	+0.8	1979-83	−10.9	+0.9	−11.8	1971-83	−6.2	−2.7	−3.5
Paraguay	1971-79	−2.0	+5.2	−7.2	1979-84	−0.9	+2.3	−3.2	1971-84	−1.5	+4.1	−5.6
Peru	1971-79	−3.7	+0.6	−4.3	1979-84	−4.6	−2.8	−1.8	1971-84	−4.1	−0.8	−3.3
Uruguay	1971-79	−8.0	+2.3	−10.3	1979-84	−5.0	−2.8	−2.2	1971-84	−6.8	+0.3	−7.1
Venezuela	1971-79	+2.3	+0.9	+1.4	1979-84	−2.2	−4.6	+2.4	1971-84	+0.5	−1.2	+1.7

Source: Most real wage data has ben calculated from the ILO: *Year Book of Labour Statistics*. GDP per capita figures (in constant 1980 US dollars) have been taken from the IMF: *International Financial Statistics Yearbook* (Washington, DC, 1986).

(columns (3) and (6)) has narrowed in 23 countries while it has widened in 14 countries. None the less, there has been a clear tendency in the 1980s for economic growth to continue to outstrip real wage improvements. This phenomenon is not evident in similar comparisons made for the 1950s and 1960s.

It does not necessarily mean, of course, that wages from regular employment are now at appropriate levels or that the trends have been inappropriate. For developed economies, the trend rate of growth of labour productivity (GNP per worker) has commonly been used as a first approximation to the "room" that may exist for real wage increases as a result of the process of economic growth. But in the developing country context there has been much less agreement on the use of this standard. Many would argue that as long as DCs are characterised by substantial "duality" and apparent underutilisation of labour in various activities, there is little scope for real wage improvements for regularly employed workers with comparatively high incomes. On this view, most, if not all, of the growth "dividend" should be used to expand employment opportunities rather than to improve the position of those already fortunate enough to be fully employed in good jobs. Hence, it is argued that it is not at all unexpected or undesirable to find real wages advancing more slowly than economic growth. All the same, the evidence presented above does suggest that if there was in earlier periods a tendency for wage levels to escalate out of control, this appears to have been checked in most DCs. Labour market distortions associated with inappropriately high wage levels have undoubtedly tended to diminish rather than increase.

2. Wage adjustments

The extent to which equity and efficiency goals of wage policy are met will depend on the pattern of wage adjustments over time. The size and frequency of wage adjustments obviously have an important influence on macro-economic efficiency: the achievement of economic objectives, such as low levels of inflation, full employment, sustained economic growth and equilibrium on the balance of payments. At the same time, on equity grounds a high priority is usually given to wage adjustments that are at least sufficient to preserve worker purchasing power, especially that of the lowest-paid groups. Moreover, adjusting wages at least approximately in line with price movements helps ensure that the relative

income positions of different groups in the community are not abruptly and arbitrarily altered through inflation. Rapid changes in real wages may also adversely affect the efficient operation of enterprises. Steep drops in real wages undermine worker motivation and commitment and may lead to greater industrial conflict. Similarly, abrupt rises may make it more difficult for enterprises to absorb the higher costs. Moreover, if changes in relative income positions are needed, a series of minor adjustments spread over a period of time is often advisable because it enables all economic agents to make the necessary adaptations as painlessly as possible. It has been considerations of these kinds that have made the preservation of purchasing power an important starting point for wage adjustment decisions.

Assessed against this standard, the pattern of short or medium-term wage movements in DCs over the last 10 to 15 years gives rise to considerable concern. In some DCs real wages have dropped by up to 50 per cent, and declines of 10 per cent or more within as short a time span as two years have been quite common. The picture that emerges from figures 5.1, 5.2 and 5.3 is one of remarkable flexibility, indeed volatility, in real wage movements. This is in sharp contrast with the experience of most IMECs and the CPECs of Eastern Europe, where despite marked changes in inflation and economic growth wages have typically been well protected (see chapters 7 and 8).

The irregular pattern of wage movements in DCs would appear to be linked in part to poorly developed wage determination systems. Where the practice of periodically adjusting basic wage scales every one, two or three years has not been firmly established through collective bargaining, government regulation or other procedures, accelerating inflation has meant that real wages for at least some categories of workers have declined precipitously. Eventually, however, pressures for some wage adjustment have accumulated to the point where they could no longer be resisted. Large "catch-up" increases have been called for, even though not easily accommodated by the economy. The result has been a disruptive pattern of irregular wage adjustments, producing medium to long-term real wage movements which have not necessarily been in line with clearly conceived wage policy objectives.

Wage restraint policies

Postponing adjustments as long as possible has been a natural reaction of governments convinced that economic conditions warrant wage restraint.

Since the beginning of the 1980s wage restraint has generally occupied a prominent place in stabilisation programmes aimed at breaking inflationary expectations, reducing pressures on government deficits, improving profitability and boosting incentives for job creation. It has also been viewed as necessary for restoring equilibrium to the balance of payments by reducing domestic demand for imports and potential exports and by improving international competitiveness in the production of export goods and import substitutes. The severity of the economic crisis that many DCs have had to cope with over the last five to ten years, particularly those in Africa and some parts of Latin America, accounts in large part for the frequent sharp falls in real wages apparent in figures 5.1, 5.2 and 5.3.

The severity of wage restraint has been further increased by several other factors. First, in some instances, the implementation of stabilisation policies has been long delayed (for example, the failure to adjust domestic incomes to a decline in a country's terms of trade). This has meant that when stabilisation measures have eventually been introduced, they have had to be all the more stringent. Second, wage restraint has sometimes turned out to be inadvertently severe when inflation has been higher than anticipated and governments have failed to adapt their wage adjustment decisions accordingly. Third, wage restraint has in some DCs been applied especially vigorously because not only has it been comparatively easy to implement (simply involving delays in adjusting statutory minimum wages or public sector pay scales) but it has also served the long-run objective of promoting employment expansion and reducing the gap between urban and rural incomes. Finally it has quite often been the result of the dire condition of government budgets and the inability to finance increases in the public sector wage bill. Moreover, preference has frequently been given to the preservation or even expansion of employment rather than to the raising of wages as the best use of a constrained public sector wage bill. This outcome has been favoured by the role played by the public sector, mainly in Africa, as the chief provider of job opportunities, particularly for the increasing numbers of secondary and high school leavers.

In retrospect, it is evident that the degree of wage restraint applied in some cases can be questioned. Sharp downward pressure on real wages, be it in the form of small and slow nominal wage adjustments or the removal of subsidies on basic goods and services,

has sometimes led to highly disruptive social conflict that might well have been avoided by less draconian stabilisation measures. Moreover, where declines in real wages have been substantial, the effects on work standards and performance have been most unfortunate. This has been particularly apparent in the public sector which has often borne the brunt of austerity measures (see box 5.1 on Sudan). Many observers have associated the large absolute and relative declines in public sector pay with the departure of the most productive employees, increased absenteeism, illicit practices, moonlighting (both during and after regular working hours) or simply low work effort.

In some cases in Africa where real pay has fallen 50 per cent or more, the effects on standards of public administration have been devastating. To cite just one example, in Ghana the purchasing power of lower level public service pay scales in 1984 was only one-fifth of its value in 1977. For higher grades it was just 6 per cent. Even though these losses may have been somewhat mitigated by promotions, payments in kind and other more or less hidden forms of remuneration, it nevertheless remains true that in seven years inflation had almost completely wiped out the motivational effectiveness of pay. From this and other cases, it is being increasingly accepted that, although the relationship is difficult to document and measure precisely, public sector performance is dependent on pay levels. Moreover, once performance standards are allowed to deteriorate substantially as a consequence of short-term financial pressures, it is bound to be a long and difficult task to raise them again. In recognition of this, public sector operational efficiency considerations appear to be receiving more attention in wage policy decision-making than in the recent past. Thus in Ghana, despite continuing financial difficulties, it was accepted that some improvement in public service pay would have to be made as part of the country's programme of structural adjustment.

Another unfortunate consequence of wage restraint has been the gradual undermining of statutory minimum wages. The 1970s and 1980s have seen a much more cautious approach to both the size and frequency of minimum wage adjustments. In sharp contrast with the experience of the 1950s and 1960s, minimum wages in most DCs have increased less rapidly than average wages and per capita income. Thus, a recent ILO comparison of the experience of Latin American countries over the period 1970 to

---

5.1   Wages and structural adjustment in the Sudan

Sudan is a poor country with vast international debts, a chronic balance-of-payments deficit and high inflation. It has recently experienced severe droughts, the inflow of large numbers of refugees, the outflow of large numbers of skilled workers seeking employment and higher wages abroad, and a resource-draining conflict in the south. External debt exceeds US$13,000 million and real GDP is lower than in 1976-77. Despite injections of large amounts of foreign loans and aid, and various rounds of IMF assistance, the economy has shown little improvement over the past decade. Government employment has risen by something like a quarter but there have been large reductions in real pay. The public sector dominates regular wage employment, providing 500,000 out of 600,000 jobs.

Civil service pay scales have been adjusted infrequently even though prices doubled between 1977 and 1980, doubled again between 1980 and 1983, and yet again between 1983 and 1985. By November 1983 civil service pay scales were one-fifth of their real level in 1970. The severe erosion of real pay has had serious adverse effects on morale and productivity. Discontent with the drastic reduction in standards of living for professional groups in public employment was one of the contributory factors to the overthrow of the previous regime and the restoration of a democratic political system in 1985-86.

The transitional Government in 1985 introduced a package of improvements in civil service pay and allowances. These had the effect of restoring real basic salaries in July 1986 to a little more than one-fifth, and real gross salaries including allowances to about one-third, of their 1978 levels. Modest though the real effects of the package may be, it imposes very considerable financial burdens on the newly elected Government.

The importance of the public sector pay bill to the Government's budget severely limits the scope for increasing real pay. But despite this, some restoration of the value of lost real income is being viewed as a precondition for effective structural adjustment as it is vitally necessary to improve morale and efficiency in the public service. Close attention is being given to improving the ability of the Government to finance wage increases by dealing with the problems of overstaffing and ineffective manpower deployment produced by former government policies. Voluntary retrenchment on special terms is seen as one possible way of reducing some of the excess staffing, and retraining and redeployment of other employees could lead to improved production and the removal of some scarcities of skilled labour.

The present Government is seeking to deal with these problems in a constructive way. In a statement of policy to the Constituent Assembly on 7 July 1986, it announced that it was seeking an agreement with trade unions on a social contract which would achieve social peace and mobilise energies to restructure and strengthen the nation. Agreement on policies and the associated obligations on both sides is regarded as the desirable as well as the most promising way forward. Trade union co-operation is regarded as particularly important, to ensure that the difficult adjustment processes are implemented as smoothly and as equitably as possible, with a minimum of hardship.

1983 showed that the purchasing power of the minimum wage had fallen over the period in 13 out of the 16 countries examined, often quite substantially. Moreover, in 10 out of 15 countries, nominal minimum wages had by 1983 risen more slowly or only at the same rate as average wages. Where minimum rates had increased faster, it was sometimes due to their relatively low rate in the base period. From the fragmentary information on minimum wages in Africa, it would appear that minimum wages have been adjusted infrequently and by comparatively small amounts. Unfortunately, in a limited but increasing number of DCs caution in the adjustment of minimum wages has led to substantial declines in their real value so that they have lost all relevance in wage determination. Thus, the modest but still significant contribution that minimum wage fixing may make to poverty alleviation through the raising of excessively low wages has been lost.

Wage restraint and stabilisation policies: An assessment

More generally, wage restraint as an element of stabilisation programmes has been questioned on the grounds that it will not necessarily be effective in bringing about the required economic adjustments, at least not within a reasonable time period. Whereas the effects of wage restraint on government budgets may be more or less direct and immediate, the effects on other economic variables in the developing country context are much more uncertain. Thus, as inflation in DCs has often been fuelled by excessive monetary growth, supply bottlenecks and escalating import prices rather than labour cost pressures, the effectiveness of wage restraint in bringing it to a halt is correspondingly reduced. With respect to the balance of payments, wage restraint is unlikely to have much effect on curbing imports where the basic consumption goods of workers do not or no longer form a significant part of what is imported. Nor will it contribute to promoting exports where their expansion is limited by the non-availability of necessary imported inputs, technology, labour force skills or capital resources rather than by international cost competitiveness.

There may be much controversy over the scope for expanding employment in the long run through real wage reductions. But the short-run effects are likely to

| 5.2 | Economic and wage stabilisation in Israel |

Spiralling inflation afflicted the Israeli economy in the early 1980s. The annual rate of inflation was 120.4 per cent in 1982, 145.6 per cent in 1983 and 373.8 per cent in 1984. Between 1978 and 1984, prices rose by more than 100,000 per cent! By the summer of 1985, the mushrooming budget deficit threatened to become unmanageable. Foreign debt reached a peak of US$24,000 million, the highest level per capita in the world.

On 1 July 1985, the Prime Minister announced a drastic austerity plan to avert "total collapse" of the economy. The plan included a devaluation of the shekel by 19 per cent, a further significant cut in government subsidies, a three-month freeze of wages and prices, a 3 per cent reduction in public sector wages and retrenchment of some 10,000 public servants (3 per cent of the public workforce).

The Histadrut (the General Federation of Labour) strongly opposed the announced plan. Intensive tripartite negotiations were held and culminated on 16 July in a new wage pact for the private sector whose principal features were suspension of the cost-of-living increment (COLA) for the next three months; instead of the COLA, payment of a supplement of 14 per cent on the July wages; payment of a supplement of 12 per cent of the July wages in August; and payment of a compounded supplement of 12 per cent, between November 1985 and March 1986, in three monthly instalments. Negotiations between the Government and the Histadrut were initially deadlocked on the public sector, with the former insisting on a 6 per cent reduction in the sector's workforce, or a 3 per cent cut plus a 3 per cent reduction in wages. Subsequently, the Government agreed to abandon the 3 per cent cut in public sector wages. For its part, the Histadrut accepted the retrenchment of some 10,000 civil servants but insisted that the lay-offs be carried out in accordance with the rules laid down in labour contracts and not through emergency regulations.

During their first year of operation, the stabilisation measures had a dramatic impact on the rate of inflation. Prices rose only 3.9 per cent in August 1985, in line with the plan's target, while in December 1985 the consumer price index actually fell 1.3 per cent, the lowest inflation rate since 1969. During the first six months of 1986, consumer prices rose at an annual rate of around 20 per cent, far below the three-digit figures of immediately preceding years. The following effects had also emerged by mid-1986: the budget deficit had fallen from 15 per cent to 3-4 per cent of GNP; the external current account balance showed a surplus; the unemployment rate had increased as a result of the stabilisation plan to 7 per cent, but was distinctly lower than the 10 per cent anticipated; and real wages had gradually begun to rise after falling 20 per cent in the first stage of the plan.

A number of factors contributed to the success of the austerity plan during its first year of operation. By and large, the major elements of the programme had been thoughtfully conceived. The interactions of its different components and the cumulative outcome, in retrospect, had been anticipated quite accurately. Reliable information was continuously given out to the public and helped to secure widespread understanding and support for the measures initiated. There was careful monitoring of the programme, and prompt, decisive action was taken to shunt the programme back on track when deviations inevitably materialised.

Of critical importance, intensive discussions and negotiations took place, at the outset of the plan and during its initial implementation, among labour, management and the Government. The Histadrut recognised that austerity was necessary to fend off economic disaster. It also accepted that a temporary reduction of income of wage earners was unavoidable. However, it objected strenuously to aspects of the original plan which would have imposed wage regulation by executive decree or emergency legislation, thereby circumventing and undermining collective bargaining. It became partner to the programme after the Prime Minister pledged not to impose those compulsory mechanisms. It also succeeded in negotiating wage cuts in both the public and private sectors which were less deep than initially announced by the Government.

be minimal owing to lags in investment decisions and may well add to the overall negative impact on jobs of austerity programmes by producing further decreases in effective demand. Typically, investigations of wage-employment relationships have found it difficult to uncover evidence of strong negative correlations in the short run. Thus a recent ILO study of wage-employment relationships in Latin American countries, covering the periods 1975-78 and 1978-81 and 12 countries, found no instances in the first period where a rise in real wages was associated with a significant rise in open unemployment. On the contrary, in six of the countries there was a negative correlation. Much the same pattern was evident in the second period. Changes in unemployment were far more readily accounted for by changes in the level of demand. More detailed examinations of the relationship between short-run employment and

wage changes over time in individual countries (Panama, Uruguay, Chile) also obtained similar results.

Controversies have also arisen from the way in which wage restraint policies and more generally entire packages of stabilisation measures have been implemented. Typically they have been introduced in an atmosphere of crisis where the deterioration in economic conditions makes it clear to all concerned that drastic measures that will affect the living standards of major groups in the population need to be taken. More often than not, decisions on the programme have been taken in great secrecy, without prior consultations with those groups potentially at risk. Not surprisingly, in these circumstances workers' organisations have bitterly opposed those elements of the stabilisation packages that have affected their members most directly, such as wage freezes, increased prices and reduced provision of basic goods and services, and cut-backs in employment. However, there are reasonable grounds for believing that stabilisation programmes would stand a better chance of success if they were not simply imposed but rather preceded by an open discussion of the practical alternatives for resolving the problems that must be confronted, and if they built on at least a measure of social consensus on how the burdens of adjustment are best shared (see the example of Israel in box 5.2). Within the limits of time and resources available, there are possibilities for elaborating programmes in ways that accommodate wage earner and other interests without undermining the basic purpose of the operation. This would involve spreading the burdens of adjustment amongst the various income groups in the community roughly in accordance with their ability to carry them, varying the degree of wage restraint directly with wage levels, providing some contingency guarantees about the size of real wage losses that would be tolerated, non-economic measures such as enhanced job security or rights to participate in decisions, and so on. Unfortunately, stabilisation programmes have not often been elaborated in this manner but rather usually in authoritarian ways that have generated much conflict. Moreover, the fear of conflict linked to stabilisation programmes, particularly by governments in a weak political position, has been a principal reason why their implementation tends to be delayed too long.

The different ways that governments have used to influence wage adjustments have given rise to their own problems. In some cases, they have limited their action to those decisions traditionally taken by governments in mixed economies, namely wage adjustments in the public sector and statutory minimum wages for the private sector. However, in DCs such action often has a much greater impact than comparable decisions in IMECs because the public sector is proportionately much larger. The pursuit of wage restraint policies through these instruments alone has also raised questions concerning the disparity of treatment between those workers most directly affected and other segments of the labour force. Concerns of this kind, along with a desire to correct income imbalances and exercise close control over labour cost movements, have sometimes motivated governments in DCs to introduce more comprehensive forms of wage controls. The experience with these broad systems of wage controls has been quite varied. In some cases (for example, Singa-

pore) wage control has appeared quite successful over a number of years in maintaining international competitiveness and widespread support amongst workers' and employers' organisations. Elsewhere the experience has been much less positive, the controls being seen as an undue infringement on collective bargaining or encountering major problems in their practical application.

In a number of DCs the governments' concern has been, not with limiting private sector wage increases, but rather with offsetting real wage declines. In sharp contrast with practice in developed countries, cost-of-living allowances have been introduced which give existing workers an entitlement to wage increases of specified amounts, generally varying inversely with existing wage rates (for example the Philippines, Sri Lanka, Mauritius, Ethiopia, Egypt, Peru). While generally meeting their primary objective of protecting real wages of low-paid workers, they have also had a number of unfortunate side-effects such as complexity in the determination of individual worker wage and fringe benefit entitlements, differential treatment of workers with similar qualifications depending on their date of hire, confusion over the respective responsibilities of private and governmental decision-making on wages and adverse effects on the voluntary development of collective bargaining. With the passage of time, these adverse side effects tend to intensify. Yet once governments have introduced cost-of-living adjustments, it has often been difficult to abandon them.

3. Wage structures

In DCs as elsewhere, an economically ideal wage structure would be one in which "every rate is just high enough to induce each kind of labour to present itself in the needed quantities, provides just enough incentive for workers to acquire skills and accept responsibility, and just enough incentive to meet required standards of performance" (Berg, 1969, p. 295). From the equity perspective as well, such a structure would have much to commend itself since wage differences would be kept to the minimum levels that are economically essential. Although the situation differs enormously amongst DCs the actual pattern of wage differences has often departed significantly from this ideal standard. In some instances these departures have led to remedial policy measures going well beyond anything attempted in IMECs. At the risk of excessive simplification, the following discussion singles out just three frequent targets for policy concern, namely inter-industry, inter-occupational and public-private sector wage differentials.

Inter-industry differences

The general expectation has been that wage differences between industries would tend to reach a maximum during the early stages of economic development and to diminish gradually thereafter. It is at the earlier stages of development that skill differentials and inter-industry variations in technical sophistication and capital intensiveness would appear to be largest. The limited empirical evidence available highlights substantial variation in the experience of individual countries but provides some support for the expected tendency. Thus, an early study of the experience of 17 developed and developing countries over the period 1948-65 found that the inter-industry wage spread was generally wider in DCs and that international differences in industrial wage structures tended to narrow over time. A more recent study of inter-industry differences in average earnings covering 19 Latin American countries and time periods of up to 40 years also found that, in spite of much diversity amongst countries, there was some tendency for wages between specific industries to narrow with time. More uniformity was found in the composition of the best- and worst-paying industries. With only a few exceptions, certain industries dominated the top-paying group (for example within manufacturing, printing, drink, transport equipment, rubber, non-electric machinery, electrical machinery and non-metal products) and those at the bottom of the wage hierarchy (for example textiles, clothing, cloth; woodworking; furniture; food processing and leather).

Whereas differences in skill content provide part of the explanation for the large inter-industry variations in earnings observed in DCs, there is evidence that other factors are typically of considerable importance as well. Although much research has focused on earnings differences between the formal and informal sectors of the economy, a number of studies have found that there are also substantial differentials within the formal sector. Thus, earnings variations amongst regularly employed wage earners have been accounted for not only by worker characteristics such as years of schooling, work experience, age, skill category and employment status, but also by the characteristics of the enterprise or industry. These include the size of the enterprise, average labour productivity (as measured for instance by value added per worker), level of skill intensity, capital/ labour ratios, profit rates, ownership, trade union organisation and degree of competition in the market for its products. These studies confirm the results of more casual observation, namely that similarly qualified workers may earn very different wages depending on the enterprises where they happen to work. While this phenomenon is not unique to DCs, it is generally thought that inequalities between firms and industries are larger than those found elsewhere.

The economic implications of these inequalities depend considerably on their origins. Where they arise because it is in the interest of the enterprise to be more selective in recruitment to obtain more motivated, committed or trainable workers, the inequalities are consistent with, indeed necessary for, allocative efficiency. Even if not essential for recruitment purposes, the inequalities may still be justified to the extent that the higher wages are associated with improved operational efficiency, that is, with better motivation, stronger commitment, more skill acquisition, lower turnover, less industrial conflict, and so on. But where the inequalities reflect simply the favourable or unfavourable market position of particular employers or the power of particular trade unions or the vulnerability of particular categories of workers owing to labour market imperfections, their legitimacy is open to serious doubt.

Even where inequalities appear unwarranted, it is not always evident that they could be removed or reduced through wage and industrial relations policies that would be considered as equitable and effective. None the less, a number of countries, particularly in Africa, have sought to reduce inter-industry and inter-firm inequalities by introducing unified national pay structures. This has been done either through centralised or industry-level collective bargaining (for example, Cameroon and many other French-speaking African countries) or by legislative decree (such as Algeria). In many countries more or less unified pay structures have also been imposed throughout the public sector, including both the public service and the public enterprise sector (for example Nigeria, the United Republic of Tanzania, Egypt).

Inter-industry and inter-firm inequalities at both extremes of the wage structure have attracted the most attention. There has been concern in some countries about the high wages paid by multinational enterprises, profitable export industries such as petroleum or mining, or firms with a monopoly position on the local market. The fear has been that the high wages paid would not only aggravate unemployment problems by inducing excessive rural-urban migration but also push up the general wage level by establishing inappropriate targets for other industries to emulate. From the equity perspective, it has been maintained that the above-normal profits generated in these sectors should be shared, not just by the workers in these sectors, but by society as a whole through government taxation. Concerns of this kind have been among the principal reasons why some DCs have introduced uniform national wage structure policies or have used other means to restrain wages in the leading enterprises. Most governments, however, have felt reluctant to impose such limitations in part because they believe that high wages in the private sector are largely financed by the profits of multinational enterprises that would otherwise be exported. Also the argument that high wages in certain parts of the private sector raise general wage levels unduly appears increasingly implausible in the context of falling or stagnant real wages. Moreover, multinational enterprises now frequently claim that they seek to pay wages that, although often somewhat higher than national employers, will not disrupt local labour markets. It is uncertain, however, to what extent they limit their pay levels for their own strategic reasons or at the unofficial behest of governments or other employers.

Governments in DCs have been more ready to attack inter-industry inequalities at the bottom end of the wage structure. Over the past 15 to 25 years they have tried to use statutory minimum wages as a means to raise what often appear as deplorably low wages. As of January 1986, 98 countries had ratified the Minimum Wage-Fixing Machinery Convention, 1928 (No. 26), making it one of the the the most widely adopted international instruments of the ILO.

The structural characteristics of these systems are remarkably diverse, there being important differences in the numbers and categories of workers covered, the scope of the rates fixed (for example, generally applicable as opposed to industry-specific rates, unique rates for all workers or different rates for occupational categories, national or regional rates) and the form of the machinery used for fixing rates. Despite this diversity it is possible to distinguish four basic roles that minimum wage fixing (hereafter MWF) plays in national systems of wage determination. The most limited role envisages MWF as a means of protecting a relatively small number of workers in low-paying industries who occupy a specially vulnerable position in the labour market. Another role is to achieve "fair wages" for particular industries and/or groups of workers. Those singled out for protection are not necessarily confined to the lowest paid or vulnerable workers but include all those for whom it is judged necessary to ensure that wages are maintained at "appropriate" levels or that the principle of "equal pay for equal work" is applied. A third role is to establish a basic floor for the wage structure. This approach views MWF essentially as an instrument for making a modest contribution to the alleviation of poverty by providing all workers with "safety net" protection against unduly low wages by applying upward pressure on the bottom end of the inter-industry wage structure. The last and most comprehensive role is to influence the general level of wages. In this view, MWF is seen as a policy instrument for achieving such broad national objectives as the promotion of economic stabilisation and major shifts in the distribution of income.

Although governments continue to use MWF in all these different roles, some distinctive tendencies are discernible. Limiting MWF to only a few categories of "vulnerable workers" in certain industries has often not proved viable in the long run, because a large number of workers are in need of protection and because a complex administrative organisation is required to fix and enforce many different rates. In practice, this approach also risks widening as opposed to narrowing inter-industry wage differentials. Such problems have also caused some disenchantment with the use of MWF to establish "fair" wages. Moreover, the trade union movement has sometimes seen such state intervention as a threat to collective bargaining. The result has been that highly selective and variegated approaches to MWF with complex structures varying by industry and occupation have been replaced or supplemented by generally applicable minimum wages of broad coverage, often with only limited or no variation of rates by region or broad sector of economic activity.

Another general tendency concerns the levels at which minimum rates are fixed. Frequently, the original introduction of statutory minimum wages was accompanied by rather ambitious expectations regarding what they might achieve in raising general wage levels and rationalising wage structures. Unlike the pattern typical of IMECs, the wages actually received by many workers have often been directly or indirectly affected by the rates fixed. However, with the passage of time, there has been a growing recognition of the dangers inherent in trying to achieve too much through MWF. If minimum wages are fixed too high, they may fail to achieve the basic objective of poverty reduction by decreasing employment opportunities and widening the gap between earnings of wage earners and the self-employed in both urban and rural areas. There has therefore been a tendency to confine MWF to providing "safety net" protection through rates that are only relevant for the lowest paying industries. Indeed, as previously indicated, in some instances wage restraint in minimum wage fixing has been carried to the point where it has lost all relevance for wage determination, and hence its role in decreasing poverty by reducing excessive inter-industry differentials has been undermined.

Inter-occupational wage differentials

The general expectation is that skill differentials will be large and perhaps rising in the earliest stages of economic development but will eventually diminish with the expansion of the national education system, facilities for vocational training and opportunities for gaining on-the-job experience. A number of studies of the experience of both developing and developed countries over several decades have given some support to this generalisation. However, they have at the same time identified the influence of some special country-specific factors such as the rate of economic development (slow expansion is less likely to create labour market pressures on skill differentials as training systems will not be placed under strain); the importance of structural changes; the size of the labour market; and the orientation of national manpower policies.

But a series of non-economic factors have been just as, if not more, influential. Thus, a number of DCs in Asia and in Africa inherited from colonial rule exceptionally unequal wage structures that reflected essentially racial patterns of employment. Even after most of the higher-paid jobs were taken over by nationals, it was not always an easy task to move rapidly towards more equality. There were still widespread skill shortages and the groups that would lose from more equal wage structures had great political and economic influence. More generally, it would appear that custom has a substantial influence in per-

petuating differentials in the face of demand and supply pressures. This, plus the fact that employers will always find ways to remunerate those categories of workers that are in truly short supply, may explain why excessive rather than too narrow wage differentials have been a more common problem in DCs. However, there are governments which – inspired by egalitarian ideals – have aggressively used statutory minimum wages or centralised systems of wage determination to achieve greater equality. Thus, in both Ethiopia and the United Republic of Tanzania, the wages of higher paid groups in the public sector have been frozen for well over ten years. In other countries the excessive narrowing of occupational differentials appears to have been brought about more or less inadvertently through incomes policy measures that have favoured the low paid during what have turned out to be extended periods of inflation.

It is therefore not surprising that amongst DCs there is great variation in occupational wage differentials. Figure 5.4 shows the wage ratios between seven main occupations and unskilled construction workers in 12 major cities. In some cities, such as Bombay, Hong Kong, Seoul, Cairo and Buenos Aires, occupational wage differentials appear relatively low and only slightly higher than those in major cities of IMECs. In other big cities, particularly in Latin America and some Asian countries, occupational wage differentials are very high. In all these cities the relative earnings of white-collar occupations in DCs are consistently higher than those in IMECs (figure 5.5).

For at least two decades there have been persistent complaints in many DCs about the shortages of skilled manual and technical workers and the relative over-supply of low-level non-manual workers, suggesting that current occupational wage differentials are respectively inadequate and excessive for these two groups. However, it is not always clear that the claimed shortages of skilled manpower represent more than normal recruitment and training difficulties for groups of workers with specialised knowledge. Even if there were shortages, one would wish to know whether they are the result of inadequate wage incentives or of limited training facilities and insufficient opportunities for gaining on-the-job experience. Workers almost always appear anxious to upgrade their skills when given a reasonable opportunity to do so. Even when the immediate financial reward may not be substantial, skill improvements may open opportunities to more pleasant, interesting and socially respected work, further occupational advancement as well as easier access to jobs and greater job security. As for jobs in apparent excess supply, wage differentials may be kept up in order gradually to improve recruitment standards and to sustain motivation by maintaining a correspondence between relative pay and social status or authority structures within the establishment. There is thus much scope for discretion in the fixing of wage differentials. Much of the substantial variation in wage differentials both within and between countries is probably due to historical hazard rather than to economic imperatives or to deliberate trade-offs of economic efficiency in favour of more egalitarian wage structures.

Nor is it evident that there has been any noticeable change in this respect with the passage of time. Judging from the debates over wage policy issues in

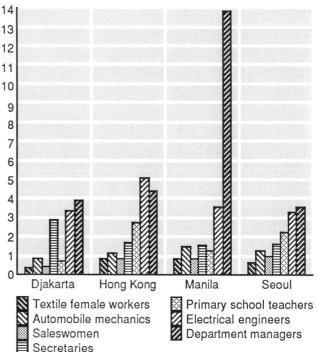

Figure 5.4. Ratio of wages between selected occupations and unskilled construction workers in major cities: Developing countries, 1985

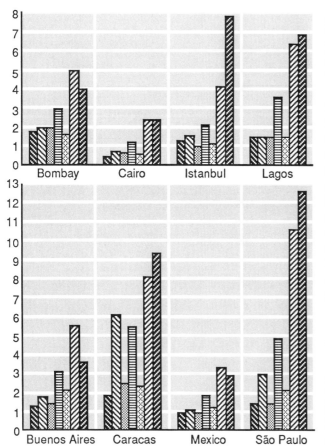

Source: Union Bank of Switzerland: *Prices and earnings around the globe* (Zurich, 1985 ed.). The survey was conducted by two unrelated organisations in each city, chiefly correspondent banks and offices of UBS, data on earnings being supplied by representative companies. Age, marital status, education and experience, as well as broad job descriptions, were specified. Wage comparisons are based on gross earnings, inclusive of all supplementary payments such as holiday pay and additional monthly salaries.

DCs, there has been no tendency during the past 10 to 15 years for labour market implications to be more effectively taken into account. On the contrary, a compilation based on the ILO October Survey has shown that over the last ten years, occupational wage differentials have tended to narrow in IMECs but not in DCs. A number of DCs appear to have experienced an increase rather than the expected decline in wage differentials for many occupational groups. In addition, the movements in these differentials have been rather erratic and evidently not the result of deliberate wage policies or consistent wage determination decisions.

Public-private sector differentials

Ideally, there ought to be approximate equivalence between rewards and effort in the public and private sectors in order to avoid imbalances in the labour market, to sustain operational efficiency in both sectors and to satisfy widely held notions of equity regarding the workers immediately concerned,

Figure 5.5.   Average ratios of wages between selected occupations and unskilled construction workers: Cities in DCs[1] and IMECs,[2] 1985

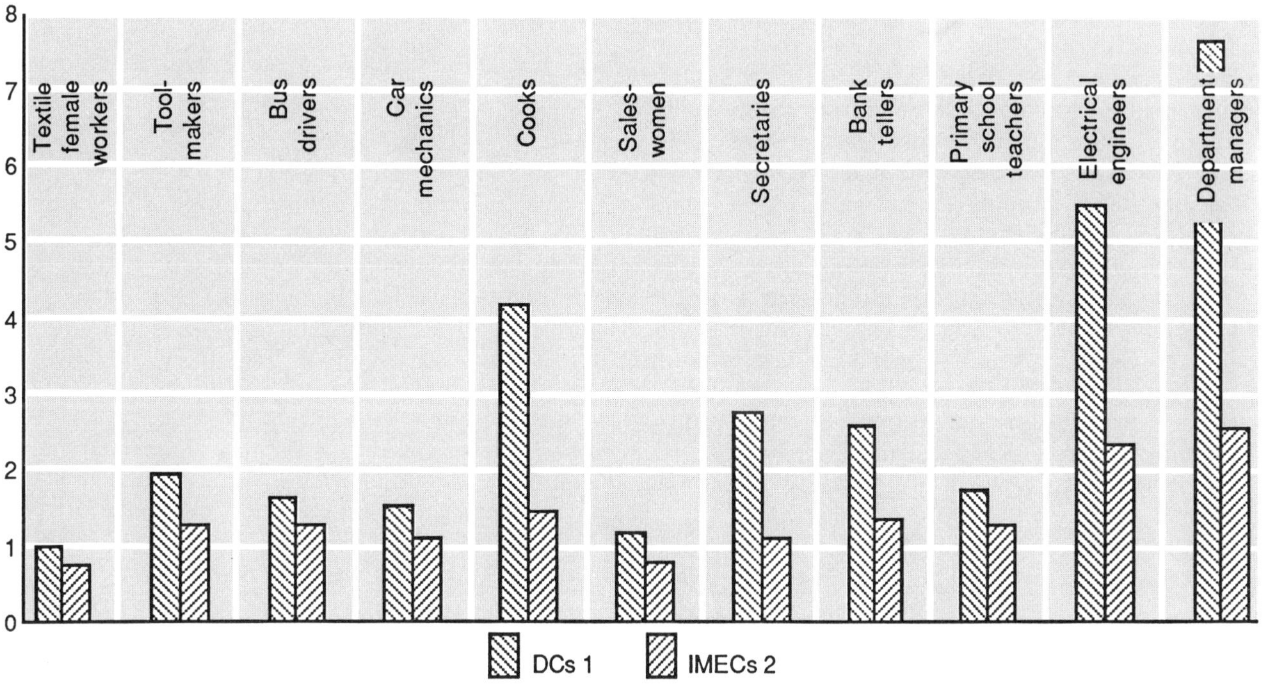

[1] Abu Dhabi, Bangkok, Bogota, Bombay, Buenos Aires, Cairo, Caracas, Hong Kong, Istanbul, Jakarta, Jeddah, Kuala Lumpur, Lagos, Manama, Manila, Mexico, Panama, Rio de Janeiro, São Paulo, Seoul, Singapore, Tel Aviv.   [2] Amsterdam, Athens, Brussels, Copenhagen, Dublin, Düsseldorf, Houston, Helsinki, Lisbon, London, Los Angeles, Luxembourg, Madrid, Milan, Montreal, New York, Oslo, Paris, Stockholm, Sydney, Tokyo, Toronto, Vienna, Zurich.

Source: See figure 5.4. The figures are based on unweighted averages.

taxpayers and the community at large. Whereas, to a greater or lesser extent, this has been the main principle accepted for public sector wage determination in IMECs it has proved much more difficult to apply in DCs. The main reason would appear to be that in a large number of DCs the public sector provides such a predominant share of regular wage employment for many categories of workers that it cannot avoid exercising a leadership role in wage determination. Moreover, public sector wage and employment decisions in DCs are often influenced considerably by many additional considerations. On the one hand, there has been a strong expectation that the public sector in DCs would serve as a model employer, not only in the terms and conditions of employment that it provides, but also in the job opportunities it creates. Pressures in this direction have been intensified by the fact that the public sector is generally where the ruling elites have obtained a significant part of their political support and where trade unions are the most extensively and strongly organised. On the other hand, the public sector wage bill often accounts for such a substantial proportion of

government expenditures, indeed of national income, that government decisions with respect to pay and employment cannot be isolated from responsibility for managing the national economy. This means that, in addition to the traditional employer concerns of minimising costs and recruiting, retaining and motivating a qualified workforce, governments have had to take into account the impact of their pay and employment decisions on the overall size of the public deficit, the division between capital and current expenditures and the availability of jobs on the labour market.

The result of these diverse pressures has been that the public sector in many DCs has gained the reputation of providing relatively high rates of pay, particularly for the lower categories of workers and in the leading public enterprises. Indeed public sector pay policies have often been identified as one of the principal causes of unduly high regular wages. A 1986 report on sub-Saharan Africa by the World Bank singled out public sector personnel policies as an important source of urban bias in these countries. Central government earnings were reported to average 6.9 times per capita GDP, whereas in Asia the ratio was only 3.3 and in IMECs much lower still at 1.7. However, such highly aggregated comparisons are not easily interpreted because they undoubtedly reflect in large part different employment structures. Comparisons restricted to earnings from employment may give quite different results. Thus, a recent IMF study shows that in IMECs the share of government wages (exclusive of public enterprises) in total wages in the economy and that of government employment in total non-agricultural employment was roughly equal, suggesting that average public service pay is not very different from average pay elsewhere in the economy. However, in DCs the government share in total non-agricultural employment was somewhat higher than its share of wages in total wages, suggesting that average earnings from regular employment in government are probably lower than in the non-agricultural private formal sector.

Rather than making such global comparisons, it is more relevant to compare public-private pay differentials for workers with similar skills. These have tended in the past to favour the public sector for the lower-paid categories but generally to favour the private sector for the higher-paid. This pattern is at least indirectly corroborated by frequent reports that the outflow from the public sector is usually low or negligible for people in lower grades, but high for top level staff.

However, in the wake of the intensifying economic crises experienced by many DCs over the last 10 to 15 years, it is evident that the relatively privileged position of the public sector has been undergoing important changes. Particularly in Africa, but also elsewhere in the Third World, severe wage restraint has often been applied to the public sector. Not only have the real incomes of public employees fallen but, more often than not, the declines have been much more substantial than in the private sector, reducing, eliminating or reversing the public sector pay advantage.

In this connection, it is interesting to note that recent results of the ILO October Inquiry do not reveal the public service as a high-paying employer, even when comparisons are confined to lower level jobs. Table 5.2 shows that for virtually all DCs and all the occupations for which a comparison may be made from the survey, the public sector pays lower wages than private sector employers. In some cases (for example, Algeria), the comparisons may reveal simply the usual pay advantage that public enter-

prises are given over the public service. However, in most instances the ratios reflect public-private sector differences, at least for the larger employers. It is perhaps most noteworthy that public/private pay differentials are not systematically different between DCs and developed economies. If anything, the public sector in developed countries appears to pay high wages more frequently than in DCs.

In recent years, the relative position of highly-paid public sector employees appears to have become particularly unfavourable. When public sector pay adjustments have had to be made they have, quite understandably, favoured the low-paid. Thus, at the time of independence, many DCs in Africa inherited extremely wide civil service pay structures. In 1963, the ratio between the bottom and the top of the civil service pay scales for six African countries (Egypt, Kenya, Nigeria, Sudan, United Republic of Tanzania, Ghana) was found to be between 1:30 and 1:64. By 1979, these ratios had been reduced generally to a range 1:11 to 1:17, with one exception – Kenya – where the ratio was 1:25. Since 1979, there has been a further marked compression in differentials with, for example, bottom to top ratios falling below 1:10 in many countries. (There are of course some exceptions. In Malawi, for instance, the ratio was still 1:25 in 1984.)

In a number of countries it is now becoming an important policy issue whether the trend towards further pay compression should not be halted or even reversed. The performance of the public sector is largely in the hands of higher-paid employees. Those in positions of authority cannot be expected to enforce reasonable performance standards when they are demotivated themselves and are forced to engage in questionable or illicit practices. The effective motivation of supervisory personnel is critical to the process of upgrading performance and restoring workplace discipline.

Another consequence of the decline in the relative pay position of the public sector has been the deterioration of pay systems and related personnel practices. As might be expected, with basic pay increases being restricted, attempts have been made to protect the relative income position of public employees in other ways such as the granting of additional annual increments, easier promotions to higher grades, further allowances and bonuses, more extensive payments in kind and other fringe benefits. These various manipulations of pay system practices, while generally not sufficient to fully offset declines in the

Table 5.2.   Private/public wage ratios in selected industries and occupations: Developing countries, October 1985 (Public service wages = 1)

Country	Wage concept	Typists				Office clerks			Computer programmer in insurance	Card and tape punch machine operator in insurance
		Printing	Wholesale trade	Banking	Insurance	Printing	Light and power	Wholesale trade		
Africa										
Algeria	mw/m	1.11	1.11	1.11	1.11	1.11	1.11	1.31	1.11	1.11
Benin	ea/m				1.43		1.29		3.43	2.01
Burkina Faso	ea/m	1.10	1.16	1.84	1.36	1.09	1.45			
Mali	ea/m	1.18	2.47			1.06	1.88			
Mauritius	ea/m	1.11		2.18	1.52	1.63	2.14			
Rwanda	mw/m	1.25	1.25	1.07	1.07	1.00	1.00	1.00	0.88	1.00
Seychelles	ea/m	1.00	1.29	1.37	1.15	1.00	1.00	1.52	1.00	
Latin America										
Chile	ea/m	2.15	2.24	3.48	2.33	2.15	2.56	2.24	1.30	2.33
Cuba	ea/m	1.09	1.09	1.00		0.65	0.91	0.77		
Guatemala	ea/h	1.77	1.32	1.87	1.25	1.00	3.55	1.62	1.77	2.19
Honduras	ea/d	0.91	1.57	1.03	1.03	1.66	2.25	0.82	1.00	0.71
Trinidad and Tobago	mw/m	1.10	1.27	1.53	1.31	0.96	1.30		0.73	
Uruguay	aw/h					2.26	1.45			
Asia										
Bangladesh	ea/m	0.87		1.00	1.00	1.50	1.00	1.17	2.12	1.00
Burma	aw/m	0.75	0.82	1.00	1.00	0.99	0.99			
Cyprus	ea/m	0.71	0.67	1.05	0.84	1.04	0.97	1.47		0.69
Developed countries										
Australia	mw/w			0.85			0.60			
Austria	ea/m	1.39		1.84	1.72	1.41	1.37		0.93	1.46
Canada	aw/h	0.89	0.86	0.73	0.76	1.26	1.42	1.28	0.92	0.87
Czechoslovakia	ea/m							1.15	1.00	0.98
Germany (Fed. Rep. of)	mw/m	0.80	0.65	0.90	0.86	0.75	1.20	0.81	1.07	0.89
Italy	mw/m	1.04	0.92	1.26	1.09	0.96	1.12			
New Zealand	mw/w	0.89	0.86	0.92	0.78	0.78	0.63	0.86	0.87	0.78
Romania	aw/m	1.04		1.00	1.00	1.09	1.19		1.00	1.00
Yugoslavia	ea/m	0.78	1.17	1.18	1.23	1.13	1.09	1.43	0.82	1.07

Abbreviations: ea = average earnings; mw = minimum wage rate; aw = average wage rate; h = per hour; d = per day; w = per week; m = per month.
Source: Calculated from ILO October Inquiry, 1985.

purchasing power of basic pay scales, have nevertheless been significant for certain workers. The result has often been that the overall logic and effectiveness of the pay system for motivating public employees has been gradually undermined. This has complicated wage policy formulation as it has meant that basic pay system reforms (scales grading, promotions, allowances, and so on) need to be undertaken along with pay increases to restore motivation. Unfortunately, such reforms are not easily carried out, particularly in a context of continuing financial restraint and overstaffing.

Finally, extreme financial pressures have prompted a number of governments to exert a close control over pay determination throughout the public sector, and not just in the public service proper. The fear has been that weak systems of financial accountability in public enterprises, the monopoly position of some of them and unbridled competition for scarce manpower would result in highly unequal and escalating wages. Consequently, governments of a number of DCs have sought to exercise much closer control over pay in public enterprises than typically has been the case in IMECs. This has taken the form of guide-lines and systems for prior approval of pay adjustments, various forms of limits on what public enterprises may pay or even the introduction of a uniform system of classification and pay throughout the public sector. These controls have engendered their own set of difficulties even though they have helped to achieve a higher degree of horizontal equity throughout the public sector, and perhaps to limit excessive mobility. They have inevitably reduced the latitude for individual public enterprises to adjust wages in line with labour market pressures and to adapt pay system practices to their needs for operational efficiency. Moreover, they have reduced opportunities for workers and their organisations to participate in meaningful ways in the determination of their terms and conditions of employment. It is difficult to assess to what extent such restrictions may impair the economic performance of public enterprises and hamper efforts to make them financially more accountable.

Chapter 6

Other urban incomes: Vulnerable groups in developing countries

For the analysis of vulnerable groups it can be misleading to divide urban economic activities into a "formal" and an "informal" sector. There is no common definition of what is meant by the informal sector. It is sometimes depicted as little more than small-scale enterprise and has accordingly been regarded as a potential source of economic growth and productive employment. At the other extreme, it is seen as mainly encompassing "survival strategies" by those who cannot afford to be unemployed in the conventional sense, so that its growth is a negative reflection of economic underdevelopment and an increasing labour surplus. Others have simply lumped in the informal sector all those not employed by government or large incorporated enterprises.

More importantly, "vulnerable" labour status cannot be adequately identified by any notion of "sector". At the simplest level, earnings differentials between workers in the so-called formal and informal sectors may be minimal or even the opposite of what is commonly suggested. Thus, one review of Indian experience found no clear evidence of consistent wage differentials between those working in "formal" and "informal" sector employment. The fact is that within enterprises of different sizes there are typically workers of diverse labour statuses, with varying degrees of vulnerability. There is growing evidence from around the world (from industrialised as well as low-income countries) that many labour practices associated with some notions of the informal sector are prominent in enterprises typically classified as formal. In short, precarious, unprotected forms of employment are not necessarily concentrated or at their worst in "informal", "unregulated" small-scale economic activities.

The focus of this chapter is on worker vulnerability in urban areas. By this is meant not simply low incomes, though that is commonly involved. Some workers may be receiving a reasonable income but be in precarious casual work, at risk of losing their job at almost any time. Others may be earning a subsistence income but be subject to indiscriminate deductions through dependency on an employer, middleman, or relative. Others may be vulnerable through their enterprise's links to other enterprises, such that their income or employment security depends on the whims or economic performance of others.

An example will show why the informal sector concept is obfuscating, and why vulnerability is so varied. In an ILO survey of business establishments in one industrialising economy, one place visited was described at the outset as a "furniture factory". The making of furniture was concentrated in and around a large house, the owner of which was an entrepreneur. In various rooms, there were about 40 workers each doing something connected with furniture making. When asked, the entrepreneur reported that he employed two workers, which strictly speaking was correct. The business was registered and the two workers were covered by labour regulations. Others in the building were close relatives of the entrepreneur, some of whom were apparently unpaid, some paid on the basis of a share of the profits. Many more were subcontractors or self-employed artisans, most of whom were essentially dependent on the entrepreneur for their raw materials or equipment or space. Some workers were reportedly in debt-bonded labour, highly vulnerable to deductions from their earnings. Finally, there were outworkers, those who were sent work to finish in their own homes. Thus, in just one enterprise there were various groups with different employment statuses and very distinctive forms of vulnerability.

As this example helps to highlight, workers may be vulnerable by virtue of their productive activity (type of enterprise and "sector") and by virtue of their labour status. There are also certain groups of workers such as migrants and women who remain trapped in low-paid and insecure employment because of segmentation and stratification.

1. Vulnerability by sector

For our purposes, productive activities can be divided into five strata. First, there is an administrative *public service sector*, which can be divided somewhat crudely into a sub-stratum of workers with salaried career jobs, giving relative income security and access to fringe benefits, and a sub-stratum of menial service wage workers. In recent years, public sector workers in many countries have been vulnerable to the erosion of real incomes (see chapter 5) and have become increasingly vulnerable to loss of employment. Indeed a sharp distinction has developed between a privileged category of public sector salaried workers and an increasingly vulnerable set of workers in temporary, low-paid jobs in the public sector.

The second stratum or sector comprises *large-scale "corporate" enterprises*, typically geared to the international economy and often dominated by multinational enterprises. Within this corporate sector one can distinguish between:

- a relatively small number of workers – "core" workers – in what may be called "progressive" jobs, with career potential, on-the-job acquisition of skills and income-earning capacity, employment security and access to fringe benefits;

- the mass of production workers – "outer-core" workers – doing process work in relatively "static" jobs, that is, with little opportunity for upward mobility and vulnerable to displacement or "skill" obsolescence through technological innovations or market changes; and

- peripheral workers in casual, short-time or outwork jobs without any employment or income security, often paid little or nothing but expected to be on standby as a "labour reserve".

There can thus be marked differences in security and vulnerability within the "formal sector", where stratified labour forces are often deliberately maintained. Electronics enterprises in many South-East Asian countries, for example, employ a small nucleus of salaried, career employees under whom work the bulk of wage workers, whose vulnerability consists not only of low wages and the absence of benefits but institutionalised insecurity of employment. Most production workers are not intended to remain in their jobs for more than two or three years. Their vulnerability arises primarily from their substitutability, which gives them a weak bargaining position for raising incomes, and from their lack of potential upward mobility within the enterprise. Even in that most economically successful of newly industrialising countries, the Republic of Korea, labour turnover in large enterprises is reportedly no different from that in the supposedly more insecure small-scale sector.

The third stratum consists of *small-scale, dependent enterprises*, producing goods or services for the local community, which are tied to large corporate enterprises through subcontracting or other regular links. Subcontracting by large, often multinational, enterprises has spread in recent years, often in response to the growing uncertainty and competitiveness in international trade. Units tied into a dependent relation to large-scale export-oriented enterprises will tend to be hardest hit by a downturn in international trade and may simply be forced out of business or obliged to operate at very low levels of capacity in recessions. Even street vendors may belong to the dependent small-scale unit "sector". Studies in several Latin American cities, for example, have shown how many street traders are part of well-organised commercial networks controlled by large-scale modern enterprises.

A fourth stratum contains *small-scale, independent enterprises* producing for local markets, which have been vulnerable to domestic economic developments, and in particular to shifts in income distribution and consumer demand. Their numbers have grown relatively fast in many low-income countries, partly reflecting the influx of people trying to eke out a petty income. The main expansion seems to have been in personal and trading services in which incomes have been relatively low. But the increase in numbers has not been accompanied by an increase in the average size of such establishments, which suggests more widespread underemployment in terms of income, time and skills. Some economies have reached something close to saturation point in this respect. For example, in the city of La Paz in 1980 there were 51,381 business establishments in an area with a population of 719,780. That represented one business for each 14 inhabitants. There were 27,606 small food stands, one for every 26 people. On average, just over one person worked in each business. Nearly two-thirds of all vendors worked in the street and 83 per cent of artisans worked in their homes. Some 65 per cent of businesses had a capital investment of less than US$100. Perhaps most telling of all, most of the so-called informal businesses had not been there for very long, a third for less than a year. This example may be an extreme case of urban involution, but it reflects the tendency for urban underemployment and poverty to be spread by the proliferation of small-scale units of economic activity.

This small-scale independent sector has been particularly important in African towns, perhaps accounting for over 50 per cent of total employment in Côte d'Ivoire, for example, nearly 50 per cent in Togo, and over 48 per cent in Benin.

Work in these units tends to be highly irregular for many of those involved. Thus a survey in Lubumbashi, Zaire, found that most of the employment consisted of day work. And wages, where they are involved, tend to be much lower on average than in the public sector or in large incorporated enterprises. In Bombay and in Coimbatore, for example, workers doing comparable work in unregistered workshops in the engineering industry receive less than half as much as those working in registered large-scale factories. In many African towns, wage earners in small enterprises typically have their incomes directly linked to the immediate economic performance of the production unit, often through some form of profit-sharing, and many receive less than the minimum wage. A survey in Abidjan found that about half of those working in industrial sectors such as textiles had incomes below a modest poverty level figure of about 1,500 Francs CFA. Indeed, more than eight out of every ten small-scale employers in textiles were earning less than the minimum wage level, reflecting the intense saturation of textile production in African towns. However, in many other sectors, small employers tend to earn more or at least as much as regularly employed wage earners.

Small "informal" production units are frequently depicted mainly as providing necessary and useful wage goods. The reality is that most provide petty services, often useful in any community but rarely contributing much to accumulation or economic growth. Thus, over 59 per cent of individual workers in Côte d'Ivoire's second biggest town, Abengourou, and about 72 per cent in Bangui, capital of the Central African Republic, were estimated to be in service type jobs. And in many towns there are an enormous number of petty auto-mechanics and the like, typically underemployed and living in considerable poverty.

Most of these enterprises face a highly precarious existence, and some estimates suggest that only if they survive at least three years do they have much chance of growing. Even then employment generation *within* small-scale enterprises tends to be fairly minimal. This results both from the reluctance of businesses based on family or kinship ties to allow strangers into the enterprise when survival depends on trust and reciprocity, and from the limits placed by competition on potential expansion. Employment growth in small-scale businesses in African towns has stemmed from increasing numbers of such units rather than the expansion of existing enterprises. For instance, surveys carried out in Yaounde in 1978 and in 1983 found that the average number of workers had fallen slightly, from 2.2. to 2.1.

There are also some notable differences between enterprises in certain industries or towns, giving rise to considerable income inequality within the small-scale enterprise sector. Those whose main or sole income comes from such activities tend to earn the least. It certainly cannot be presumed that small-scale production constitutes a stable source of livelihood. It can be argued that small-scale production is a way of spreading poverty, to allow more people to avoid absolute misery and severe malnutrition, that such production enables the poor to obtain goods and services at a price they can afford, and that these activities help to create a domestic market, essential for capital accumulation. However, as an avenue to socio-economic development, no country has succeeded in industrialising by means of small-scale independent "informal" production. Many such activities would surely disappear or be absorbed by the corporate sector or its surrogate of dependent smaller-scale units if the production became reasonably profitable. The cruel dilemma is that if workers in these enterprises were effectively protected from harsh working conditions, low incomes and employment insecurity, the activities would probably either cease to be done or be taken over or be pushed out by larger enterprises.

The surplus population

The fifth stratum in the urban economy consists of the most vulnerable group of all, those with marginal attachment to any productive unit, sometimes described as a *"marginalised mass"* or a *"surplus"* population. Here, the most prevalent form of vulnerability is simply the likelihood of complete detachment from the labour market through loss of morale, capacity, physical strength, or appeal to potential employers. This surplus population can be analytically subdivided into five categories, as shown in table 6.1, each with distinctive forms and degrees of vulnerability.

First, there are those who could be described as constituting a *latent* labour reserve for urban areas, that is, those mostly outside the urban labour force who could be attracted into it if the circumstances warranted. This category includes potential rural-urban migrants and many women, married or not, who work outside the labour force in or around their home. The existence of this latent labour reserve may put downward pressure on wage rates because the potential workers can easily be drawn into the labour market.

The second category is the *floating* labour reserve, those intermittently in the urban labour force, who may mix casual employment with periods of economic inactivity or unemployment, or simply withdraw from urban areas when not required. The existence of this type of labour reserve also intensifies the vulnerability of other groups whose niche in the labour force is under constant threat from a mobile category of workers, most of whom are in an extremely weak bargaining position and are resigned to low earnings and poor working conditions. As with the latent reserve, this category is often not counted as part of the unemployed. But it fulfils the same role in so far as it helps put downward pressure on urban wages and working conditions.

The third vulnerable category of the surplus population is the *active* labour reserve, that is, the openly or job-seeking unemployed, as measured by most censuses and labour force surveys. As shown in chapter 1, open unemployment has risen considerably in many low-income and industrialising countries, in which the concept of unemployment has become increasingly appropriate, despite the absence of government-funded unemployment benefit systems. A conventional view among some economists is that in these circumstances the jobless must be "voluntarily" unemployed and thus require no special policy action. This view is unjustified theoretically and has not been supported empirically. Clearly, the unemployed are dependent on the good will and ability of relatives and neighbours to support them, but with the growth and increasing duration of unemployment, this support becomes increasingly tenuous. It has been argued that because unemployment is concentrated among youths and other house-

Table 6.1. Different categories of the surplus population (or the labour reserve)

Category	Work status	Main groups
Latent	Inactive	Rural residents, married women
Floating	Intermittently active	Labour circulants, migrants
Active	Job-seeking unemployed	Youth, landless
Employed	With job, little work	Migrants, youth
Stagnant	"Unemployable"	Uneducated

hold dependents rather than "household heads", transfers of income and other means of subsistence are secure. This ignores a consequence of having one or more household members unemployed – a general lowering of living standards of all household members, pushing not only the unemployed but the whole family into poverty. Thus, in an urban survey in Costa Rica, the poorest households had the highest dependency rates and the highest unemployment rates among "non-heads of household", as well as relatively low household labour force participation rates. In urban West Bengal, the poorest households were the most likely to have at least one member unemployed (table 6.2). The fact that some surveys have suggested that non-heads of household constitute most of the unemployed could give a misleading impression of the voluntariness of that unemployment, since those who are unemployed are least able to set up an independent household and are the most likely to join or remain in an income-earning household. Moreover, in urban areas the poor are particularly prone to recurrent short-spell unemployment. In short, the active unemployed are a highly vulnerable group, and grow more so with rising overall unemployment and declining incomes of poorer sections of society.

The fourth surplus population category is best described as the *employed* labour reserve, which has been quite significant in many industrialising urban labour markets. It consists of extra workers hired, or put on unpaid stand-by, typically in circumstances in which the large-scale nature of production and the detailed division of labour allow enterprises to substitute easily one worker for another. Typically, such surplus workers will only be paid for the actual time worked or the output produced, yet they have to be ready for work at short notice. During early industri-

Table 6.2. Unemployment rates of non-farm service and production workers in the current labour force by expenditure classes in urban West Bengal, 1977-78

Unemployment rate (rupees)	Per capita monthly expenditure (percentage)	
	Male	Female
0-25	8.7	4.7
26-55	5.9	3.3
56-75	4.6	3.5
76-100	2.8	3.9
101-250	2.1	1.5
Above 250	5.3	0.0
Total	3.5	2.9

Note: A person is defined to be in the current labour force if he/she was in the labour force for at least one hour on at least one day during the reference week. The unemployment rate is defined as the ratio of the number of person-days spent in the current labour force in the reference week divided by the number of days spent in wage work over the same period. The service and production workers include street vendors and exclude farmers, fishermen or forestry workers. The very small sample size for the expenditure size classes Rs.0-25 and above Rs.250, means that the corresponding estimates have large margins of error.

Source: P. Bardhan: "Poverty and employment characteristics of urban households in West Bengal", in G. Rodgers (ed.): *Trends in urban poverty and labour market access* (Geneva, ILO, forthcoming).

alisation, when "commitment" or habituation to wage labour is limited, or where there are low wages and poor, unregulated or under-regulated working conditions, enterprises will be inclined to "employ" a reserve which can be used to compensate for high absenteeism, high turnover or erratic work intensity of existing employees. Pools of surplus workers may be hired for a nominal fixed cost, paid mainly on a piece-rate basis if required, so earning little or nothing if "permanent" workers are in the jobs or if there is a slack business period. In large enterprises surplus workers may be hired on a temporary or probationary basis for many months or even years before perhaps being shifted into regular posts. In the interim, they will be subjected to a gradual induction process while visibly posing a threat to the jobs and incomes of other workers. As an example, in the textile industry of Bombay, high absenteeism in the factories (no doubt at least partly due to low wages and poor working conditions) led to the practice of keeping a "Badli pool" of surplus workers, accounting for perhaps 20 per cent of total employment. This type of labour practice is not widely documented, but anecdotal evidence is widespread. Those concerned may experience a prolonged and uncertain period of poverty, having to rely on relatives to support them while they wait hopefully

for the nod of opportunity. For the workers and their families it represents a cruel dilemma, and for those in work supporting them an unenviable source of tension and foregone earnings.

The final labour surplus category is sometimes described as the *stagnant* surplus population, sometimes as the "lumpenproletariat". It is a large group in many urban areas, particularly where overall rates of unemployment have been high for many years, as for example in many Caribbean countries. It encompasses the long-term unemployed, those no longer able to obtain or retain employment, and those seen as or actually "unemployable" (at least in the short run) doing what in Jamaica is aptly called "scuffling". In part, this lumpenproletariat comprises those unable to come to terms with new work relations or forced by repeated failure in the labour market into crime, vagabondage, prostitution, alcoholism, drug addiction or long-term social illnesses, phenomena which are fostered by rapid urbanisation and high unemployment. Many in the lumpenproletariat are part of the surplus population but scarcely part of the labour reserve for development; their poverty and precarious survival are extreme. When recession hits an economy it invariably boosts the numbers who fall into this category, a status from which they subsequently have little chance of escape. Thus one analysis found that in four high-unemployment Indian states about half of the illiterate urban unemployed had been out of work for more than a year. In such circumstances it is extremely unlikely that they have any chance of getting paid work again, let alone the chance to escape from abject poverty.

In sum, all groups in the surplus population are relatively vulnerable, and there are adequate data to show (see chapter 1) that in many parts of Latin America, the Caribbean, Africa and South Asia, the numbers involved have grown substantially in recent years, particularly since the end of the 1970s. The overall vulnerability of those in the surplus population has probably also increased, since there is ample evidence that the latent reserve has been largely converted into a floating reserve – shown by the increase in migration out of rural areas and the growth of female labour force participation rates in many parts of the world. Moreover, the active labour reserve has grown, as shown by rising urban unemployment rates, bringing with them larger numbers of victims pushed into a demoralised, impoverished state of unemployability.

Trends in relative wages and earnings

By no means all the poorest workers are outside the public and large-scale enterprise sectors. For example, while low-income earners in Costa Rica are concentrated in small establishments some very lowly paid workers are found in the relatively "protected" or "formal" sectors of the economy (table 6.3). But there is also some evidence of growing differentials and inequality within urban areas. Wages or earnings in small-scale units have fallen in many places, often below the average income levels prevailing in rural areas.[5] For instance, real wages in small manufacturing units in Calcutta in the early 1980s were lower than they had been in the early 1970s. And in Madras, earnings of the self-employed and employees in the "unorganised sector" – as the analysis described those living in the slums – very probably fell during the 1970s. Almost three-quarters were earning less than 150 rupees per month, which was equivalent to about 2 kg of rice a day. They were earning about half as much as comparable workers in large-scale enterprises. Stagnating or falling real incomes have also been observed in other Indian cities, such as Ahmedabad. In Africa income inequalities in urban areas have also widened, because of the drop in wages for relatively unskilled workers.

Finally, as noted earlier, the size of the surplus population has been growing, partly because of falling incomes, saturation of small-scale economic activities and thus the inability of some petty producers to survive as such. Its numbers have been swollen by workers drifting from the public sector and from the large-scale enterprise sector, who have been unable to enter the small-scale sector due to lack of skills, contacts, savings, abilities or opportunities. Increasingly, labour vulnerability has been reflected in the growth of open unemployment and of income inequalities. Not only has urban unemployment been rising since the 1970s, but in many cities long-term unemployment has been growing as a proportion of the total. In Panama, for example, those seeking work for over six months rose from 47.9 per cent of all jobseekers in 1978 to 59.1 per cent in 1983. Chronically high unemployment in many growing urban areas represents an aspect of impoverishment of mounting significance for policy-makers.

2. Vulnerability by labour status

Workers may be in large or small units of production but have very different labour statuses

Table 6.3. Costa Rica: Urban poverty profile by household head's sector of employment, 1982 (per cent)

| Employment | Household status | | | |
	Destitute	Poor	No-poor	Total
Public	3.6	17.5	31.3	27.3
Employer, large-scale	0.0	0.3	2.9	2.2
Wage worker, large-scale	20.7	28.1	33.2	31.6
Self-employed, professional	0.0	0.6	0.9	0.8
Self-employed, non-professional	40.2	23.8	14.6	17.6
Employer, small-scale	3.0	5.9	4.9	5.0
Wage worker, small-scale	32.6	23.8	12.2	15.5
All employment	100	100	100	100

Note: Destitute households were defined as having a per capita monthly income of zero to 714 colones (extreme poverty income); the poor had a per capita income of 714-1,428 colones. Incomes are adjusted for number of children and payments in kind. Large-scale establishments were defined as having more than five employees.
Source: M. Pollack: "Poverty and the labour market in Costa Rica", in G. Rodgers (ed.): *Trends in urban poverty and labour market access* (Geneva, ILO, forthcoming).

involving quite distinctive forms of vulnerability. The conventional fourfold classification of employer, self-employed (own account), unpaid family worker and wage worker does not capture the situation adequately. For identifying the most vulnerable groups we need at least to consider in more detail the categories covered by the term wage worker.

One common procedure is to divide wage workers – and other groups for that matter – into those who are "protected" and those who are not, where protection means being covered by government labour regulations. The problem here is not only that the term covers rather a wide range of situations but that formal protection may be virtually meaningless if it is not enforced. The critical point is that the status of casual labour implies a basic lack of security, with debt-bonded labour, at the beck and call of an employer, perhaps the most insecure group of all. As one detailed empirical examination in India showed, debt-bonded labour is by no means found only in backward rural areas. Such workers may count as wage labour, and receive a nominal wage, but the extra-economic coercion to which they are subject is an extreme form of exploitation and oppression. Whether or not groups of workers are subject to regulations and formal "protection" is little guide to their economic and social vulnerability.

Each labour status category faces some common and some unique economic risks. For example, the self-employed and small-scale employers in most developing countries are vulnerable to rapid techno-logical change, market fluctuations and other devel-opments. This may force them to save high proportions of their net revenues. For many, their position is made more precarious by lack of credit on reasonable terms or any other institutional assistance. They will therefore be reluctant to make long-term employment commitments or to make fixed money wage payments if they can avoid them. Thus, in the recessionary conditions of the early 1980s there was a shift from the use of wage labour to non-wage labour by small-scale enterprises in many urban economies, in both industrialised and industrialising countries.

Casual wage earners

Wage labour can involve very different work statuses. At the top are workers in regular "perma-nent" employment doing jobs that are progressive in the sense that they gain on-the-job experience and technical skill that raises their incomes and status the longer they stay. This has always been the lot of only a minority of workers. For most, work has been "narrower" in terms of the range of tasks to be performed, less "autonomous" in terms of personal discretion and timing of work, and more "static" in terms of income and occupational mobility. Below them are workers who have only a "casual" labour status, that is, who do not have regular or stable employment.

Various distinctions can be made between types of casual labour. A useful starting point is between those hired on a short-term, temporary basis by public or large-scale enterprises and those hired by small-scale enterprises which normally entails unprotected or insecure employment, that is, uncovered by protective legislation. While there are differences between these two insecure groups, casual workers in large-scale firms have more in common with "reg-ular" workers in small-scale units than with other groups in the large-scale sector. Some observers would add, as a third category of casual workers, those who are dependent self-employed, that is, working on a contract basis or even as part of a "gang" of workers employed under a collective subcontract, as is common in the construction indus-tries in many parts of the world.

Not all casual workers face the same types of vulnerability. Short-term and "temporary" workers (those subject to firing without notice and thus without employment security) are more vulnerable

Table 6.4. **Wage rates for non-farm service and production workers by general education categories, urban West Bengal, 1977-78**

General education categories	Daily wage rate			
	Casual work		Regular work	
	Male	Female	Male	Female
1. Illiterate	6.32	3.45	9.46	4.06
2. Primary and below	8.10	3.65	10.76	4.40
3. Middle and secondary	7.74	3.80	14.21	6.39
4. Above secondary	–	–	24.88	–
All workers	7.36	3.50	12.01	4.17

Source: See table 6.2.

than permanent wage workers because they are not covered by government-backed regulations and/or union-negotiated collective bargains. As such, they may be subjected to lengthened working days, increased intensity of work, removal or non-appli-cation of safety standards, and so on. These forms of vulnerability are endemic. But dependent casual workers, including debt-tied workers and out-workers, are vulnerable also because they can be exploited through the provision of raw materials, premises in which to work, and equipment. More-over, casual workers are, almost definitionally, very unemployment-prone. They also have lower wage rates than those in regular wage employment, as a survey in urban West Bengal showed, for both men and women and whatever the level of formal schooling (table 6.4). In Kenya, the mean wage differential between casual and unskilled manual regular employees was over 20 per cent. Casual workers are also concentrated in the poorest strata. In Coimbatore, it was found that the lowest per capita incomes were those of casual and other short-term wage workers. Thus, casual workers accounted for 43 per cent of the lowest expenditure quintile in urban areas of Gujarat and 58 per cent in Maharashtra, though they only accounted for 22 per cent of all workers in both of those Indian states. Across urban areas in all Indian states, there was also a strong positive correlation for urban male workers between person-days of unemployment and the percentage of casual workers in the labour force. In sum, casual workers not only have low earnings when employed but have lower incomes due to their repeated unem-ployment.

Many other workers have only the opportunity for

day work at irregular intervals, and could be said to belong to the employed labour reserve. More generally, evidence of a shift towards small-scale units of production, both as a response to recessionary circumstances and as a strategy of decentralisation by large enterprises, has been associated with a general *casualisation* process, removing many workers from any semblance of regulated security. In Zambia, for example, it was found that any shift to small-scale firms implied increased casualisation. Large-scale enterprises employed weekly paid casual workers, who stayed only as long as there was extra work to clear; general workers, normally the first to be laid off in difficult times; and skilled craft workers with fairly secure positions in so far as the enterprise could not afford to lose them even when business was thin. In the small factories, however, the first two categories tended to be absent, and even the position of craftsmen was not secure.

Above all, it seems that the biggest single cause of casualisation of labour in recent years has been the desire of employers to bypass minimum wage and other labour regulations. For example, since the 1970s casual employment has increased enormously in Zimbabwe, which has been attributed to increases since independence in minimum wages for permanent employees. The same trend was documented for unskilled urban and rural workers in Latin America (see chapter 4).

Apprentices

Another vulnerable labour status is that of "apprentice". Apprentices are often little more than unpaid workers, who receive no recognised and little informal training. In many African towns apprentices and family workers make up from 70 to 80 per cent of all workers in small-scale enterprises, and apprentices account for 60 to 70 per cent of these. In Yaoundé most workers in enterprises surveyed in recent years have been classified as apprentices. Such apprentices often receive no money incomes; their families pay the employer during a long period of apprenticeship. Thus, in French-speaking African towns surveys suggest that at least a third of apprentices pay employers for their apprenticeships. Moreover, over three-quarters of apprentices were in enterprises where the employer himself had only manual education or training.

Conceptually, an apprentice is a worker undergoing training while in employment, the training being designed to produce an identifiable and socially recognised set of skills. At the end of the period of training the apprentice should qualify (or fail to qualify) as a technically skilled worker in that type of work. Unless the resultant "qualification" is recognised by other workers and by consumers, the apprenticeship can hardly be described as valid. But in small-scale enterprises in particular, many forms of apprenticeship are not widely recognised and are certainly not registered with any administrative body, either industry-based or governmental. None the less, as chapter 1 showed, apprenticeship may be a better preparation for work than more formal types of training.

Domestic workers

Another particularly vulnerable category are "domestic workers", that is, those employed by urban households to do domestic work. This category should be separated from other wage workers, simply because of the personal or familiar labour ties involved. They are dependent on the employer household, both for their immediate subsistence and for their continuing employment. In developing countries domestic workers are by no means always employed by wealthy households and often receive very low or insignificant money wages, so making them both dependent and vulnerable to loss of job. In a survey of ten cities in Colombia, men and women working in domestic service jobs were found to have the lowest average incomes, with the exception of self-employed (non-professional) women. And in metropolitan Lima, domestic service workers were earning less than two-thirds the average income of the next lowest-earning group, wage workers in small-scale establishments. In San José City, Costa Rica, domestic servants in 1982 were receiving less than two-fifths the average income of that second-lowest group. In short, domestic workers remain an unprotected and impoverished group in urban labour markets, to which governments have insufficiently addressed themselves.

"Contract workers" and "outworkers"

Finally, two groups apparently expanding in many countries are "outworkers" and "contract workers". They should not really be described as either wage workers or self-employed. While anecdotes abound, their plight has only rarely been the subject of detailed empirical investigation in urban economies. With labour contracting, there is an oral or written contract between an enterprise and an intermediary, or middle-man, the latter being responsible for mobilising a labour force for a job of work. This commonly means that the workers receive only a fraction of the money paid out for their work. To the extent that they receive less than the prevailing market wage, this usually implies that extra-economic methods are being used by the contractors to obtain and control the workforce. Labour contracting is particularly common in the construction industries, and at least in some countries there may have been a shift from direct to labour-contracted employment, as table 6.5 indicates for Malaysia. In many cities, the major construction companies retain only a small supervisory and clerical staff and subcontract through linked layers of enterprises and individuals, as has been documented in such cities as Bogotá, Mexico City and Dakar. Even in India, where a National Commission of Labour report showing how contract labour was used to bypass labour legislation led to the Contract Labour (Regulation and Abolition) Act of 1970, there is evidence that the use of such workers has increased.

Just as large-scale enterprises have increasingly contracted out part of the production process to small-scale firms, so employers have used subcontracting to individual workers as a way of reducing overhead costs and as a means of labour control. This was the explanation, for example, for a modern paper-producing mill in Cali, Colombia, subcontracting the work of providing raw materials to garbage-pickers. From the employer's point of view it was less costly than wage labour. For the garbage-pickers it meant greater insecurity of work and income.

Another well-known case of labour-only subcontracting is the ambulatory labour system in Hong Kong. This is a floating labour reserve, consisting of a mass of casual workers with various skills who move between manufacturing establishments to do job work. It is a system that has suited the flexible requirements of the many small-scale manufacturing plants in Hong Kong, while also lowering labour control costs. There and elsewhere the disadvantages for the workers essentially stem from their lack of employment contracts, so that they have no protection through safety and health regulations, social security or other labour laws. Commonly, contract workers have no access to medical or other benefits and are too insecure to press for whatever legitimate rights they might have.

Contract labour is very closely related to domestic

Table 6.5. Employment in construction, Peninsular Malaysia, 1975-83

	Employed through labour contractors	Per cent of total employment
1975	68 767	64.4
1976	67 914	61.8
1978	75 478	61.1
1979	88 735	62.5
1981	121 571	64.5
1982	142 334	64.3
1983	186 095	62.5

Source: Government of Malaysia, Department of Statistics, *Industrial Surveys* (various issues).

outwork, which has also grown as a response to surplus labour conditions, the influx of women to urban labour forces, technological change and, perhaps most importantly, increasing international competitive pressures that have driven employers to try more assiduously to cut labour costs and the costs of abiding by labour regulations. Industrial homework has even spread at a rapid rate in highly industrialised urban economies. Studies by the New York and New Jersey Departments of Labour and by independent researchers have documented a proliferation of industrial homework in those States, from the garment industry to such unexpected activities as explosives manufacturing and photo engraving. It should not be presumed that vulnerable types of labour status will disappear with industrialisation and development.

By no means all labour contractors subject workers to poor working conditions and low pay. But usually the principal employer is absolved of the responsibility for recruitment, establishment of terms and conditions of employment, assignment of work, provision of tools, raw materials and working premises, supervision and discipline, observation of safety and health regulations, and the provision of welfare and other fringe benefits, if they exist. This means that in many "formal" or "regulated" enterprises much or all of the labour force is effectively "informalised", and thus made much more vulnerable than might be expected. Of course labour contracting as a widespread phenomenon can only really exist if workers collectively are in a weak bargaining position.

In sum, contract labour, outworkers, casual wage workers, domestic workers and apprentices are

Table 6.6. Composition of urban non-agricultural employment, by work status, Brazil, 1981-83 (per cent)

Regions and years	Brazil 1981	Brazil 1983	Southeast 1981	Southeast 1983	Northeast 1981	Northeast 1983
Employee:	75.9	74.9	78.2	76.7	70.0	70.2
Protected	69.2	64.7	72.0	68.0	58.0	52.0
Unprotected	30.8	35.3	28.0	32.0	42.0	48.0
Employer	3.2	3.4	3.7	3.9	1.8	1.7
Self-employed	19.2	19.8	16.6	17.9	26.0	25.3
Unpaid family workers	1.7	1.9	1.5	1.5	2.2	2.8
Urban non-agricultural employment	100.0	100.0	100.0	100.0	100.0	100.0

Note: A wage worker is considered protected if he/she has a labour contract and is therefore covered by labour legislation.

Sources: J. Jatobá: "Urban poverty, labour markets and regional development: The case of Brazil", in G. Rodgers (ed.): *Trends in urban poverty and labour market access* (Geneva, ILO, forthcoming).

Table 6.7. Incidence of poverty among urban workers, by work status, Brazil, 1981-83 (percentages)

Regions and years	Brazil 1981	Brazil 1983	Southeast 1981	Southeast 1983	Northeast 1981	Northeast 1983
Employee	23.5	29.0	18.8	23.7	41.5	48.8
Protected	11.0	16.3	8.5	13.9	22.2	28.4
Unprotected	51.4	52.2	45.0	44.7	68.2	70.8
Employer	0.6	1.4	0.5	1.7	0.6	1.0
Self-employed	31.9	31.8	28.7	30.1	43.5	43.9
Unpaid family workers	100.0	100.0	100.0	100.0	100.0	100.0

Sources: See table 6.6.

forms of urban employment, with different forms of insecurity. As a result, within-sector differences in security of income and employment are often greater than those between sectors. As noted earlier, recent trends in many urban economies suggest that the use of casual labour has increased relatively and absolutely, whether as a result of recessions or because of a desire by enterprises to avoid minimum wage and labour regulations. It is by no means concentrated in small-scale "informal" enterprises. For instance in Guadalajara, Mexico, a recent survey found that over a third of all workers in large food industry firms were employed on temporary contracts, without any welfare benefits, whereas 28 per cent of workers in smaller food firms were similarly unprotected. In large-scale construction materials firms the ratio of unprotected temporary workers was even higher. Moreover, in both large-scale and small-scale enterprises rising urban unemployment and competitive pressure may well accelerate the trend towards the use of more temporary and unprotected workers. This has been observed in urban areas of Brazil, where the ratio of "unprotected" workers to total employment increased quite sharply in the early 1980s (table 6.6). And as table 6.7 shows, over half of all "unprotected" wage workers were earning only the minimum wage or less, a proportion that was rising. This raises basic questions about the direction and efficacy of labour market regulations.

Earnings and incomes by employment status

The incomes of workers and their families are affected both by their labour status and by the "sector" in which they are working. Small-scale employers may earn much more than casual workers in large-scale enterprises or in the government sector. In Montevideo in 1984, small-scale enterprise employers on average were earning twice as much as the average wage worker in enterprises registered with the official social security system. And as table 6.8 shows, employers were earning over four times as much as full-time "informal workers", defined as those whose principal and, if any, secondary activity was non-professional self-employment, unpaid family work or wage work without social security coverage. If "informal sector" employers and "informal" wage workers were lumped together it would appear, erroneously, that "informal" and "formal" sector earnings were similar. In reality, there were extreme differences within the informal sector. The same pattern was found in Lima, Peru. And as table 6.9 shows, in Colombia, Costa Rica and Peru, income differentials between groups of workers within "sectors" were also greater than those between sectors.

Many households have avoided poverty through what is sometimes called "occupational multiplicity", whereby one or more household members combine two or more income-earning activities of different labour status. This not only secures subsistence incomes through combining low-productivity and low-earning part-time activities but is a form of risk reduction. The Montevideo survey found that most of those whose main jobs were "formal", as defined by

Table 6.8.   Individual and household incomes by employment status, Montevideo, 1984 (US dollars)

| Status | Individual income | | Household income |
	All individuals	Household heads	Head employed
Individual			
Full-time formal worker	143.69	186.39	
Part-time informal worker	169.16	154.81	
Full-time informal worker	80.30	88.30	
Informal employer	346.52	360.55	
No occupation	70.27	86.25	
Household			
Fully formal			242.95
Part-time informal: Head formal worker			281.42
Part-time informal: Head informal or part-time informal worker			213.55
Fully informal: Workers			109.19
Informal employers			356.90

Note: Figures are average monthly incomes in US dollars calculated at the rate of US$1.00 = 36.7 new Uruguayan pesos.

Source: A. Portes, S. Blitzer and J. Curtis: "The urban informal sector in Uruguay: Its internal structure, characteristics and effects", in *World Development* (Oxford), 1986, Vol. 14, No. 6, p. 734.

Table 6.9.   Income differentials by sectors in three developing countries (wage earners in the informal sector = 100)

| Sector | Costa Rica[1] | Colombia[2] | | Peru[3] |
		Males	Females	
Formal sector	204	176	151	209
Public	251	201	193	n.d.
Owner, formal		614	422	558
Self-employed professional	359			
		340	264	253
Worker, large firm	180			
Worker, small firm	136	151	130	139
Informal sector	138	123	91	140
Owner, informal shop		273	250	332
Self-employed	163	123	71	146
Worker, informal shop	100	100	100	100
Domestic services	39	87	87	61

n.d. = no data.

[1] San José City.   [2] Ten cities.   [3] Metropolitan Lima.

Source: V. Tokman: *The informal sector: Fifteen years after*, Paper presented at the Conference on the Comparative Study of the Informal Sector, Harper's Ferry, West Virginia, 2-6 October 1986, p. 15.

registration with the social security system, only had such jobs, and that other family members were either doing similarly registered jobs or were economically inactive. Only one in ten households where the "head" was in registered employment included someone in non-covered ("informal") work, whereas by contrast 71 per cent of households headed by someone in informal work had nobody in registered employment. Spreading income sources seemed to entail continued labour market segmentation, with households either in registered employment or concentrating on non-registered, informal activities. Such segmentation seems bound to accentuate household income inequality. Interestingly, in Jakarta an experimental survey divided work activities into formal sector, informal sector and subsistence labour, where the third category was own-account work designed for household consumption. It found that through combining different activities many people worked very long work-weeks. But only a small minority of households had members in both "formal" and "informal" work, as table 6.10 shows. And combining work statuses was not so much a way

to wealth as the means of avoiding poverty. Those who were solely in "formal" wage employment had by far the highest average household income; those who were doing informal work, even if combined with wage labour, were much poorer. In Bangkok, Thailand, it was estimated that wage labour contributed about 50 per cent of the consumption needs of the average household, "informal" (own account for sale) work accounted for about 30 per cent, and subsistence work for about 20 per cent.

3. Vulnerable groups: Segmentation and stratification

If opportunities exist for labour to move from low-income, low-status to higher-income, higher-status positions, policies could concentrate on enabling workers to take advantage of them, for example, through education and training. However, if there is extensive segmentation, so labour mobility is very restricted or non-existent, policies need to focus on altering the fundamental structure of the labour process. The existence in many urban economies of unprotected casual labour, small-scale unregistered units of production and so on indicates considerable labour segmentation.

Table 6.10. Distribution of types of labour combination, Jakarta, 1980

Type	Per cent distribution of households
Formal, wage only	6.9
Formal and subsistence	39.3
Formal and informal and subsistence	18.8
Formal and informal	3.4
Informal and subsistence	31.6

Note: If subsistence work accounted for less than 10% of total household labour then it was ignored.

Source: H.D. Evers: "Trends in urban poverty and labour supply strategies in Jakarta", in G. Rodgers (ed.): *Trends in urban poverty and labour market access* (Geneva, ILO, forthcoming).

First, there seems to be little movement from the small-scale business sector to large-scale enterprises. In Coimbatore, for example, it was found that such inter-sectoral mobility was highly restricted. It is therefore difficult for workers to move into regular wage employment from low-level, low-paid jobs in small enterprises, or from the marginalised surplus population. This point will be further elaborated in the sections on migrant labour and women workers.

Second, while in some urban economies there is a pattern of movement from wage to own-account employment, in most there is little mobility between labour statuses. The Montevideo and Coimbatore surveys illustrate that quite clearly. In Coimbatore it was rare to find household members in different labour statuses, primarily because of social stratification which restricts labour force participation in different types of work. Only 21 per cent of the casual and self-employed workers could name someone from a wide circle of kin employed in permanent wage jobs. In Kuala Lumpur, however, it was found that Chinese men often moved from wage to own-account status, whereas Malays rarely made that change. Thus labour status mobility may vary according to the social group in question.

Third, mobility from casual to regular employment is generally limited. Thus in Bombay, very few workers make the transition from casual work to regular employment in small establishments or factories. Similar findings have been reported from other Indian cities, in which the ethnic stratification of such forms of employment is particularly pronounced. In sum, labour segmentation in urban economies means that many workers find themselves permanently trapped in low status, low-paying and insecure forms of activity.

In addition, some groups are far more likely than others to be in such vulnerable situations as a result of labour force stratification. This is not the same as segmentation. Social stratification determines entry to particular labour statuses and sectors; segmentation determines mobility between statuses and between sectors. In that connection, for example, in one Indian city caste background was not surprisingly found to be a more important determinant of entry to permanent wage employment than level of schooling, and that caste precluded subsequent change. The analysis concluded:

"We see ... the determining effects of caste, occupational and residential backgrounds in the case of the Pallans of Ammankulam as well as of the Chakkiliyans of Kamarajpuram. A rather high proportion of the members of both these communities is in the 'labour elite'. In both cases it is because of a particular history including the fact that members of these castes were recruited into factory employment in the early days of factory employment in Coimbatore. They have been able to build on this partly through education and the possibility of making use of education in order to enter public sector employment. The importance of personal contacts and of recommendation in entry to permanent wage work have tended to create self-reinforcing networks which may be restricted to people from particular caste and residential background. But it is not only to permanent wage work that this applies. In all the five slum areas we studied, where special circumstances such as those we have just described do not apply, the lowest ranking Madharis and Chakkiliyans are most likely to be casual workers or highly dependent sellers of kerosene (if they are not pursuing their hereditary occupations as leather workers). Muslims, on the other hand, are more likely to be petty traders in plastics, cloth, vegetables and fruit, or scrap, than are the other historically low-ranking urban groups. ..." (Harriss, 1986, p. 49).

The caste system is a particularly strong example, but there are many socially vulnerable groups and social characteristics that mark out individuals for discrimination or economic insecurity. Moreover, economic and social vulnerability is related to somebody's position in the life cycle. The initial point of entry to the urban economy is critical, and many young workers never recover from being lured or forced into low-level jobs and exploited labour statuses. Clearly, in urban as in rural economies the worst affected of all are child workers, many of whom go to the cities alone to work, many in little more than bonded labour. The remaining part of this section concentrates first on vulnerability over lifetime and then on three vulnerable groups that are found in all urban economies throughout the developing world: labour circulants, migrant labour and women workers.

Vulnerability over lifetime

Wage employment of the youngest children commonly involves work as part of the family group. For example, this was observed in carpet making in Pakistan and the brickmaking industry in India. Children may work as assistants to adults in factories and shops and be paid little or nothing for doing so. In some countries children are sent to urban areas as domestic servants of distant kin, with the extent of oppression and exploitation being inversely related to the closeness of kinship.

Probably child wage labour is more frequent in small-scale units than in large industrial enterprises because the latter can less easily ignore government regulations. But confirmation of this is difficult because of an obvious reluctance to report child employment among employers, parents and children alike. Moreover, there is evidence of the use of child labour in some large enterprises, as in Morocco, where extensive employment of young girls in large carpet factories was reported. Child labour in many urban economies is still pervasive.

Most low-income urban workers are in jobs where income does not increase with age. Accordingly, those who marry and have children almost certainly experience a big drop in living standards. Thus in Madras workers in unskilled or manual occupations, such as rickshaw puller, construction worker, barber and vegetable-fruit vendor, could only expect an annual rise in earnings of 1.6 per cent in the 1970s compared with a 10 per cent per annum increase in consumer prices at the time.

On the contrary, most workers in most sectors are highly vulnerable to the simple withering fact of age, and in the absence of protective measures start to suffer declining income power at a fairly early age. In Madras, it was found that "semi-skilled" construction workers' earnings peaked in their thirties, craftsmen's in their late twenties, all self-employed at about forty

and a tailor at about thirty. Beyond those ages, implicitly, labour market vulnerability grows increasingly severe. Older workers in urban areas tend to lack the support network, or informal social security system, represented by the extended kinship system more typically found in rural areas. In other words, the nuclearisation of households in urban areas accentuates the vulnerability of older workers. The result is that households headed by older people are often in great difficulties. In Costa Rica 48 per cent of the destitute and poor households were headed by people over the age of 55, whereas only 18.9 per cent of non-poor households were headed by people in that age bracket. But the main problem is that with rising urban unemployment older workers can often become easily detached from the labour market altogether. In Panama rising overall unemployment resulted in many older workers aged fifty and over being pushed out of "modern" employment.

Labour circulants

In most urbanising economies labour migration plays a major role. According to some estimates, urban in-migration on average has accounted for about 40 per cent of urban population expansion in recent years in developing countries as a whole. Migrants not only constitute a large part of urban labour forces but collectively are often vulnerable to various forms of exploitation and abuse. There is, however, an analytical difficulty in ascertaining whether the plight of migrants is due primarily to their being migrants or to the structure of labour market or to the characteristics common among the migrant population.

Perhaps the most vulnerable group of all migrants is what could be called *labour circulants*, those who move between the countryside and towns, between towns or between rural areas to ensure their livelihood. Probably the most typical pattern is for a worker to leave his or her family in a rural household while moving to the city for a short period of wage employment. There are other cases where there is no usual place of residence, as with migratory labourers, who move from town to town or to wherever there is the prospect of casual employment. An example is the *torrantes* in Chile, workers who follow a regular trail in search of seasonal and other temporary work. And there are other groups who usually reside in urban areas who supply labour for part of the year to agricultural areas far from the city. In the case of the

Strange farmers of Senegambia, urban workers go periodically to labour as groundnut farmers along the Gambia river on plots lent to them by their village hosts in return for a predetermined number of days of labour.

Some have a life-style of migratory labour, some possess limited or partial control of a piece of land or occupational niche that is insufficient to provide subsistence for them and their families, and some are landless and essentially at the beck and call of potential employers wherever jobs arise. This third type includes the *boias-frias* in Brazil, poor workers who eke out a survival in the urban slums of Sao Paulo and attend morning auctions for labour in a traditional spot. If hired they are carted off to work in the fields of a distant agricultural estate or on a construction site in the city or in a new township being constructed in the interior of the country.

Circulants have an unenviable existence. Above all, they have been used as a cheap source of labour, paid enough only to cover their immediate consumption requirements rather than a "family wage". Often they are paid at low rates because it is presumed that their living expenses are subsidised by other family members outside the urban economy or that their other activities enable them to clothe and feed their families, if they have them. Labour circulants are often hired for low-wage, insecure jobs because their wage and job expectations and aspirations are relatively low. They are frequently hired to do jobs for which a stable wage labour force is not required. This is particularly so in construction industries around the world, which generate a seasonal or short-term irregular work pattern. They are also often used in "static" jobs, that is, those that have low turnover costs and require little specific skill training. In terms of sectors of production, they are usually found in large numbers in the "outer core" and "periphery" of large-scale enterprises, and as casual workers in small-scale units.

Labour circulants are essentially a floating labour reserve, and their vulnerability arises not only from their poverty and need for income but from their ignorance of prevailing market wages and socially accepted working conditions. They also tend to relate urban money wages to incomes they could receive in rural areas, which usually means they have lower aspiration wages than other urban workers. In many places they are able to find jobs more easily than migrants who have moved to the city with the intention of staying there "permanently", or at least for their working lives. This is partly because their supply price, or aspiration wage, is lower and partly because they tend to have less of a network of social support in the urban areas. This was found, for example, in Jakarta, where permanent migrants from surveyed villages in West Java mostly took longer to obtain their first job than temporary migrants from the same villages. This was attributed to the fact that permanent migrants came from more prosperous backgrounds than the circulants, so enabling their families to support them through a period of unemployment. The long-term migrants also typically had more formal schooling than the circulants and hence had stronger aspirations for large-scale enterprise jobs. Many more labour circulants were to be found in small-scale enterprises with labour-intensive low-productivity employment. Most circulants had little margin to be selective about the job they took in the city and were prepared to accept low incomes in low-status, hardworking, time-consuming activities. The necessity for some income gained them access to the margins of the work force as cab drivers, cigarette-butt scavengers, kerosene and water carriers, day labourers, and so on.

Labour circulants are also, perhaps surprisingly, often hired from outside the city even though there are plenty of unemployed or underemployed workers available in the urban areas. One reason for this may be that circulants are more resigned to low wages and can be used to exert disciplinary pressure on urban workers reluctant to accept low or falling incomes and worsening working conditions. In the early 1980s, in Kuala Lumpur, Malaysia, construction contractors were known to rely heavily on the use of illegal immigrant workers brought to the city for short periods from Thailand and Indonesia. They were used primarily because they could be paid very low wages and subjected to harsh discipline without having recourse to the law.

Migrants hired for specified periods and brought from their villages by labour contractors are effectively controlled by their isolation from other elements of the emerging working class in the cities and by such devices as small advances and the withholding of wages until the end of the period of employment. Temporary migrants into the Bombay construction industry, for example, have long been manipulated in that way, being paid meagre weekly living expenses during the work period, the rest of the wage being paid on their return to the village. After the deduction of advances and interest, and taking account of their living expense payments, such workers often receive very little.

Circulation has also played a role in fostering ethnic or racial divisions of labour, with one racial, ethnic or caste group in the rural areas supplying short-term labour to an enterprise or industry while another makes up the major part of the workforce. Commonly, ties develop between certain villages and a type of urban job, with groups of workers being separated into cells in the workplace. Such stratification may foster an illusion that one group benefits from the relative disadvantage of another; it is an illusion because all strata can be prevented from developing a collective bargaining position. In some places, labour circulants have been hired in supervisory positions because they are less likely to identify with production workers; in others, probably the normal case, labour circulants will be in the lower-level jobs. In Manila, small contractors in the construction industry rely on a pool of labour circulants, typically drawn from the foreman's own village. There are several possible patterns, but labour circulants tend to be in the most low-paid and insecure jobs.

Labour migrants

The second and related disadvantaged group in urban labour markets consists of *labour migrants*, that is, those who move to live and work in or around the city. An assessment of their position is complex, but ILO and other recent research has helped to document recent trends and has indicated where policy intervention would be most promising and is most needed.

Concentration in low-paid jobs

A popular model of rural-urban migration postulates that migrants join a queue for urban wage jobs, so that as urban unemployment rises the flow from the migration tap is reduced to a trickle. The picture is somewhat more complicated than this model implies (see also chapter 5). Some observers have claimed that migrants make up a large part of the stagnant surplus population in urban areas and have used such epithets as "marginal mass" to describe them. And in the occasional study, migrants have been shown to be prominent in certain types of marginalised activities, as was the case of scavengers (Madharis) in Coimbatore. However, there are reasons to believe that migrants commonly circumvent the unemployment pool, partly because they

have low aspirations and expectations, as was found in Kingston, Jamaica. Various surveys have found that migrants do not have above-average urban unemployment rates, and there is tentative but not conclusive evidence that they have a lower propensity to be unemployed (see below). In the Indian Punjab, most urban in-migrants who looked for work after arriving in the city of Ludhiana had found employment within a month of arrival. This pattern is repeated elsewhere in many places.

Another reason why migrants may avoid unemployment is that many only enter the urban labour force once they have been informed of a job, and more often than not secure a job through relatives already working in the city. Thus, in a survey in Kuala Lumpur, Malaysia, in 1982, over a third of all men migrants and over two-fifths of all women obtained their first jobs in the city through relatives or friends. There is a further factor, noted earlier and widely cited in analysis of labour migration to South Africa, but applicable elsewhere. It is that migrants, and labour circulants most of all, are more easily paid sub-subsistence or "non-family" wages, partly because of their relative isolation, partly because of their presumed lack of urban relatives to support and partly because they are expected to get part of their subsistence from rural family production. In effect, the migrant is paid the bare minimum to survive the period of wage labour. Moreover, migrants are commonly seen by employers and their agents as unlikely to join unions or to agitate for higher wages or better working conditions.

Migrants may thus avoid a lengthy initial period of unemployment. However, they may be used as an employed labour reserve for a very long time; in the Bombay textile industry most of the Badli pool of surplus workers were in fact migrants to the city. It may also be true that migrants are overconcentrated in casual employment, which means in effect that many of the poorer migrants are in unemployment-prone jobs.

In comparison to the urban unemployed, migrants are often preferred for low-level jobs on grounds of docility or even intentional stratification of a factory workforce. Indeed, as has been documented, in certain circumstances employers will institutionalise labour instability by allowing workers prolonged leave, in return for a commitment to return when required, or by ensuring their return by locking the migrant workers into a job through indebtedness. In Peru, the form of debt recruitment known as *enganche* (the hook), involving petty cash advances to migrants, has been one extreme form of this practice.

Migrant workers thus comprise a large part of the floating labour reserve, as well as the employed labour reserve. But beyond that, migrants have been widely observed to be concentrated in the most insecure, lowest-paid and lowest-status urban forms of employment such as casual jobs. In Tehran a survey found that recent migrants to the city were far more likely to be in temporary jobs than were other groups. In some cities, migrants can only get part-time jobs, and many survive by combining two or more such jobs, as was found to be the case of 12 per cent of male adult migrants in Jakarta. Migrants may lack such basics as identification cards, birth certificates, work permits or social security cards, all of which undermine any minimal bargaining position they might have in surplus labour markets. For example, it was found that migrants in Rio de Janeiro received few social benefits because they had no work cards, for which they needed a birth certificate, usually unknown in rural areas. Some employers in the city were known to insist on workers *not* having a work permit so as to enable the employer to avoid paying social security contributions. Another practice, widespread in African towns, is for youthful migrants to be hired in jobs as pseudo-apprentices, provided with lodgings but paid little or nothing, being left to receive part of their subsistence from rural or urban relatives. And not surprisingly, various surveys have shown migrants in urban areas to be earning somewhat less than other groups, as in Seoul, for example.

Lack of upward mobility

The status of the initial jobs taken by migrants may not be that important if they have subsequent opportunities to move into more skilled, more secure, higher-income employment. This leads us back to the question of labour segmentation. One of the central arguments of the segmented labour market model is that mobility is limited between segments or strata or labour statuses or occupations. A basic methodological difficulty in interpreting available data is to determine when a change of job is evidence of "upward" mobility; another difficulty is that cross-sectional data may be inadequate if migrants who fail in the urban labour market are the most prone to leave the area, thus giving an upward bias to the observed pattern. Some observers believe migrants are generally upwardly mobile or are no less mobile than other workers. Studies have been carried out to

support the view that they face no discrimination or other barriers to mobility in Brazil, Mexico, Peru, Bombay, the United Republic of Tanzania, Zaire and the Republic of Korea. But the observed mobility may have reflected other characteristics, such as the level of schooling, age of labour force entry, and social background, that were not taken into account. Thus, a survey in Chile, taking these factors into account, suggested that migrants experience "less upward and more downward mobility" than non-migrants.

Other studies have pointed to a more general lack of mobility, with migrants faring no better and possibly worse than other workers. Thus, in the Rio de Janeiro *favelas* it was reported that more than half of all job changes by the men studied entailed no change in skill level, and less than a quarter had made upward changes. While many had managed "to escape unskilled positions at one time in their working lives, they were as likely to fall back as to move up" (Perlman, 1976, pp. 159-160). In Kingston, Jamaica, migrant women continued to earn relatively low incomes and remained in low-status, relatively unskilled jobs because they had *entered* the urban labour market in such jobs and because there was a general lack of upward mobility. In Mexico City, a survey of low-income neighbourhoods found that only 35 per cent of migrants had improved their occupational status compared with their pre-migration jobs.

Labour segregation

In Coimbatore in South India migrants were reportedly trapped in small-scale units of production or in casual, poorly remunerated work such as dependent commission selling. But the reality was that there was very low probability of upward mobility for any workers in the low-status social groups. In Bombay, it was found that casual work was mostly taken by poor, landless, low-status, poorly educated migrants from specific villages who were stuck in these jobs, so that labour segregation could be said to have originated in the villages. In Ahmedabad in the Indian state of Gujarat, a study of the construction industry indicated a high degree of segmentation. Building construction has long been organised in that city through a complex contracting system in which, according to one estimate, general building constructors have been responsible for recruiting 97 per cent of workers in the industry. The socio-economic profile of the typical construction worker is a poor, illiterate, unskilled migrant who sticks to the first job he gets and tries for another only when he loses it, in view of the relatively poor chance of getting another job in conditions of chronic labour surplus.

In Calcutta too, the stratification of workers has meant that migrants enter and remain in low-level jobs, and one analysis has suggested that this tendency has increased with the long-term stagnation of Calcutta's economy. And in many countries, there has been a pronounced tendency for certain jobs or even industries to be dominated by streams of migrants from particular areas or with particular ethnic, caste or religious characteristics. This has been commonly observed in Jakarta, where occupational specialisation is legendary. As one study noted:

"There are probably three related reasons for such specialisation in what are essentially unspecialised occupations: the preference given by those already employed or in a position to give jobs to relatives, friends and others from the same group; the information provided to newcomers by established acquaintances; and the greater ease of allocating work or territories in a group with a common background. The bus recruiters are young men from the Batak area of Sumatra, and a number of bus companies are owned by Bataks. Some ex-*becak* drivers from the Cirebon area have become *becak* owners and prefer to rent their *becaks* to those from the same area. In both occupations, and in some trades, a degree of mutual trust is obviously desirable, as is the possibility of sanctions against those who violate that trust. Trust and sanctions are more readily extended to those with family or at least ethnic and regional ties than to those from entirely different backgrounds. Word of how to get into an occupation also spreads most readily among migrants, or potential migrants, from a particular area with close ties of family and friendship ... Finally, observations confirm that some informal market or territory sharing is worked out among those who sell (kerosene, petty trade) or collect (cigarette butts, waste paper). Social connections obviously facilitate informal sharing arrangements.

"Of course, the stronger the influence of regional ties in determining occupations, the less occupational mobility and the greater the persistence of income disparities." (Papanek, 1975, pp. 15-16)

This process was further illustrated in an account of the Jakarta *pondok*, which is a "lodging-house-cum-enterprise", in which typically single migrants, commonly from the same village or area, live together and work in one particular trade, such as making and selling ice cream or preparing and selling cooked food. The *pondok* are owned by individuals who are often relatively successful migrants from the area from which they draw their "lodgers-cum-workers".

Women workers

Despite a common misconception to the contrary, women constitute a majority of rural-urban migrants in many developing countries, and many teenage girls enter the urban economy through low-level, low-paid and insecure forms of employment. The plight of such women can be a desperate one. Thus, for example, in India it has been widely reported that hard-pressed rural families have sent wives and daughters to cities to support them through prostitution. And in Thailand, every year thousands of young girls leave their village families to flock to Bangkok to work as masseuses and the like, remitting what little they can until their charms fade. In less severe situations, many young women enter the urban labour market through domestic employment, often for little pay and often unknown to any labour authorities. And whatever the sector, women earn on average much less than men.

As far as the sectoral distribution of urban employment is concerned, young women are often pushed into the "outer core" of large-scale enterprises in export-oriented industries. They have been entering the major corporate enterprise sector in increasing numbers in recent years, especially in the newly industrialising countries. The most well-known case is the electronics industry, which in many countries has relied overwhelmingly on young, single women workers, many drawn from distant villages and expected to work for low wages and very long work weeks (50-60 hours being common) for two or three years. The vulnerability of women workers in the large-scale sector is compounded by their general lack of opportunity for training and upward occupational mobility. In export production zones women workers have been made more vulnerable to poor incomes and working conditions by the non-enforcement of labour standard laws and the ban on union activity. Some studies have suggested that the wages paid to young women in such conditions are insufficient to meet even their basic subsistence needs.

In some urban industries the introduction or strengthening or enforcement of minimum wage

Table 6.11.   Typical subcontracting chain, Mexico City

Productive unit	Productive character	Worker characteristics
A. Producer of electrical appliances	Multinational; draws on a list of 300 regular subcontractors; sends out 70% of its production	3 000 workers; regular work; high wages with benefits
B. Producer of radio/TV antennas for A	Mexican capital; subcontracts 5% of production. One of various units linked to firm A	350 workers; lower wages, fewer benefits than A
C. Producer of electronic coils for firm B	"Sweatshop" operates illegally in basement of owner's house	6 young workers (aged 15-17), providing homework for fluctuating number of homeworkers
D. Homeworkers producing electronic coils for C	Homeworkers duplicating some tasks carried out in C	Women working individually at home

Source: L. Benería: *Subcontracting and employment dynamics in Mexico City*, Paper presented at the Conference on the Comparative Study of the Informal Sector, Harper's Ferry, West Virginia, 2-6 October 1986, p. 8.

regulations has led to the replacement of male permanent workers by women casual workers, as in Zimbabwe. Underpayment persisted through the conversion of permanent employees to casual or contract piece-workers, since these were not covered by the labour and minimum wage regulations. This, however, was far more likely in small-scale units than in large-scale enterprises. Most of all it affected the sexual distribution of employment, leading to a widespread substitution of women for men.

Women are disadvantaged by their heavy concentration in small-scale production units, in which many are unpaid for their work. For instance, in urban areas of Indonesia in 1980 women accounted for over a third of all those with "informal" work statuses (self-employed, self-employed with family workers, and family workers), while they accounted for only a quarter of those in the "formal" sector (employers and wage workers). In small-scale enterprises in Penang, Malaysia, women were concentrated among the lowest earners. But in general they are also vulnerable to being pushed into the labour statuses that have the lowest incomes and most insecure employment. In urban India women spent twice as large a proportion of the time they were in the labour force in casual employment as men did. Conversely, a far smaller proportion of women were in regular wage employment. It has been suggested that female urban unemployment rates are typically higher because, in part at least, women are more often able only to get casual jobs.

Perhaps the most worrying aspect of the continuing growth of female employment in urban economies is that much of their increased labour force participation has been of a precarious and low-income nature. For example, in small-scale businesses in African towns women are overwhelmingly concentrated in petty commerce and are very rarely in wage or manufacturing employment. Outwork and contract labour have pushed many women into positions of dependent and impoverished insecurity. An example is the case of vertical subcontracting in Mexico City known as *maquila*, or domestic *maquila* when it involves home work. In essence it consists of processing or production work carried out by firms for others under specific contracts, and it has mostly covered labour-intensive tasks resulting from an ability to fragment the production process. A typical vertical chain is illustrated in table 6.11, which is based on a real situation. Each rung down represents a smaller unit of production, the lowest being homework distributed from a workshop operated illegally in the basement of the owner's house. The proportion of women increased with each rung down. In the bottom two strata not only were most workers women but work was irregular and incomes often well below that required for a minimial subsistence. Workers in firm C were receiving the bare minimum wage without fringe benefits, while the homeworkers were receiving an average wage equivalent to one-third of the minimum wage. As this example illustrates, if enforced, regulations and policies to control labour contracting more effectively would have considerable benefits for women workers.

Similarly, women are far more likely to be permanently trapped in poverty than men. That is partly because of labour segmentation, which means that once in low-level, low-paying forms of employment they have little opportunity for escape, and partly because they face wage and benefit discrimination in whatever sector or labour status category they find themselves. As most women seem to enter the urban labour process through unprotected or casual wage labour or in small-scale units, they tend to have little chance to move up into regular protected wage employment. In Montevideo, for example, it was found that not only were women far more likely to enter the urban labour market as unpaid family workers or wage workers without social security coverage, but were also far more likely to remain in those statuses. In terms of income the women's disadvantage was double, first through the means of labour market entry, then by earning less than men in similar types of activity status. And no doubt there and elsewhere, so meagre and insecure are their earnings in wage employment that they seek ways of shifting into own-account employment rather than remain in the so-called "formal sector".

The most vulnerable group of all women are those who live alone or those who are primarily responsible for their household income and subsistence. In Costa Rica, although only 15.7 per cent of urban households were headed by women, more than 37 per cent of destitute (the poorest) urban households had a female head. In Sudan, a quarter of the low-income households were headed by women. Similarly, those households in which the husband or father are unemployed propel women members into the labour market, at times when they have to accept whatever work they can find rather than "search" rationally for somewhat longer.

Certain economists argue that women's lower wage rates and earnings reflect their preference for certain jobs and types of work that result in a crowding of supply for certain occupations, which thereby lowers wages. This assertion amounts to little more than blaming-the-victim. It presumes that women's labour supply behaviour is autonomous and a matter of preferences rather than an adaptation to perceptions of employer demand for female labour and the type of work they can obtain. The reality in most urban labour markets is that choices for women are extremely limited and limiting. As a study of women workers in the Indian city of Lucknow concluded: "The long established fact of non-employment of women in certain jobs, for whatever reasons, influences the supply behaviour of women to the extent they also tend to accept the notion that they are not suitable for these jobs. Another factor

may be women's low valuation of their capabilities …" (Papola, 1983, p. 23).

Women's economic vulnerability is compounded by the vicious circle of low incomes restricting the access of girls to schooling and training, which reduces their ability to escape from the lowest rungs of the urban labour market. The training women are given tends to be informal and is often an extension of their subordinate position in the family, so that gender relations perpetuate the sexual stratification of income-earning opportunities.

As with migrants, labour segmentation intensifies the economic vulnerability of women workers as much as initial forms of discrimination (social stratification) in determining their access or entry to various sectors and labour statuses. Women have far fewer opportunities for "promotion" and other forms of occupational and income mobility in urban labour markets. Not only are women concentrated in low-income positions but their avenues out of them are more likely to be blocked.

4. Concluding points

In urban areas, households in poverty are generally those without someone in a regular wage or salaried job. In West Bengal, for example, this applied to no less than 40 per cent of all households. And the majority of poor households did not have a single regular wage earner. Moreover, in most countries it is the absence of male workers in the household that is most strongly associated with poverty.

Among the worst causes of lifetime economic vulnerability are the entry level difficulties and initial barriers faced by specific groups in urbanising labour markets. The groups most affected include women in general, labour circulants and labour migrants and, almost certainly most vulnerable of all, child workers. To that extent, as urbanisation proceeds it becomes increasingly urgent to develop more effective policies to help particular disadvantaged groups overcome such barriers to entry that prevent them gaining access to relatively decent forms of employment. Although they are insufficient in themselves as a means of dramatically altering earnings differentials, the degree of inter-group inequality could be reduced if some labour protection and labour regulations were extended to the types of activity in which the most socially vulnerable groups are concentrated. Thus, to take just one example, workers in small shops suffer from employment instability, inability to join trades unions, lack of access to social security, and wages that typically are not guaranteed by law. Unfortunately, the lack of pressure for social security from the workforce itself contributes to the perpetuation of its economic vulnerability, and often reflects the fear that social security coverage would mean even lower wages rather than a statutory contribution from employers. Social protection would help particular groups, such as domestics, outworkers and wage workers in small-scale businesses, while many forms of protective action by the State would not be costly, merely representing a determination by the authorities, local probably more than national, to combat the worst forms of abuse in the labour market. But beyond that, the actual forms and mechanisms of labour stratification and labour market segmentation need to be combated. Restricted mobility between sectors, labour statuses and income-occupational levels means that the entry-level disadvantages are accentuated by the expansion in numbers of those groups, such as women and migrants, who are squeezed into the most insecure and exploited forms of employment. That ultimately is a structural problem, requiring an employment strategy adopted and carried out at the highest government level, if a significant reduction in labour force vulnerability is to be achieved.

Chapter 7

Wages in the industrialised market economies

The main wage issues arising in industrialised market economy countries (IMECs) over the last decade and a half have been closely linked to general macro-economic developments. Many commentators have identified the rapid growth of real labour costs during the 1970s as a fundamental cause of stagflation and, as a consequence, governments have made their moderation a major policy objective. As can be seen from figure 7.1, most IMECs experienced a substantial growth in real earnings (hourly earnings in manufacturing deflated by the consumer price index) throughout the 1970s. Even during the recession which followed the first oil crisis in 1973-74, only in the United States did real earnings decline. Since the early 1980s, however, the growth in real earnings has moderated significantly and the upward trend of the previous decade has been reversed in a number of countries. For example, real earnings declined by over 10 per cent in Sweden between 1979 and 1983 and Norway witnessed a fall of about 5 per cent over the same period. In the United States and Canada real earnings also declined, but by a smaller magnitude.

The moderation in wages growth in the 1980s is no doubt primarily the result of a prolonged period of slow growth and continuing deterioration in labour market conditions. However, some observers have attributed it, at least in part, to changes in wage determination. In some countries employers have sought to make labour costs more responsive to macro-economic conditions and firm or industry-specific circumstances. Governments have also acted to make wages more flexible by altering institutional arrangements and encouraging decentralisation of wage fixing. In other countries the degree of centralisation has increased as governments have unilaterally implemented wage freezes or guide-lines. A few countries have eschewed such policies and instead have sought a consensus on wage moderation on either a bipartite or tripartite basis.

1. Wage levels and employment

Over the last two decades economic conditions within the IMECs have undergone a fundamental change. In the 1960s, economic debate was largely concerned with the distribution of the benefits of growth, and governments were confident of their ability to handle the economy. Most economists believed that a strong negative relationship existed between inflation and unemployment, and that governments, by varying fiscal and monetary policies, could choose appropriate combinations of the two. In retrospect, this trade-off – if such a trade-off actually existed – appeared reasonably acceptable. Most countries were able to keep unemployment to relatively low levels without paying too high a price in inflation. However, matters changed dramatically in the 1970s. Rates of economic growth slowed and in some cases turned negative while the apparent relationship between inflation and unemployment deteriorated or disappeared, with increasingly high levels of unemployment coexisting with abnormally high rates of inflation. Comparing 1974-81 with 1966-72 for the 24 member countries of the Organisation for Economic Co-operation and Development (OECD), the average annual growth of national product was halved while the average annual inflation rate doubled. By 1982 the unemployment rate was twice the average rate for the earlier period.

In the wake of the deterioration of the macro-economic environment, all governments have in recent years pursued policies aimed at moderating income claims, especially wages. This reflects, inter alia, their belief in a positive relationship between changes in real wages and unemployment. In the short run, higher real wages stimulate consumer demand which may lead to more investment and employment. But in the longer run, the effects may be negative. If labour is expensive, enterprises may

Figure 7.1. Real hourly earnings, wage earners in manufacturing: Industrialised market economies, 1971-86 (1976-80 = 100)

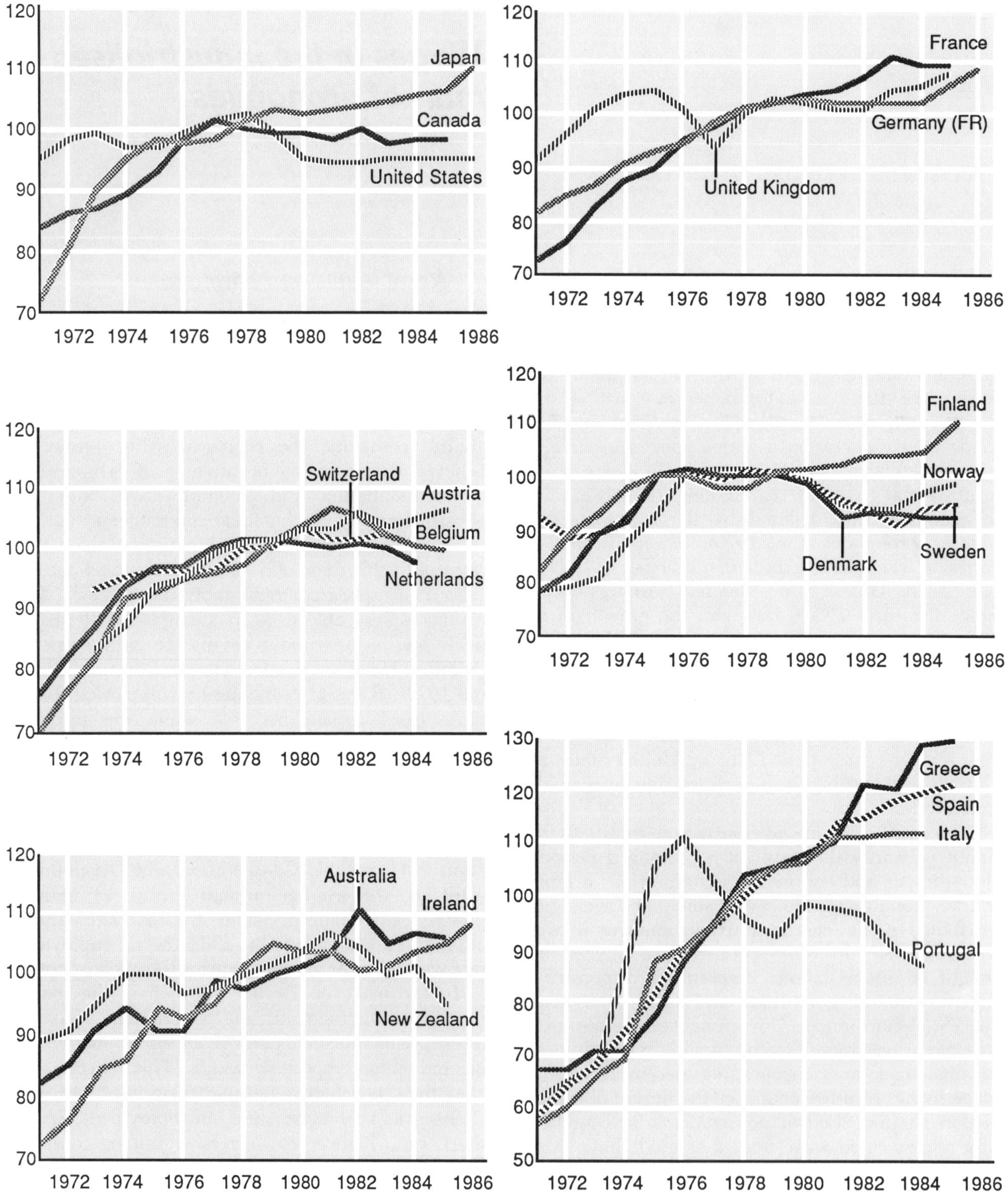

Source: ILO: *Year Book of Labour Statistics.*

invest in capital-intensive equipment. High labour costs compared with those in the main trade partner countries may reduce jobs in export and import-competing industries. High labour costs may also reduce profitability and thereby investment. Finally, rising wages can cause inflation that may have a dampening effect on output, profits and investment.

Two measures have been used to substantiate the claim that excessive real wages may increase unemployment. One is the real labour cost gap – increases in real labour costs over and above the growth in labour productivity. The second, discussed later, is the share of profits in national income or the level of profitability. Referring to the first measure, the OECD argued in its 1985 *Employment Outlook* that:

"... real labour costs have grown much more rapidly in Europe than in the United States: over the whole period since 1970, they grew at an annual rate of nearly 3 per cent. Since the growth of real labour costs was more rapid than the growth of labour productivity, a so-called 'real labour costs gap' emerged. The emergence of this gap in Europe was especially noticeable over the period until the second oil shock and the subsequent recession." (p. 34)

By comparison, in the United States real labour costs and productivity grew in parallel at an annual rate of about 0.5 per cent over the period 1970-84. With this disparity in real unit labour costs went a strongly contrasting employment performance between North America and Europe. Over the entire period between 1970-84 total employment expanded by 33 per cent in North America compared to a gain of only just over 1 per cent in Europe. Based on such evidence, the European Economic Community has claimed (in *European Economy*, November 1984):

"This confirms that the spread of classical unemployment is mainly associated with the failure of real wages to adjust to the levels warranted by the crises in productivity and the terms of trade that occurred during the 1970s." (pp. 99/100)

This view has, however, been strongly contested by, for example, the European Trade Union Institute (ETUI). It argues that there is no direct correlation between movements in the real labour cost gap and employment performance, since the two countries with the worst employment performance have seen the "gap" move in opposite directions. In the United Kingdom, the Institute figures show that the "gap" diminished substantially between 1975 and 1981 while in Belgium it expanded.

European employment performance has in fact varied greatly. In a few of the largest countries, such as Spain, the Federal Republic of Germany and the United Kingdom, employment in 1984 was below its 1970 level. Yet many of the smaller countries, such as Austria, Finland, Greece, Iceland, the Netherlands, Norway, Portugal and Sweden, all recorded significant employment growth over the same period. Employment growth in Norway, at an annual rate of 1.8 per cent, was not far below the United States growth rate of 2 per cent. More importantly, since 1983, which roughly corresponds to the trough of the last recession, employment performance among European countries has remained diverse and does not necessarily appear closely correlated with wages growth.

Among the countries recording the largest gains in employment over the period 1983-85 are the United Kingdom and Turkey, both of which exhibited above-average wages growth. Finland, Denmark and Norway, which have shown considerable wage restraint, are also among this group. At the other end of the spectrum, employment continued to fall in Ireland, Portugal, Switzerland, France, the Federal Republic of Germany and Spain for this three-year period as a whole, and the last three countries are among a small group for which nominal wage growth is currently well below that in the 1960s. Moreover, in Japan, real labour costs grew faster than in either Europe or the United States throughout the 1970s. As a result, a substantial real wage gap opened up and persisted alongside continuing growth in employment. Between 1979 and 1984 real labour costs continued to increase at an average annual rate of about 3 per cent, thus maintaining the wage gap. Despite this, employment in Japan increased by 13 per cent over the period 1970-84. These developments suggest that in the short run at least there is no clear predictable link between employment and changes in real wages and productivity.

The changing share of profits and its impact on the quantity and composition of investment is also used to support claims that excessive real wages cause unemployment. Profit share is usually defined as the ratio between companies' gross operating surplus and gross value added. Generally speaking, movements in the profit share will mirror trends in the real wage gap. For the seven largest OECD economies, profit share has returned to the level prevailing in 1968, from only 80 per cent of that level in 1982. This improvement has been attributed to wage growth moderation over the last four years and rising productivity, due in part at least to labour shedding. The one country where the profit share has not rebounded to the late 1960s level is Japan.

Despite the pick-up in profit shares for Europe as a whole, the rate of return on investment remains low. The explanation for this – advanced by both the OECD and the EEC – is the substitution of capital for labour. As capital intensity has increased, given profit shares yield lower rates of return on investment. The EEC estimates that the average net rate of return on net capital stock in the Community was 4.2 per cent in 1984 compared with 11 per cent in the 1960s. The rate of return declined throughout the 1970s and although this trend has been arrested as real wages moderated, the current rate remains inadequate.

The EEC claims that the investment mix has been biased against the use of labour. High real wages have encouraged labour-saving investment (capital deepening) rather than capital widening. As a result, labour productivity in Europe has risen strongly while capital productivity (output per unit of capital stock) has been declining since 1960. In the United States changes in the productivity of both labour and capital have been less dramatic. The EEC argues that comparing the rise in labour costs with increases in productivity can be misleading in a period when labour productivity growth is due largely to greater labour-saving investment – hence the failure of the recent reduction in the real wage gap in Europe to boost employment.

This proposition has again been challenged by the ETUI, which notes that there are serious methodological difficulties involved in using the rate of return as a measure of capital cost. In particular, it reflects the return to owners of capital, not the cost of capital to firms wishing to invest. The ETUI has drawn attention to attempts to measure costs to capital users that take into account interest rates and government taxes and subsidies. Results from two of these studies are summarised in table 7.1.

These figures indicate that a falling ratio of capital to labour costs over the 1970s was experienced in the United States and Japan as well as Europe. The ETUI argues that there is little evidence of a close relationship between changing capital/labour costs and employment performance, since rising relative real labour costs have been accompanied by rising or falling employment in different countries. There is also considerable debate over whether firms adjust their use of labour and capital to changes in relative prices in the short or medium term or whether invest-

Table 7.1. **Estimates of real capital costs relative to real labour costs: Industrialised market economies, 1970s and 1980s (1973 = 100)**

	Kopits (1982)		Snessens (1983)	
	1973	1978	1973	1978
Belgium	100.0	46.0		
France	100.0	54.7	100.0	78.4
Federal Republic of Germany	100.0	90.9	100.0	81.8
Italy	100.0	36.3	100.0	96.1
Netherlands	100.0	34.5		
United Kingdom	100.0	98.0	100.0	94.7
United States	100.0	67.7	100.0	89.2
Japan	100.0	67.1		

Source: Based on ETUI: *Flexibility and jobs – Myths and realities* (Brussels, 1985).

ment decisions are related more to current technological developments, expectations about future demand and the behaviour of competitors.

The ETUI has concluded that labour-saving investment in Europe has more to do with the recessionary environment than with labour costs, as firms concentrate on technological innovations that reduce costs rather than expand output and employment. The implications are that more expansionary monetary and fiscal policies are needed to boost aggregate demand and capital-widening investment.

The precise impact on employment of real wage increases through the agencies of a profit "squeeze" or capital/labour substitution remains problematic. But the prevailing view appears to be that when these two factors plus the impact on international competitiveness and labour supply are taken into account, real wage behaviour has been partly responsible for increases in unemployment since the early 1970s. However, it is equally clear that other factors have also been involved. As a report by the High-Level Group of Experts to the Secretary-General of the OECD (the Dahrendorf Group) recently noted:

"Historically, there can be little doubt that rapidly rising labour cost is related to the emergence of labour market imbalances, including unemployment. Even this relationship is not simple. While rises in unemployment between the two oil shocks can, to a considerable extent, be accounted for by increases in labour costs, other factors, such as sluggish demand growth and high level interest rates, must be adduced to explain developments since 1980." (OECD, 1986a, pp. 9/10)

Indeed, most IMECs have exhibited considerable real wage moderation since the early 1980s, yet unemployment has remained stubbornly high. Acceptance of a positive relationship between real wages and unemployment does not necessarily imply that real wages must fall further before a more robust labour market will emerge. There may be long lags before reduced real wages and the concomitant improved profitability are translated into capital-widening investment and employment-expanding output. Long lag periods are all the more likely in the current environment of uncertainty, excess capacity, depressed output expectations, high interest rates, unstable currencies and fears that inflation may again accelerate. There may be a danger of "over-shooting" the desirable degree of real wage moderation and thus unnecessarily reducing aggregate demand and worsening income inequalities.

At a recent meeting, OECD Labour Ministers agreed that "Real wages can and should grow in most countries, but for the nation as a whole within what is earned by productivity gains, and reflecting changes in the terms of trade between countries. The key is to maintain moderation in the growth of nominal wages, so that, without rekindling inflation, real incomes can continue to rise and contribute to the recovery." The European Commission suggests that, for the time being, (average) real wages should grow more slowly than the overall rise in productivity, the difference being available for increasing investment and employment. It recommends a larger difference for countries with high unemployment and a smaller one for those with low unemployment. However, it would seem logical to link the degree of wage moderation with the demand policies that governments follow in the future. If these policies are selectively expansionary, then wage moderation will be relatively more important to keep inflation in check. In this view, a more active demand policy is a *quid pro quo* for continuous wage restraint.

2. Wage adjustment

The failure of wages to adjust quickly or sufficiently to changing economic conditions, notably the supply "shocks" associated with the first (1973-74) and second (1979-80) oil crises, as well as to rising unemployment, has been identified by many commentators as an important cause of the deterioration in macro-economic performance in recent years.

The measurement and extent of wage flexibility

It has often been contended that, in response to the macro-economic disturbances of the 1970s and 1980s, the United States adjusted largely through real wage reductions while in Europe real wage rigidity resulted in lower employment levels. However, the concept of wage "rigidity" or "flexibility" is not as simple as it might first appear. In fact, a number of authors have challenged the view that real wages are significantly more flexible in the United States than in most European countries.

The ETUI, for example, using a number of relatively simple wage flexibility measures (such as a comparison of the standard deviation of changes in real and nominal wages over the period between 1960 and 1982), found that the United States had "the lowest real wage flexibility" of five countries examined. Japan and the United Kingdom exhibited the highest degree of flexibility on this measure, while Australia and Canada were third and fourth respectively.

An important study on this issue by Grubb, Jackman, and Layard (1983) measured wage rigidity by the increase in unemployment necessary to return inflation to its original level following a "shock", such as a fall in productivity or a deterioration in the terms of trade. The more responsive nominal wages are to the unemployment rate, the less the degree of wage rigidity. They found that the average real wage rigidity was about unity, meaning that a "shock" which increased inflation by one percentage point would require an extra percentage point of unemployment to remove the additional inflation. Countries with very low real wage rigidity were Switzerland, Japan, New Zealand, Sweden and Austria. In a middle grouping were the Netherlands, France, Canada, Belgium and Finland; and with a measure of unity or above, in ascending order, were Australia, United States, Italy, Norway, Spain, Denmark, the Federal Republic of Germany, Ireland and the United Kingdom. This would suggest that, in terms of aggregate wage responsiveness to unemployment, the United States has performed below par, although some European countries have been even worse.

A more recent study by Coe (1985) has developed short- and long-run measures of real wage rigidity for 11 countries. The methodology in this study follows the approach adopted by Grubb et al. in that it measures the responsiveness of nominal wages to changes in both inflation and unemployment rates.

At the beginning of the 1980s a considerable proportion of the unionised workforce in the United States accepted lower or frozen nominal wages in so-called "concession bargaining". This appears to have begun in 1981, when 5 per cent of private sector unionised workers who negotiated new agreements, or had their contracts reopened, took pay cuts while 3 per cent agreed to wage freezes. Contract modifications were at first generally confined to firms in financial difficulty with a recent record of low profitability. However, as the recession continued, wage cuts and freezes became more widespread. In 1983, 15 per cent of unionised workers in the private sector took pay cuts and 22 per cent had their pay frozen. By 1984, this process seems to have slackened with only 5 per cent of unionised private sector workers negotiating wage reductions while 17 per cent negotiated pay freezes.

One particular feature of concession bargaining was the reduced impact of cost-of-living adjustments (COLA). Unions in some industries agreed temporarily to forgo or defer COLA payments, reduce the frequency of review periods, or divert some of the accrued payments to other forms such as the maintenance of fringe benefits.

The incidence of concession bargaining varied across and within sectors but was generally concentrated in industries such as automobiles, steel, rubber, airlines, railroads, trucking, meat

packing, supermarkets and construction, and within those firms and industries experiencing unusually sharp reductions in product demand, leading to imminent threats of closure and/or lay-offs for the majority of union members. In other industries, union money wage settlements also moderated after 1981 but the moderation was far less dramatic.

Some observers believe that concession bargaining is a sign of fundamental changes in the wage determination process in the United States. Others see it as an essentially transitory phenomenon that will disappear once economic conditions improve sufficiently. They point out that concession bargaining was never widespread but largely confined to certain distressed manufacturing industries. However, it is probable that the widening of union/non-union wage differentials during the 1970s greatly contributed to concession bargaining at the beginning of the 1980s.

Many of the union workers who subsequently accepted wage cuts or freezes were among those who received the largest wage increases during the 1970s. Union wages in automobiles, steel, rubber and trucking climbed from a level 30 to 40 per cent higher than the average wage for all private non-farm production workers in the late 1960s to a level 50 to 80 per cent higher in 1981.

According to this definition, real wage rigidity is high when nominal wages strictly and rapidly follow the pattern of inflation and when they are unresponsive to changes in unemployment rates.

In the longer term money wages and inflation tend to increase in parallel – so differences in the long-run measures of real wage rigidity between countries are primarily caused by the responsiveness of wages to unemployment. For example, it is estimated for Japan that the growth in wages is reduced by over 3 percentage points when the unemployment rate increases by 1 percentage point. As a result, the long-run real wage rigidity estimate for Japan is very low. Wage levels in Finland and Australia also appear to be very responsive to increases in unemployment. However, in the United States wages growth slows by only about 0.3 percentage point for a 1 percentage point rise in unemployment which is comparable with France, Switzerland and the Federal Republic of Germany and less than Canada, Italy, the Netherlands and Austria.

In the short term there is greater scope for divergence between movements in nominal wages and prices; thus, the short-run real rigidity measure is dependent on the sensitivity of nominal wages to prices as well as to unemployment. Coe's results indicate that nominal wages respond more slowly to inflation in the United States than in any other

country considered in the study. In the short run therefore, real wages are more flexible in the United States than in virtually any of the European countries. A number of observers have attributed this high flexibility of real wages towards inflation to various factors. For example, Bruno and Sachs (1985) note that:

"... in economies such as that of the United States, with desynchronised bargaining, low wage indexation, and long-term contracts, nominal wages will tend to lag behind prices when inflation is increasing. In such a case, real wage moderation after a supply shock will be achieved automatically by a temporary jump in inflation." (pp. 217/218)

This attribute facilitated a reduction of real wages in the United States around the time of the first oil crisis. The increase in commodity prices between 1972 and 1974 brought about a fall in real wages since nominal wages were by and large determined prior to the increase in prices. In the 1980s, the United States has again witnessed a significant slowing in real wage growth but this time with a deceleration in inflation (see figure 7.2). This is further explained in box 7.1.

However, Japan, Finland and Australia still stand out as countries with the most flexible real wages in the short term because wages in these countries are very responsive to unemployment.

Wage moderation during the 1980s

The OECD has tested the hypothesis that recent wage moderation is "unusual" in some sense through two types of tests. The first involves using a nominal wage equation (similar to that used by Coe to measure real wage rigidity) estimated on the basis of data up to 1979 to forecast wage growth in the 1980s. This is then compared with actual wage movements. The United States equation tends to overpredict wage growth starting in the second quarter of 1983 by an average 0.5 percentage point per half-year. There is thus prima facie evidence of a change in wage behaviour. The second set of tests examines the stability of the wage equations, focusing on possible changes in mid-1979 – around the time restrictive monetary policies were adopted in the United States – and in late 1982, about the trough of the recession. The United States equation failed virtually all tests and the results suggest that nominal wage growth has reacted more rapidly to reduced inflation in the recent past than in the 1970s and that the sensitivity of wages growth to unemployment has increased. A second United States equation which makes provision for changed wage behaviour from mid-1983, through the inclusion of a constant shift variable, passed the various stability tests. This supports the view that there have been significant changes in the bargaining process. However, the analysis does not indicate whether such changes are temporary or permanent.

Some authors then sought to establish whether a change in behaviour has occurred in other countries (Chan-Lee, Coe, Prywes, 1987). Wage equations estimated up to mid-1979 for the seven largest OECD economies overpredicted wage growth in the 1980s for every country except the United States and Japan. This could suggest changed wage behaviour; however, the results were not confirmed by stability tests, except for the United Kingdom. For the other major countries examined the hypothesis of changed behaviour was largely rejected. Thus, it can be concluded that the wage moderation of the early 1980s was mainly related to non-accommodating macro-economic policies resulting in high rates of unemployment and reduced inflation. However, the study shows that in some smaller OECD countries, such as Austria, Finland and Spain, wage behaviour seems to have significantly changed since the mid-1970s.

Bruno and Sachs have constructed an index of nominal wage responsiveness to inflation, based on

Figure 7.2. Hourly earnings and inflation in the United States, 1971-86: Wage earners in manufacturing

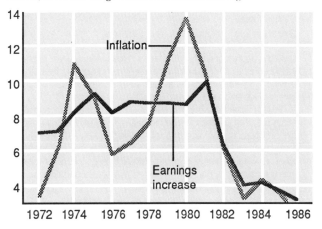

Source: ILO: *Year Book of Labour Statistics.*

the duration of wage agreements, the degree of explicit wage indexation, and the extent to which wage setting is highly synchronised. The countries which rank high on the responsiveness index include Australia, Denmark and the United Kingdom while the United States, Canada and Switzerland are at the other end of the scale.

It can be argued that the responsiveness of money wages to inflation had two major effects on macro-economic performance after the supply shocks of the 1970s. First, nominal wage stickiness tends to moderate the adverse repercussions of a terms of trade deterioration, while a greater degree of indexation tends to worsen the consequences of a price shock since the initial jump in prices is passed through to wages. This situation will be exacerbated if the terms of trade deterioration leads to an inflation-inducing domestic currency devaluation. Consequently, it has been argued that countries with low nominal wage responsiveness were better able to avoid the sharp profit squeezes that afflicted several countries after the first oil crisis. Second, it has been suggested that these same countries were well placed to pursue expansionary aggregate demand policies, since price increases engendered by increased demand in the goods market would only be translated into higher wages after a considerable lag.

3. Wage adjustment policies

Over the past 15 years many IMEC governments have intervened in the wage formation process. The main reason for their intervention has been to reduce

7.2   **Indexation and inflation**

The inflationary impact of indexation will be determined by several factors: the extent to which indexation establishes a link between price and wage changes; the extent to which indexation alters the degree of wage movements in response to price changes and vice versa; the nature of the price index used; and the degree to which indexation acts as a substitute for, rather than a complement to, other sources of generalised wage increases.

It is important to note that wage indexation does not create the nexus between price and wage increases; it merely institutionalises the process. In the absence of indexation, other methods of compensating for price rises are used. In some circumstances, a policy of wage indexation can in fact act as a "circuit-breaker". One view suggests that when inflation achieves a certain momentum, wage earners demand anticipatory pay increases to protect themselves against future price rises. If expectations are high, inflation may accelerate. Indexation of wages may avert this effect by giving an assurance for the future. Moreover, an indexation system which adjusts wages simultaneously and uniformly prevents relative distortions and dampens wage escalation through "leap-frogging". It may also reduce the cost of industrial disputes over wage relativities. Proponents of indexation argue in addition that the price index provides governments with a means to wind down the rate of price and wage increases, through cuts in sales and excise taxes, reductions in public sector charges, subsidies for essential services and price control over commodities such as food and steel. Sheehan (1974), for example, has claimed that this helps generate a "virtuous circle in which lower rates of price increase lead to lower wage increases which in turn moderate subsequent price increases, and so on".

However, even though individual or sectoral wage indexation adjustments may be justified, they may lead to inflation for the economy as a whole if the adjustments are generalised (see *World Labour Report*, Vol. 1 (1984)). Under normal economic circumstances, wages and salaries are affected by fluctuations in the cost of living, pressures for a gradual increase in real wages, the movement of relative wages and, of course, the state of the labour market. The role of collective bargaining and trade unions in wage trends is often stressed but, while collective agreements formalise wage adjustments, the general movement responds to considerations of fairness and reason. The employee and the employer have a strong common interest in maintaining a stable work relationship and avoiding the costs and bother that go with separation: finding a better job on the one side, and hiring and training new workers on the other. Such mutually beneficial relationships are maintained more easily when each party feels that it gets a proper deal from the other: a reasonable work performance for a fair remuneration. However, this situation does not necessarily lead to price stability, full employment and adjustment to changing economic conditions.

In all events, in times of recession when productivity rises slowly, systematic full adjustment of wages to rises in the cost of living can lead to inflation. This is particularly true when workers consider that it is only right and proper for their remuneration to keep pace with that of others: between them and others within the same enterprise, between major sectors (public and private sectors or services and goods-producing sectors) and at times even between countries. These emulative effects have led not only to inflation but also at times to reduced employment opportunities.

inflation, which flared up after both oil shocks. But, as explained in the first section, they were also concerned that high wage levels would hamper the creation of new job opportunities.

Wage policies during the 1970s tended to emphasise the achievement of a more equal distribution of income. Several countries, including France, the Netherlands, Greece, Spain and Portugal, increased minimum wages faster than average wages. In various other countries, such as the United Kingdom, Australia, Canada, Ireland and New Zealand, low-paid workers were often excluded from the various wage restraints. Finally, many wage policies reinforced the trend towards more equal pay for men and women.

Governments stepped up intervention in wage fixing in the early 1980s when, according to one study, they:

"... played a more active role in affecting the outcome of collective bargaining than ever before in peace time. There were several wage freezes, or statutory limitations on increases, of varying duration. Almost everywhere that there was a

national practice of indexing wages or prices, the mechanism was halted, or its consequences limited, or its implementation postponed." (Clark, 1984, p. 19)

The aim and nature of government wage intervention also changed during the 1980s. Governments were less preoccupied with distributional goals than during the 1970s, but they were alarmed by rapidly increasing unemployment and high wage levels, particularly in Europe. Since a number of governments had large budget deficits, they were obliged to take a strict line in wage negotiations in order at least to maintain previous employment levels in the public sector. They tended therefore to concentrate on two issues: public sector wages and various indexation mechanisms. As will be shown in the next section, public sector wages in the 1980s generally rose more slowly than private sector wages. In many countries, the automatic link between private and public sector wages was broken, and governments started to bargain more aggressively with public sector employees. In effect, in some countries such as the Netherlands and the United Kingdom, the government sector attempted to act as a "wage leader" for the private sector. The possible effects of indexation on inflation are discussed in box 7.2.

Many European governments have tried to reduce the impact of wage indexation. Between June and October 1982, the French Government applied a general wage and price freeze. Between 1982 and 1987, various Danish Governments suspended automatic indexation schemes. The Luxembourg Government restricted the impact of full indexation in 1982 and 1983. The Dutch Government threatened to impose a wage and price freeze which indirectly contributed to the conclusion in 1982 of a bipartite central accord on wages and working time reduction. Similar policies have also been pursued in Australia, Belgium and Greece. Their experiences will be analysed in greater detail below. The Australian and Greek examples are particularly interesting because the governments of these countries reintroduced a system of wage indexation.

In the late 1970s and early 1980s successive Governments of *Belgium* sought union agreement on changes to the wage indexation system in order to reduce labour costs and inflation. Wages, based on legally binding collective agreements, are adjusted according to changes in the consumer price index – a major feature of private sector pay determination in Belgium for several decades. Union agreement to alter the system was not, however, forthcoming and in 1982 the Government suspended indexation by Royal Decree for the period 1 March 1982 to 31 May 1982 for all employees except those on the minimum wage. From 1 June 1982 flat-rate indexation based on the standard minimum wage level was introduced for all employees. Indexation in this restricted form was originally expected to expire on 31 December 1982 but was eventually extended until September 1983. Full indexation was to be permitted thereafter; however, this was shortlived. In April 1984 a further Royal Decree resulted in indexation adjustments for 1984, 1985 and 1986 being reduced by 2 percentage points a year. As a *quid pro quo* for wage restraint the industrial relations partners were required by law to conclude collective agreements on increased employment levels and reduced working hours.

Government intervention in Belgium has produced a considerable decrease in inflation and wage increases since 1982. But, despite restraints, some companies with relatively healthy financial positions have granted employees increased benefits such as luncheon vouchers, increased end-of-year bonuses, stock options, fringe benefits, grading reviews and the

promise of pay increases in 1987. This has been used by some to suggest that state intervention has reached untenable levels and that a general policy of restraint cannot be more than temporary. Perhaps in response to such arguments the Government has recently reduced the degree of direct intervention. In September 1986 employers and unions reached a central agreement on wages, employment and working conditions to be implemented in the private sector during 1987 and 1988. The agreement reintroduces indexation and also contains a commitment to the principle of free collective bargaining. However, it would be premature to interpret this as a clear indication of diminished state intervention as the Government had threatened to impose a framework for sectoral and company level bargaining, had a central agreement failed to materialise.

Moving against the trend in 1982 the Government of *Greece* introduced a system of indexation which provided for pay increases every four months in the form of full indexation of earnings up to a certain level, partial compensation for price movements above that level and no indexation adjustments above a given earnings ceiling. However, in 1983 the system was modified by legislation to limit the growth in wages. Earnings of employees up to a certain threshold received compensation for 50 per cent of price index movements with lower levels of compensation applying to higher incomes and no adjustments above a ceiling. The system was again altered in early 1984, and thereafter applied automatically only to the public sector although the Government recommended that the same guide-lines be followed in the private sector. The new system provided for increases every three months and the extent of compensation which employees receive for movements in consumer prices is limited to their basic pay rates as defined in collective agreements rather than total earnings. Full compensation was reinstated for the lowest paid employees with a graduated scale of indexation payment for pay levels above this, up to an income ceiling beyond which no compensation applies. Agreement was reached between employers and trade unions to extend indexation in a similar form to employees in the private sector.

Wage indexation as part of a comprehensive incomes policy

The arguments in favour of wage indexation (see box 7.2) have persuaded a number of governments to

7.3   Australia: The Prices and Incomes Accord (1983-87)

The Australian Labour Party elected in early 1983 had as a major plank of its economic and industrial relations platform a Prices and Incomes Accord with the trade union movement. This provided inter alia for the full indexation of wages and salaries at six-monthly intervals providing there were no exceptional or compelling circumstances. In return, the trade union movement agreed not to seek wage increases additional to those obtained under the Wage Principles regulating the system. Each individual union was required to give a written commitment to seek "no extra claims" outside these Principles. The Labour Party claimed that previous experience showed that policies of inflation control, based on the use of monetary and fiscal restraint to control income claims, did not achieve their anti-inflationary objectives and exacted considerable costs in terms of lost production, lower living standards and high unemployment. The new Government therefore decided to adopt stimulatory budgetary and monetary policies in combination with a consensus-based incomes policy as a direct means of limiting income claims. For the trade unions the Accord involved a shift away from the traditional focus on wage increases towards an appreciation of the wide range of factors which determine living standards and which can be influenced by government policy.

The result has been an impressive moderation in real wages growth. In the first instance, the introduction of indexation facilitated an orderly transition from a wage freeze without the expected plethora of catch-up claims; in fact, there were no wage increases between October 1982 and October 1983. Secondly, the introduction of a national medical insurance system produced a one-off downward shock to the consumer price index of about 2.5 percentage points and as a result there were no wage adjustments between April 1984 and April 1985. Thus the Australian economy was provided with a breathing space of two full 12-month periods

without wage increases in a period of three years. The growth of average weekly earnings fell from 12.8 per cent in 1982-83 to 4.7 per cent in 1983-84 and the share of profits rose markedly. Meanwhile, the inflation rate was halved, falling from 11.5 per cent in 1982-83 to 5.8 per cent in 1984-85. This was accompanied by a substantial improvement in economic growth. After virtual stagnation in 1982-83, non-farm gross domestic product grew by 3.5 per cent and 4.6 per cent in 1983-84 and 1984-85 respectively, and the level of industrial disputes, measured by work-days lost, fell to 40 per cent of the average annual level for the preceding ten years.

However, the more rapid growth of the Australian economy relative to that of the rest of the world sucked in imports faster than exports could be expanded. This, combined with depressed world prices for Australia's major exports, produced a significant balance of payments problem and a substantial devaluation of the Australian dollar. This has recently necessitated a tightening of monetary and fiscal policy which has slowed the rate of economic growth and made necessary a substantial lowering of expectations about future growth and employment expansion. However, the Accord has provided the necessary framework to mitigate the inflationary consequences of the devaluation. In late 1985, the Government concluded a deal with the Australian Council of Trade Unions (ACTU) in which the unions agreed to discount the next national indexation rise by 2 per cent (which was the estimated impact of devaluation on the consumer price index in 1985) in return for income tax reductions to be implemented in 1987. At the time of writing, the Government, unions and employers were in the process of negotiating details for the introduction of a "two-tiered" wages system, under which flat-rate indexation would apply up to a certain income threshold with increased scope for collective bargaining on sector-specific increases beyond this.

build indexation arrangements into their incomes policies. For example, Australia has operated a consensus-based incomes policy since 1983 which contains a commitment to the indexation of wages, though flexibility exists for wage/tax trade-offs and pay restraint in return for improvements in social security. This highly centralised system has provided a remarkable degree of real wage moderation which until the second half of 1985 facilitated the simultaneous achievement of declining inflation, increased profits, a substantial improvement in economic growth, increased employment and relative industrial relations stability. However, along with these developments emerged a growing weakness in the external sector which has since reversed many of these trends and made necessary modifications to the wage-fixing system (see box 7.3 for further details).

The recent experience of Australia suggests that wage indexation does not necessarily produce wage outcomes incompatible with economic circumstances.

If indexation forms part of a comprehensive incomes policy, the framework exists for drawing the magnitude and implications of economy-wide shocks to the attention of those responsible for determining wage movements.

In a bargaining environment that stresses consensual wage norms, negotiators are more likely to absorb a terms-of-trade shock by a shared reduction in the real incomes of capital and labour. Further possibilities for wage restraint are afforded by a trade-off involving taxation and/or social welfare benefits. For example, the Government of Finland has used tax-linked incomes policies since the late 1970s to moderate domestic wage cost pressures. Previously, the share of non-wage labour costs had increased sharply. However, in incomes policy settlements since 1978 payroll taxes and employers' social security contributions have been steadily reduced. These adjustments have increased both nominal and real labour cost flexibility and have been one of the factors enabling Finland to achieve steady and sustained economic growth; GDP growth hardly deviated from 3 per cent per annum over the period 1982-85. In Italy, the Government, employers and trade unions agreed upon a similar trade-off, after a long battle over the so-called "scala mobile".

Experiences with central consultation and negotiation

It was shown earlier that countries such as Austria, Norway and Japan were among those with the greatest degree of real wage flexibility. However, this was due more to the responsiveness of real wages to unemployment than to unresponsiveness of nominal wages to price movements. Unlike the United States, the normal length of collective bargaining contracts in many IMECs is about 12 months and bargaining tends to be more synchronised and centralised, giving rise to some degree of informal wage indexation. Moreover, countries like Austria tend to be characterised by employer and employee organisations which are powerful and highly co-ordinated. A number of writers have used the term "corporatism" to describe political industrial systems which, inter alia, include these characteristics. The term covers countries where trade unions and employer associations co-operate in a number of economic and social policy areas, where no incomes policy is imposed by the State, and where the incidence of blatant and open conflict, for instance strikes and lock-outs, is very low. In such a system, hereafter referred to as "central consultations and negotiations", the formulation of economic and social policy has placed greater emphasis on direct consultation, mediation and consensus amongst major interest groups in society.

Countries such as Australia (since 1983), Austria, Norway and Sweden have intensively used central consultations and negotiations, either at the tripartite or bipartite level. Some other countries, such as Japan, the Federal Republic of Germany, the Netherlands and Switzerland have at times used central consultations, but these did not generally lead to central negotiations.

Countries with no central consultations or negotiations are usually characterised by: a less unified union movement; collective bargaining mainly at the plant level; lower rates of unionisation; and high levels of strikes or lock-outs. Examples of such countries are Canada, the United States and the United Kingdom, while France, Italy, New Zealand and Australia (prior to 1983) are also included in this group by some authors. An intermediate group of countries might contain Belgium, Denmark and Finland.

Bruno and Sachs (1985) attempted to assess the importance of central consultations and/or negotiations for macro-economic performance by relating the post-1973 increase in the "misery index" (which measures the rise in inflation plus the slowdown in real GDP growth) to an indicator of corporatism for 17 countries. They found a strong negative and statistically significant correlation. Using an OECD wage-gap measure, they show that those countries with a highly centralised system exhibited greater real wage moderation after the first oil shock. Looking at the wage gap for 1973-79, these countries had an average value of 0.2; the medium group, 4.7; and the remaining group, excluding the United States, 5.1. The US is an important exception, with a very low wage gap. This anomalous result can be explained by the unresponsiveness of nominal wages to prices mentioned previously.

Schott (1984) has also linked economic performance to measures of central consultations and/or negotiations. She found that among 17 industrialised market economies those which suffered the greatest deterioration in inflation and unemployment over the course of the 1970s were Italy, Ireland, the United Kingdom, United States, Canada, France and Australia, and in none of these countries was central consultation and/or negotiation practised in the period under review. On the other hand, in countries where she considered that to be the case, such as Switzerland, Japan, Austria, Norway and the Federal Republic of Germany, inflation and unemployment rates were far more favourable, whereas the medium group like Denmark, Belgium, Finland and the Netherlands had an economic performance which was middling. Based on this analysis Schott concluded that:

"... there is a rather clear linkage, perhaps not surprisingly, between the economic performance of developed countries in terms of inflation and unemployment and their system of interest intermediation. Those nations which are identified as having weak 'corporatism' have performed rather poorly and those where strong 'corporatism' is practised have done much better." (p. 48)

Overall therefore, the most desirable combination of labour market structures would appear to consist of intensive central consultations and negotiations and a low responsiveness of wages to inflation. Traditionally, these two characteristics have to some extent been mutually exclusive, which is hardly surprising, given that the institutional requirements of the two structures are vastly different. There are strong theoretical arguments to suggest that either structure can be consistent with relatively rapid economic and employment growth. The contrasting approaches yet similar outcomes in the United States and Australia between 1983 and 1985 lend practical support to this view.

4. Wage structures

Industry and occupational wage differentials

Part of the labour market flexibility debate within the IMECs has focused on whether or not wage differentials between occupations, enterprises, industries and regions have been sufficient to induce workers to move from declining to expanding sectors.

As part of its work on this question, the OECD has examined the dispersion of inter-industry wage differentials, the micro-economic determinants of changes in relative industry wages, and the relationship between relative employment changes and changes in industry product wages. This research covers changes in sectoral wage relativities since the late 1950s and early 1960s, within the manufacturing sector of Canada, France, Japan, Sweden, the United Kingdom and the United States.

The results show that in all countries industry wage rankings have moved considerably and that in the United States industry differentials have increased. Throughout the 1960s and 1970s it was generally taken for granted that economy-wide influences, as opposed to industry-specific variables, were the dominant forces behind changes in inter-industry differentials. However, with the exception of France, the investigation revealed that sector-specific influences have been important, although the strength of the evidence differs across countries. Labour productivity at the industry level, in particular, was positively related to industry wage changes in Canada, Japan, Sweden and the United States. This result holds across countries with very different collective bargaining arrangements, although it

appears stronger in countries with more decentralised wage-setting mechanisms.

However, the key issue is whether industry wage flexibility, in the sense of wage movements being sensitive to industry-specific changes in labour productivity, is necessarily beneficial for overall employment growth. While increasing sectoral wage flexibility could reduce competitive pressure on low-productivity industries and thus improve their short-term employment performance, it may also inhibit the capacity of high-productivity industries to exploit new innovations and markets and hence to generate long-term economic growth. So long as labour mobility is sufficient to accommodate these changes, and hardship is avoided, stability of the sectoral wages structure may in fact be broadly consistent with the needs of the economy. On balance, overall employment will only increase if relative wages in low-productivity growth sectors fall more than relative wages in high-productivity growth sectors increase. On testing this hypothesis the OECD found the necessary change in relative wages in three of the six countries (Canada, Sweden and the United States). But Japan exhibited behaviour that was inconsistent with the hypothesis. The degree of centralisation of the wage-fixing mechanisms clearly does not explain the presence of sectoral wage flexibility in a particular country.

Economic theory and some empirical evidence suggest that flexibility in the wage structure is desirable, other things being equal. But other things may not necessarily be equal. For example, in those countries which have made aggregate wage restraint a priority and are pursuing this objective through incomes policy, greater flexibility may well undermine wage restraint. It should also be recognised that there are trade-offs in efficiency at both the macro-economic and micro-economic levels. A more stable labour force may be more efficient at the macro-economic level, because it promotes the development of task-specific human capital. Greater intersectoral labour mobility, on the other hand, may be more efficient at the enterprise level because it ensures better adaptation of skills to technical and structural change. In addition, it should be kept in mind that labour supply is responsive to signals other than relative wages, such as job opportunities and employment security. Employers may also change their policies towards hiring, recruiting, training, overtime, retirement and promotion, thereby reducing the need for relative wage responses.

Figure 7.3.   Female earnings as a percentage of male earnings: Industrialised market economies, 1971-85: Wage earners in manufacturing

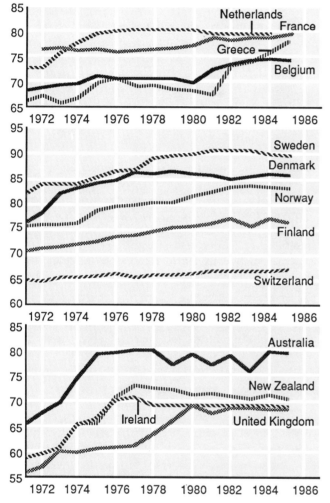

Source: ILO: *Year Book of Labour Statistics.*

Public/private sector pay differentials

Equity considerations, which often take the form of comparisons with the private sector, tend to play an important role in determining the pay of public employees. However, governments are often tempted or compelled to depart from this equity principle because they wish to maintain fiscal restraint, to avoid increasing public service prices or to influence private sector wage movements. In recent years, IMEC governments have come under increased pressure to pursue policies of wage restraint, as mentioned earlier, which have tended to focus primarily, at least in the first instance, on their own employees. Whereas earlier, public employees were considered to fare well in comparison to private sector counterparts, this trend has generally been reversed during the 1980s.

Thus, public employees in Italy tended to earn on average more than their private sector counterparts until the end of the 1960s. By the end of the next decade the balance had been reversed, a consequence of successful collective bargaining in the private sector and in particular the system of indexation which until 1979 was more favourable to private employees. This trend continued into the 1980s, even though public service unions started to press for larger pay increases in an attempt to catch up with the private sector.

In the United Kingdom, there has been a desynchronisation of public-private sector pay relativities since the late 1960s, in a cyclical process largely determined by various government pay restraint policies and consequent industrial action. Many public service employees suffered a relative decline in pay at the beginning of the 1970s, followed by a considerable improvement in the period 1974-76, as a result of special pay inquiries and high cost-of-living payments (applicable to both private and public sectors under incomes policy). This was largely reversed by the end of the 1970s. Subsequent widespread industrial action, followed by reports from the newly established Comparability Commission, then led to a relative improvement in 1980-81. In the ensuing years, by comparison with the private sector, most public service employees have suffered both from a relative deterioration in pay and from losses in real disposable income.

In Sweden, wage increases were higher in the private sector (98 per cent) than in the public sector (75 per cent) for the period 1970 to 1976. The trend reversed in the period 1976-79, when wages in the public sector increased by 39 per cent and those in the private sector by 31 per cent. Since 1979, there has again been another shift to a slight relative advantage for the private sector. In the Netherlands, the purchasing power of earnings in the private and public sector was at par in 1979. But by 1986 the public sector had suffered a relative decline of 4-5 per cent. In the Federal Republic of Germany, public service wages increased by 11 per cent more than the private sector wages in the period from 1969 to 1975, since when they have lagged behind.

Within the general category of the "public sector"

there are of course variations between state and local government employees, public corporations, and so on, as well as between different categories of public employees. However, in general it appears that public employees at the bottom of the pay scale have tended to enjoy higher pay increases than colleagues in the same establishment higher up the scale, as well as in comparison to their counterparts in the private sector. In most countries women's wages in the public service tend to be above those in private employment. Certain special groups such as postal workers, police and firemen have recently won larger pay increases than other public employees in a number of IMEC countries.

On the other hand, by comparison with the private sector, white-collar workers and higher officials in public service have suffered from compression in wage differentials. In the United States, for example, where comparability is well established for most manual workers, federal non-manual employees have seen considerable erosion in their pay since the end of the 1970s. A recognition of the negative effects of this situation on public sector efficiency has prompted, at least in some countries, recent attempts at widening wage differentials within the public sector.

Male/female pay differentials

Over the past 15 years, male/female pay differentials have diminished in most Western European countries. As figure 7.3 shows, in 1971, female wage earners in manufacturing earned between 65 and 75 per cent of male wage earners' pay; by 1985 this range had moved up to 75 to 85 per cent. For the ten countries with data for both years, the unweighted average increased from 68 per cent in 1971 to 77 per cent in 1985. Towards the end of the 1970s, however, male/female pay differentials in some countries either stabilised or even began to increase (United Kingdom, New Zealand, Ireland, Netherlands and Denmark). In Greece, exactly the opposite happened: male/female pay differentials were practically stable during the 1970s but have decreased very sharply since the beginning of the 1980s, mainly due to the policies of the new socialist Government. The overall improvement in women's relative earnings in manufacturing is generally in line with findings for the economy as a whole, but there is evidence that male/female differentials tend to be smaller for manual than for non-manual occupations.

There is considerable variation in male/female pay differentials between countries. Of the countries shown here, the three Scandinavian countries had the smallest gap (between 10 and 20 per cent) in 1985. The middle group, where the gap ranges between 20 and 30 per cent, comprises Australia, Belgium, Finland, France, Greece, the Netherlands and New Zealand. Countries with a relatively large wage gap are Ireland, the United Kingdom and Switzerland.

Broad comparisons like these are inadequate because they do not make allowances for characteristics such as age, work experience and education; nor do they take into account the structure and functioning of the labour market, and male/female work roles. For example, female workers tend to be concentrated in the younger age-groups, and pay is relatively low for young workers of both sexes. For the EEC taken as a whole, 22 per cent of working women compared to 15 per cent of working men were under 25 years of age in 1981. Experience and length of service are clearly associated with age, and the distribution of the female workforce by the length of service is likely to act to the disadvantage of women because of the age factor alone. In addition, women tend to have a faster job turnover than men. This means that it is more difficult for them to establish sufficient seniority to compete on an equal basis with their male counterparts for promotion and accentuates their disadvantage. One mitigating factor might be expected to be educational attainment. The median level of education of the female workforce tends to compare relatively favourably with that of the male workforce. Yet, in every educational category, women's average earnings are considerably lower than men's. It has been suggested that this unfavourable effect results from the subject areas chosen rather than the length or level of studies.

These factors are, however, insufficient to explain the entire earnings gap between males and females. The most widely accepted reason for the low average pay of women compared to men is the difference in enterprise and occupational composition. Women are over-represented in small plants or shops where average pay tends to be lower than in larger ones. They accept jobs in small enterprises near their home in spite of higher pay elsewhere because they have more flexibility to combine family responsibilities and paid work.

The best way to measure male/female pay differentials, while making allowance for the various "human capital" factors, is to compare male and female earnings within the same occupation. From the available data, it appears that the pay gap within individual occupations is usually quite small, and the narrower the definition of occupation, the smaller the pay gap. However, this overlooks the problem of "occupational segregation", namely the fact that women are concentrated in different types of job. The narrower the occupational definition, the more likely it is to be either a "male" or a "female" job. One interpretation advanced to explain such developments emphasises the role played by custom and practice in explaining the existing division of labour and structure of pay. For example, one study found that:

"most managers did not consciously consider different options for organising the production process … until forced to do so by a change in the product market, or by a decision to introduce a new technique … Thus, women are allocated to particular jobs and excluded from others primarily because this has always been the case, as far as the current management could remember." (Craig, Garnsey and Rubery, 1983, pp. 143/144)

On the other hand, such action by employers may be analysed in the context of dual labour market models, which divide jobs into primary and secondary categories. Primary jobs are associated with stability, long or costly training and a quality of performance having a direct influence on the financial results of the company. Employers try to give these jobs to the most productive, promising candidates they can find and afford. The top-ranking candidates are more likely to be men than women because they are supposed to show greater attachment to the company. The other shortlisted workers then take the remaining primary jobs, whether or not they are in fact less productive or less able. The persistently lower rank attributed to women goes a long way towards explaining their lower return on human capital factors and lower relative earnings. Secondary jobs, on the other hand, can be offered to the lowest bidder, quality of performance being on the whole less important than cost. The lowest bidders are largely women. A sufficient supply of women willing to take employment on these terms is a condition for the continuation of the pattern.

The improvement in relative female earnings does not appear to have been linked to a reduction in occupational segregation, and the problem of remuneration in predominantly female occupations remains the key obstacle to equal treatment to be overcome at present. An important recent step in a number of countries has involved the comparison of dissimilar jobs, but of comparable worth, held by men and women. Advocates of this procedure claim that job evaluation, if freed from some past drawbacks, could provide a basis for establishing a system of comparable value for male and female jobs. However, job evaluation presents many practical difficulties and it has been argued that such schemes would interfere with the functioning of the labour market in assigning prices to jobs. An increase in women's salaries, according to some, could raise the level of female unemployment or simply lead to wage inflation. Nevertheless, given women's persistently weaker position in the labour market, there can hardly be an escape from pay discrimination without some practical system of evaluation (or revaluation) of women's jobs.

Accordingly, many governments have given increased attention to applying in practice the principle of equal pay for work of equal value, as established in ILO Convention No. 100 (1951). Most EEC countries have adopted new legislation to ensure conformity with this Convention and with the 1975 Equal Pay Directive of the EEC which is formulated in similar terms. Since the late 1970s, the Nordic countries have also taken significant action in the legislative field, as have other countries such as Austria and Canada. In some cases (for example, Canada, the United Kingdom and the United States) the legislation attempts to spell out in general terms the conditions of equality, always a thorny issue. Another tendency noticeable in recent legislation is the placing of the burden of proof on the employer, thus reversing the traditional pattern in which plaintiffs have to provide material evidence of discrimination. Such provisions are found in the legislation of France, the Federal Republic of Germany and Sweden. Finally, it is noteworthy that recent equal pay legislation tends to devote special attention to enforcement procedures. Specialised bodies have been set up for this purpose in Austria, Canada, Ireland, New Zealand, Norway, Sweden, the United Kingdom and the United States.

5. Pay systems
Remuneration and performance

Although public debate in IMECs has increasingly focused on remuneration packages that establish a link between pay and economic performance, there has been a continued movement away from traditional forms of payment by results (PBR) where earnings depend on measures of individual output. An important part in this trend has been played by changes in technology and production arrangements that have made it more difficult to measure the contribution to output of individual workers and more essential to encourage co-operative, flexible, innovative and reliable behaviour at work. With rising capital investments in technology, employers seek effective, rational utilisation of machinery, stabilisation of effort and predictability of overall performance, rather than stimulation of increased individual output. There has thus been a move towards incentive pay designed to promote such behaviour. This has involved increasing use of either time payment systems (sometimes combined with some form of merit rating and explicit performance standards) based partly at least on non-output related measures of performance (such as machine utilisation, savings in raw materials and energy, attendance, and so on) or on group or enterprise indicators of performance. Where individual payment-by-results schemes have been retained the variable portion of the pay packet has generally been reduced.

The shift pointed out above is well illustrated by the example of Sweden, a country with a long and varied history of experiments with different forms of pay administration. The variable element of pay linked to performance has grown in the 1980s while the use of traditional piece-rate schemes has declined considerably. The interest has been mainly in new forms of bonus pay and group-based PBR schemes.

In the United Kingdom the proportion of manually employed males receiving PBR declined from 48 per cent in 1963 to 38 per cent in 1980; there was a sharp increase in the proportion of non-manual workers covered by such payments between 1974 and 1985 (from 8.3 per cent in 1974 to 22.2 per cent by 1985 for males, and from 5.1 per cent to 17.5 per cent for females). The survey from which these results are derived includes a variety of bonus systems, profit-sharing and commissions under the heading of PBR and it is presumably these types of pay systems rather than traditional PBR which are applied to the non-manual workers.

In the interests of greater flexibility, there has also been an emphasis on pay administration techniques which encourage workers to develop their skills and to assume a variety of tasks and responsibilities. In addition to changes in bonus systems and a greater reliance on techniques of merit-rating and performance appraisal, pay structures have been changing as well. For example, the introduction of new technology and the requirements of workforce flexibility have altered the relative importance assigned to the factors of job evaluation schemes. In the Federal Republic of Germany, the weight given to the factor "stress due to work environment" has been lowered, and increases accorded to the factors of "mental stress" and of "responsibility", especially responsibility for work organisation, quality and care of machinery and premises. For the "skill" factor, the value of "on-the-job training" is often given more importance than the theoretical education gained at school. In some cases the very concept of job requirements (the basis of job evaluation schemes) has been displaced by the importance of skills and attitudes brought to the job by the worker. In the United States, for example, "skill evaluation schemes" advance workers by one pay grade for each job learned, the top rate being paid to those who master all the jobs in the plant. Such schemes have been particularly successful in process production (such as chemicals and bulk food) where jobs are highly inter-related and there is a mutual advantage in employees knowing a number of jobs and understanding the enterprise as a total system.

There has been increasing criticism in some circles of the egalitarianism inherent in wage structures based on the requirements of the job (as opposed to the performance of the individual in his work). One way of correcting this is through PBR schemes. Another way is through various types of performance appraisal. In France attempts are under way to overcome the compression of wage differentials through what is popularly termed the "individualisation" of pay, or more precisely, of pay increases, linked to merit and performance. This system is increasingly applied to supervisors and technicians, but also to a lesser degree to semi-skilled and unskilled workers. In the Federal Republic of Germany too, performance appraisal, often combined with some form of bonus pay, designed to reward flexible and dynamic behaviour from workers, is used to differentiate pay increases.

Financial participation and profit-sharing

There is an increasing trend towards the financial participation of employees in the enterprise's overall fortunes. Employers in a number of countries (France, the Federal Republic of Germany, Japan, the Netherlands, the United Kingdom, the United States) have introduced various forms of profit-sharing, stock-ownership or savings schemes. Although the main goal of most of the schemes is to improve worker motivation, they are also viewed as a means of ensuring a wider distribution of wealth, improving employer-employee relations and promoting greater savings and investment.

In the United States profit-sharing schemes have received considerable publicity and attention from policy-makers, due in no small part to the work of Weitzman. However, despite the media coverage that may have given a false impression regarding their proliferation, only 10 per cent of workers in large bargaining units in the United States were covered by profit-sharing schemes in 1983. In the United Kingdom 15 per cent of large companies operate share-ownership schemes for their employees while a further 15 per cent operate some form of profit-sharing arrangement. However, one-third of the companies with share-ownership schemes offer shares only to executives.

The economic and industrial relations implications of financial participation schemes remain a subject of considerable debate. A recent study by Estin and Wilson (1986) on the effects of profit sharing in a sample of British metalworking companies concluded that their corporate performance and industrial relations profile was superior to that of a non-profit sharing group. Profit-sharing firms were found to have higher productivity and rates of return on capital, lower quit rates and working days lost. Moreover, the study tested for the independent effects of profit-sharing on remuneration and employment levels while controlling for enterprise-specific and labour supply characteristics. The results suggest that employment was about 13 per cent higher and wages 4 per cent lower than one would predict in the profit-sharing group given their other characteristics. While these findings are significant the authors warn that they are preliminary and shed no light on the question of how profit-sharing firms adjust through the trade cycle.

On the other hand, some observers have questioned the implications for employment growth of profit-sharing schemes, since workers with jobs would have a strong incentive to oppose new recruitment. Moreover, the growth of real costs might accelerate in the short run if employers conceed ordinary pay rises on top of profit-share payments to secure union agreement to longer term changes in the payment system.

The establishment of large-scale capital funds (usually termed "wage-earner funds"), collectively owned by wage earners and financed through profit-sharing and payroll levies, are also the subject of current debate. These schemes are seen not only as vehicles for substantially augmenting savings and investment and redistributing wealth but also as a way of providing workers with a more meaningful participation in enterprise-level decisions. In Sweden, five wage-earner funds were established in 1984 and now own more than 20 per cent of the share capital in three large firms. But employers, who remain strongly opposed to such schemes which in their opinion would lead to socialist ownership of enterprises, complain that the funds have mainly bought equities instead of providing risk capital for new ventures. In France, the idea of wage-earner funds under a 1984 law appeals to some trade unions, while others are strongly opposed to them. The creation of similar funds is still debated in the political forums of Denmark, Finland and the Netherlands.

6. Conclusions

Wages have played a key role in labour cost developments over the past 15 years. During the 1970s, real wages, particularly in Western Europe, did not in general adjust quickly or sufficiently to changes in productivity and terms of trade. During the 1980s, wages growth moderated in most IMECs, but this has not yet led to a significant decrease in unemployment. This may be due to long lags before reduced real wages and the concomitant improved profitability are translated into capital-widening investment and employment-expanding output. More active demand policies could contribute to more employment creation if continued wage restraint is observed.

Wage policies pursued by IMEC governments during the 1970s tended to emphasise equity considerations such as the achievement of a more equal distribution of income. Several governments increased minimum wages faster than average wages; in various countries low-paid workers were often excluded from wage restraints; and in almost all countries the pay gap between men and women was considerably reduced. During the 1980s, many governments – alarmed by increasing unemployment – began to be more concerned by efficiency considerations. As a result, they frequently intervened in wage determination, particularly by reducing the impact of wage indexation. They also took a harder line on public sector wages, so that public sector wages have grown more slowly than those in the private sector. Moreover, in some countries, male/female pay differentials stabilised or widened. In countries where central consultations and/or negotiations are, or were, practised, real wages have usually adjusted better to changes in economic circumstances than elsewhere. An exception to this is the United States where real wages have proved highly flexible.

Pay systems in enterprises have moved away from traditional forms of payment by results towards more complex remuneration packages. With rising capital investments in technology, employers seek effective, rational utilisation of machinery, stabilisation of effort and predictability of overall performance by workers. One development has been the growth of financial participation schemes. Usually, the main goal of these schemes is to improve worker motivation, but they may also serve other purposes, such as wider distribution of wealth, better employer-employee relations and greater savings and investment.

Chapter **8**

Wages in the centrally planned economies

Two important sets of considerations need to be borne in mind in trying to understand wage policy in the Eastern European centrally planned economies (CPECs). One relates to the ideological basis for socio-economic policy, the other to the changing economic conditions in these countries.

In a socialist society, ideology concerning wage policy is generally based on the Marxist axiom: "from each according to his capacity, to each according to his work". Enshrined in the constitutions of Eastern European countries, this principle is translated into a national policy of remuneration based on the quantity and quality of work provided to society. This has to be complemented by policies relating the growth of wages to the rate of productivity growth, in order to achieve the planned balance between investment (accumulation) and consumption.

Until the mid-1960s economic development of the CPECs relied to varying degrees on the mobilisation of additional factors of production – capital and labour. This so-called "extensive" phase of development has progressively faced resource limitations, and has had to be gradually replaced by the "intensification" of production based on technically more advanced machinery, increases in labour productivity and savings in raw materials, manpower and financial resources. As will be seen, a number of modifications have been made to the wage system in order to reflect this shift in economic development strategy.

1. The level of wages and incomes

In planned economy countries, national income is divided into two parts – the consumption and the accumulation fund. The accumulation fund includes mainly the investment resources for production development and construction. The consumption fund consists mainly of wages and social security

benefits but also includes current expenditure on goods by the public sector. Living standards have been improved over the years in line with increases in economic efficiency but in addition governments have increased the proportion of national income spent on consumption (see figure 8.1). This trend has been more marked in some countries than in others in the last decade (for example, Czechoslovakia, German Democratic Republic and Hungary); in some instances (as in the case of Poland for 1981), socio-political reasons may have determined certain sudden shifts. But the trend is likely to change as a result of the increasing investment needed to achieve the planned acceleration of economic growth and to speed up the transition to a more intensive pattern of economic development. In Bulgaria, Hungary, Poland and the USSR, the share of accumulation in national income is set to rise in the plan period of 1986-90. In the USSR, this altered trend was already discernible in the plan period 1981-85, when policies to improve economic efficiency, a continuing deceleration in the growth of the labour force, and the high cost of raw material extraction, all made it necessary to increase investment.

Consumption is in turn divided between personal and social consumption. Personal consumption broadly corresponds to wages and social benefits while social consumption includes current expenditure on science, education, health, art, state administration and defence. The share of personal consumption has grown in the German Democratic Republic and in Hungary in the 1980s, while in Bulgaria, Czechoslovakia, Poland and the USSR, social consumption increased slightly. In the future social consumption is planned to grow faster than personal consumption in most of these countries.

Increases in real income per capita since 1970 generally indicate a stable rise in consumption, though with some variations between countries. From

Figure 8.1. Consumption as a percentage of national income: Centrally planned economies, 1970-86

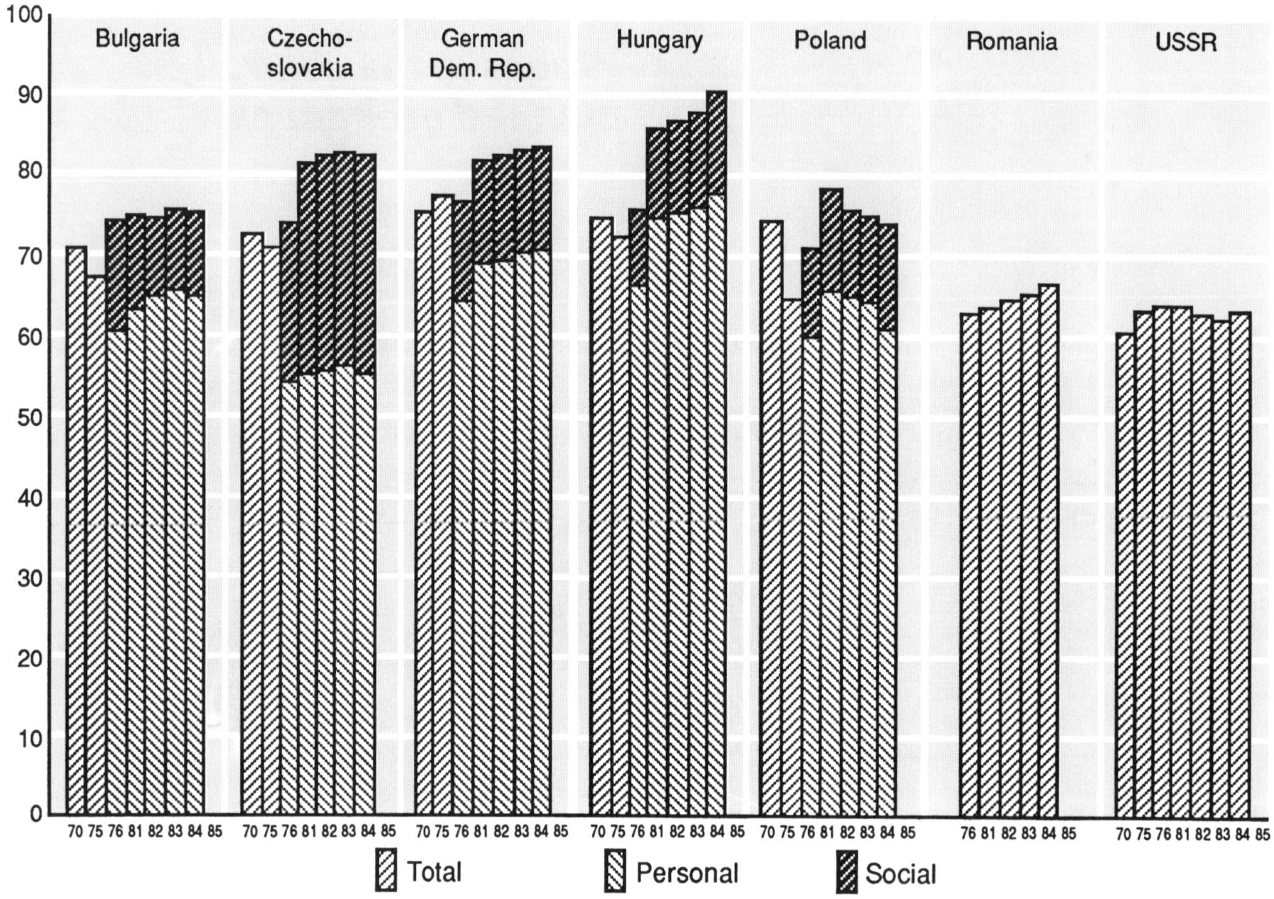

Source: National statistics, plans and plan-fulfilment reports; CMEA: *Statistical Yearbook* (Moscow), various issues; Economic Commission for Europe: *Economic survey of Europe in 1985-86*, various issues.

1981 to 1985 real incomes rose by 20 per cent in the GDR, by 19.5 per cent in Bulgaria, by 11.8 per cent in the USSR, by 7.5 per cent in Hungary and by 5.2 per cent in Czechoslovakia. In Poland, real incomes fell by about 8 per cent. (No data were available on Romania.) The decrease in Poland may be attributed to the political disturbances of the period, in particular during 1982 when real incomes fell by 18 per cent and real wages per capita by 25 per cent.

Between 1970 and 1980, real wages grew steadily in all CPECs, rising 16-17 per cent in Czechoslovakia and Hungary and by more than 50 per cent in Poland (figure 8.2). During the 1980s, there was continued steady progress in Bulgaria and the GDR. But in the other countries real wages increased more slowly and in some countries decreased in certain years. In Poland, largely due to the exceptional circumstances of 1982, real wages fell by 14.5 per cent

during the 1981-85 period; in Hungary, real wages in 1985 were just 3 per cent higher than four years earlier. The slowdown in the growth of real wages seems to have been strongest in countries where inflation was highest. However, the main contributory factor was probably the slackening of economic growth in 1981-85, a matter of considerable concern to all these countries.

In spite of slower growing or declining real wages in the 1980s, real incomes have continued to rise steadily. Apart from wages, real incomes also include incomes from social consumption funds. The social consumption funds are designed to improve national living standards according to the needs of the population, as opposed to wages from the wage fund which are paid in accordance with the quantity and quality of work done.

Social consumption funds, financed mainly from

Figure 8.2. **Monthly real earnings in the non-agricultural economy: Centrally planned economies, 1971-85: Employees in the socialised sector**

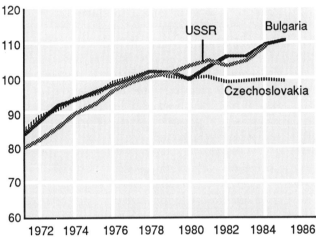

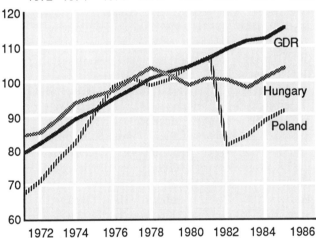

Source: ILO: *Year Book of Labour Statistics.*

the state budget, have grown considerably over the years in Eastern Europe. Between 1960 and 1982, social consumption funds per capita increased in Bulgaria by 6.7 times, in Hungary by 4.5 times, in the GDR by 2.7 times, in Romania by 5.7 times, in the USSR by 4.6 times and in Czechoslavakia by 3.8 times. Further expansion of social consumption funds – at a rate higher than the growth of wages – has been one of the priorities of socio-economic strategies in CPECs in the 1980s.

It appears that on the whole the CPECs have managed to establish appropriate general wage levels without suffering as high inflation as IMECs and many developing countries (although Poland is an exception in this regard). Nor have they experienced the degree of conflict that has typically characterised

the issue of appropriate wage levels in other parts of the world. This has been due to the close relationship that exists between the ruling party, the State and the trade unions in the CPECs.

However, this success has also entailed costs in the form of low productivity and shortages of labour as well as of various services and commodities. Some of the side-effects of centrally established general levels of wages may have been instrumental in encouraging CPECs to shift towards more decentralised systems, as discussed below. These shifts have in turn brought with them some of the problems associated with lack of central control, such as inflation, and this is true not only of Poland. These problems have to be dealt with through the wage adjustment methods peculiar to the CPECs.

2. Wage adjustment

Wages are expected to be the main element in motivating workers, as reflected in the principle of distribution of wages according to quantity and quality of work. This role is assigned to the wage fund and the way it is determined and distributed. The total wage fund – that is, the national amount available for wages and salaries – is apportioned to the economic branches (industries). Within each branch, parts of the fund are allocated to enterprises and again, further down the chain, to establishments within enterprises. The problem for the central planners is to keep a balance between control of the wage fund within the national plan, and the relative autonomy allowed to managers of establishments and enterprises. Managers are responsible for using the resources available to them to the best advantage in order to fulfil or exceed the targets set in the plan, in consultation and agreement with the trade unions and the party organs.

Wage-bill determination

A few words regarding the principles relating to determination and distribution of the wage bill (the enterprise wage fund) are necessary in order to understand the changes that have taken place in this area.

Traditionally, the wage bill of an enterprise has been assigned by the centre as an absolute sum. In calculating this sum, the centre takes into account the output target, the planned number of employees, their qualification mix, and allows for average wage increases depending on the planned growth of productivity. The growth of the wage bill used to be linked to the gross value of output; if the target in gross value was fulfilled, enterprises received the planned wage bill, while over-fulfilment of the target resulted in an increase in the wage bill. This practice was followed in most of the CPECs.

Changes began to be implemented from the early 1960s onwards. By this stage, it was becoming evident that gross value of output as an indicator of plan fulfilment tended to encourage the use of more energy and more expensive materials in fulfilling planned production. Various means have been used to overcome these tendencies. In Czechoslovakia, for example, the wage bill is assigned as a fixed proportion of the planned sales target. This illustrates an attempt to avoid another side-effect of the use of gross value of output as an indicator, which is to encourage output sometimes at the expense of marketability of products and of meeting consumer demand. In addition, linkage of wage-bill growth to centrally planned output targets can induce enterprises to conceal their real potential and reserves, as well as to avoid the adoption of demanding new production plans.

Another variant seeks to overcome some of these drawbacks by linking the growth of the wage bill to improved performance over the previous year. In Poland, for example, between 1973 and 1982 the annual growth of the wage bill was linked to the increment in value-added over the previous year. For every percentage point of increase in value-added the wage bill was increased by a coefficient assigned from the centre.

Making wage-bill growth dependent on performance can go further, as illustrated by the practice in Hungary after the major economic reforms of 1968. Since 1971, increases in average wages in enterprises have depended on increases in gross income (wage plus profits) per employee. For every percentage point increase in gross income per employee wages can be increased by a certain percentage, provided that the enterprise can afford to pay a tax amounting to a certain proportion of increased wage costs. The principle here is that the more efficient an enterprise the larger the gross income, and the more funds available for paying taxes for wage increases.

As a result of the 1982 economic reform in Poland, the growth in average wages of industrial enterprises is also regulated through taxation of those increases that go beyond a stipulated threshold. The rate of increase in average wages is set at 0.5 per cent of the rate of growth in labour productivity, but this can vary according to market requirements. For example, the actual coefficient in 1985 was close to 0.9 per cent of the rate of growth in labour productivity. Further flexibility is being sought through the use of different taxation formulas, which vary according to the activity of the enterprise in question, and factors such as the relative share of labour costs in net production value, possibilities for increasing value-added, and so on.

Different methods of wage-bill regulation can have a direct impact on personnel and pay practices within the enterprise. Where the size of the wage bill is planned in relation to average wage indicators and the number of workers employed, enterprises have a greater interest in having more workers than in raising labour productivity. The existence of a ceiling or of a tax on average wage growth can lead to labour hoarding. In this case, enterprises may seek to circumvent the ceiling or taxation by hiring new workers who can be paid below-average wages. This leaves management with the necessary resources to pay increases for certain key staff who may otherwise look for jobs elsewhere.

Recent trends indicate that those CPECs that have depended on a more centrally regulated wage policy are seeking greater decentralisation in order to promote enterprise efficiency and a mobilisation of hidden reserves of productivity. Since 1984 in the USSR, for example, enterprises participating in a major experiment seeking to improve management and productivity through providing them with more autonomy, have had the growth of their wage bill linked to growth of their real net output rather than to plan fulfilment. Where previously growth in wages was financed out of budgetary appropriations, the 12th Five-Year Plan (1986-90) expects enterprises to provide the necessary funds by increasing production and efficiency, and by mobilising all available internal reserves. In this connection, it is interesting to note that the new plan envisages that virtually all the increase in national income during 1986-90 will be obtained through higher labour productivity. Similar drives are being made in other CPECs. Such experiments seeking to promote "efficiency" can lead to problems of "equity" in wage distribution. When greater autonomy was provided to enterprises in Czechoslovakia to link growth of wages to their economic results, the relevant new wage regulations were introduced earlier in the production sector than in others. Production sector wages were already higher than elsewhere and this difference was accentuated.

8.1   Yugoslavia: Self-management and social contract

Yugoslavia, in its passage to "self-management", illustrates some of the problems inherent in the decentralisation of an originally centrally planned economy.

Central direction of the economy was abandoned after 1965, when macro-economic investment planning was abolished, foreign and domestic markets liberalised, and more freedom to differentiate earnings granted to enterprises. By 1975, however, this lack of prior co-ordination was deemed to have led to structural problems such as duplication of production, increases in the disparity of development between regions, excessive differentiation of earnings and incomes, difficulties in foreign trade, and so on. Inflation, in particular, has proved a major problem which is still far from having been solved.

Various measures have been taken to overcome some of the problems of decentralisation. Since 1976, the national plan has been based on plans originated from below by the self-managing organisations. The plans of the enterprises worked out on the basis of a common methodology, common assumptions, and common length of planning period are aggregated and reconciled with the national plan in terms of intersectoral and macro-economic consistency. They are then returned to the self-managing unit for approval. The signature of approval by the enterprise to a part of the plan is a commitment to a certain investment policy, to a certain price and personal income level, and to a certain distribution pattern. It is, as the Yugoslavs put it, a "social contract" between the State and the self-governing unit. The objective of the "social contract" is to reduce the uncertainty that was present in the market mechanism. Although the new planning principles do not

represent a return to traditional central planning, they constitute in one form or another an *ex ante* co-ordination of social goals. For example, the social contract contains guide-lines for minimum and maximum differentials between and within occupations. These guide-lines, though formally voluntary, in reality are a re-emergence of a form of central control over earnings.

However, profit still plays an important role. It is the essential source of enterprise income and of self-financing, in terms of both the production development fund, the wage bill and the material incentive fund.

The income is divided between these funds by the organs of workers' self-management, and profits made by the collective determine the level of wages. Despite workers' self-management, the distribution of wages in Yugoslavia has posed, as in other Eastern European countries, a number of problems in the attempt to reconcile concerns of equity with efficiency.

Experiments in implementing the principle of pay according to actual work accomplished and the quality of performance in these tasks are being carried out in Yugoslavia, in order to overcome the rigid application of the principle of pay according to the post occupied. This can give disproportionate weight to what is brought to the job in terms of qualifications, as opposed to what is actually *done* in the job. Through the application of a similar method of job evaluation to both production and non-production jobs, there has been a move away from the tendency towards compressed wage differentials. This has made production jobs more attractive, stemming the tide towards service occupations which had featured in the 1970s.

The material incentive fund

In the series of reforms that took place in the mid-1960s, the wage bill of enterprises in many CPECs was complemented by the so-called "material incentive fund", fed by a part of the profit of the enterprise. The material incentive fund, used in conjunction with the wage bill, is intended to play an important role in the process of achieving greater efficiency while maintaining equity. These funds were established largely with a view to providing bonuses for improved performance; the size of the fund is based on profit, either as the sole success indicator or in combination with other qualitative indicators. This was in order to counter the tendency of quantitative indicators used for regulating wage-bill growth, such as gross value of output, to induce enterprises to maximise output without paying due respect to considerations of cost, quality and demand.

The material incentive fund is not very large in comparison with the wage bill. What is important, however, is the differential share of bonuses in the employment incomes of individual groups of

employees. Generally, bonuses have the heaviest weight in the incomes of top managers to encourage them to improve enterprise performance. This may also be seen as a policy aimed at widening earnings differentials for the same reason.

In Poland, a different principle applies to distribution of the material incentive fund. It is established solely for paying bonuses to senior salaried employees. All other workers receive bonuses from the wage bill, the growth of which – as discussed above – was based until 1982 on value-added as an indicator. This and subsequent changes are designed to ensure that adjustment of the wage bill motivates workers to better performance. They illustrate the fact that methods for adjusting and distributing the wage bill and the material incentive fund are quite pragmatic and complementary. In other words, where the centre plays a more direct role in assigning the wage bill, as in the USSR, the GDR and in Czechoslovakia, the material incentive fund plays a key motivating role. Where there is a more indirect form of wage-bill regulation, as in Hungary and Poland, the regulation of basic wages tends to play a greater role in this function.

Some recent experiments
with wage-bill regulations

Many CPECs have recently tried to improve the stimulative role of wage regulation by reducing dependence on quantitative indicators of success and enhancing the autonomy of the enterprise. In the USSR, a series of changes between 1979 and 1983 went a long way in moving away from quantitative indicators used to plan the increase in the wage bill. Since 1983, for each additional percentage point in labour productivity growth beyond the planned figure, the wage bill is increased by 0.4 per cent. When an enterprise honours all its production orders according to schedule, it is authorised to increase its material incentive fund by 15 per cent. However, if it fails, this fund is proportionately reduced.

In the above-mentioned experiment for improving economic management in the USSR, the growth of the wage bill of the participating enterprises is linked to the growth of net output and the fulfilment of contractual obligations, rather than to the percentage of plan fulfilment. Furthermore both the wage bill and the material incentive fund can be increased or decreased as a result of a corresponding change in labour productivity. The enterprise can also carry over any savings in wages made in the previous year.

In Romania, a 1984 Decree permits, for an experimental period of two years, an increase in the proportion of operating profits that can be retained by an enterprise. If the plan targets are exceeded and the raw material and energy consumption is below a certain rate, the enterprise can retain 50 per cent of profits in the first year, and 25 per cent in the second year. In Bulgaria, the wage bill of enterprises since 1982 has been linked more closely to factors such as gross incomes, profits and saving of material resources. For example, for every 1 per cent increase in the gross income of the enterprise, the wage bill is increased by 0.2 to 0.5 per cent.

3. Changing wage structures

Wage structures in the CPECs are governed by the central "tariff" (classification) system which establishes occupational grades and pay scales on the basis of a national system of job evaluation. Detailed "tariff books" or wage rate and occupational classification manuals play an important role in these systems for harmonising wage rates and skill categories between industries. Most grading is industry-wide, and each

branch of activity generally decides on its own wage scales, within the framework of national wage policy directives. The trade unions participate in drafting and examining new general basic rates and schedules of grades, as well as the sectoral wage rates proposed by the respective ministries.

Sectoral wage differentials

Certain distortions in the working of the tariff systems have given rise to difficulties in meeting changing labour market needs in CPEC countries. One contributory factor is the slow and cumbersome process of revising tariff scales. Another has been the preferential wage treatment, introduced in earlier development plans, given to the so-called "material sphere" and, within it, to mining, some manufacturing subsectors and construction. Figure 8.3 illustrates this tendency for wages in the material spheres of industry (mining, quarrying, manufacturing, and public utilities), construction and transport to be higher than the average for the total economy. The only exception to this is Hungary, where the average wage for industry has been consistently lower than the average for the total economy. Agriculture is a rather special area in the material sphere of production. Since 1970 average wages in this sector have tended to be below the average for the total economy. Only in recent years has special effort been made to raise average wages in agriculture, so that they are now closer to the average for the socialised sectors (state enterprises and co-operatives).

The non-material sphere of trade, housing and community services, education, culture, health, social security, sport and tourism, pays wages below the average. Within the non-material sphere, only the science and research sector pays more than the average for the total economy, and even here wages are often lower than in construction and transport.

Table 8.1 provides greater detail on industrial wage differentials in Czechoslovakia, Hungary, Poland and the GDR for 1980. The relatively high wages in the traditional "heavy industries" (mining and metallurgy), and the low wages in textiles, clothing and food, help to explain, for example, the below-average wages of the sector termed "industry" for Hungary in figure 8.3. The table shows that the industrial branches with low or high wages tend to be much the same in each country, with the engineering industry coming closest to the national average wage. The level of wages is conspicuously high in mining, metallurgy and the energy-producing sectors; in

Figure 8.3.   Wage differentials in the socialised sector: Centrally planned economies, 1970 and 1985 (average wage in the total economy = 100)

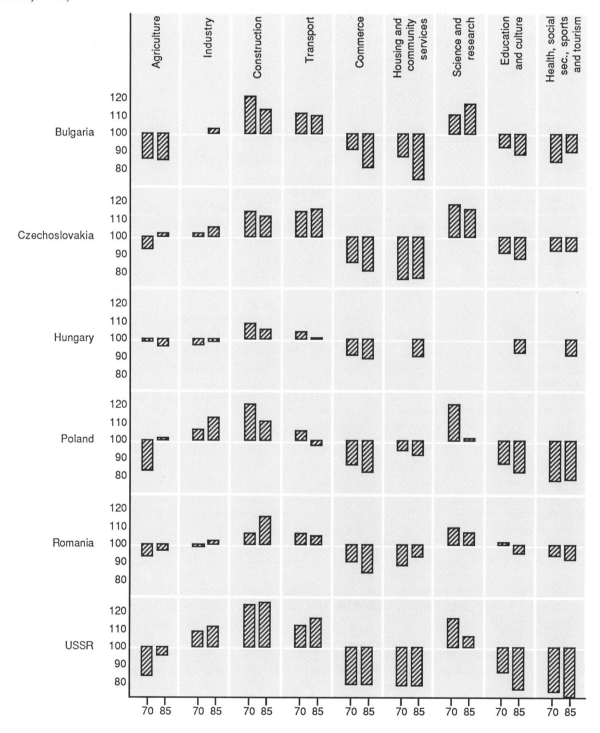

Source: CMEA: *Statistical Yearbook*, various issues.

Table 8.1. Wage differentials between industrial sectors: Centrally planned economies, 1980 (average industrial wage = 100)

	Czecho-slovakia[1]	Hungary[2]	Poland[3]	German Democratic Republic
Fuel and energy			153	111
Coalmining		148[5]	170	
Fuels	137		104	
Electricity production	112	103	103	
Basic metal industries		112	131	111
Iron and steel	119		128	
Engineering	101	95	96	103
Metal products	91[4]	90	90	
Machinery	105	97	100	
Electrical and elec-tronic products				101
Chemicals and rubber	101			
Chemicals		104	93	105
Construction materials	102	94	93	99
Wood products	90	87	84	
Textiles	82	88	87	87
Clothing	77	78	80	
Food	91	98	86	95
Light industry (without textiles)				90

[1] Gross wages in industry. [2] Earnings in state industry. [3] Net wages in socialist industry. [4] Including electro-technical industry. [5] Mining.

Source: G. Kertesi and G. Kövári: *Real wages in Eastern Europe* (Budapest, 1986; mimeographed), p. 52.

Table 8.2. Earnings differentials by occupation and sex: Centrally planned economies, 1980 (male professional earnings = 100)

	Bulgaria	Czecho-slovakia	Poland	Hungary	GDR
Men					
Professionals	100	100	100	100	100
Administrative and clerical workers	83	93	86	80	85
Skilled workers	90	85	82	78	85
Unskilled workers	80	82	77	69	72
Women					
Professionals	78	73	79	77	83
Administrative and clerical workers	62	60	65	59	58
Skilled workers	73	56	57	61	71
Unskilled workers	66	50	57	53	58

Source: G. Kertesi and G. Kövári, op. cit., p. 60.

Poland, wages in coalmining are 70 per cent higher than the industrial average. It should be noted that those branches of industry that are important employers of women workers – textiles, clothing and food – pay wages some 15 to 20 per cent below the industrial average. Figure 8.3 similarly indicates lower than average wages in the sectors of the non-material sphere, which are also large employers of women.

Over the past 15 to 20 years wage differentials between different sectors of the economy have generally narrowed, in line with policy in the CPECs to improve the living standards of the lowest paid. In the USSR, for example, the average wage in industry rose 1.8 times in the period from 1965 to 1980, with a trend towards a narrowing of differentials between light and heavy industry. In 1965, the average wage of workers in the highest-paying industry, coalmining, was 2.7 times higher than in the lowest-paying, the sewing industry; in 1980, this difference had fallen to 2.2 times. As already mentioned, agri-cultural wages were raised, particularly at the beginning of the 1980s. Moreover, wages in most non-material sectors have not fallen any further behind those in the material sector.

Occupational and other wage differentials

A 1979 survey of inequalities in income in the CPECs, in considering the combined effect of sex and occupation, found that the income of men surpassed that of women in every stratum, and also that the differences according to sex were considerably higher than those based on occupation. Table 8.2 indicates that in general, within the same occupation, the income of men exceeds that of women by 20 to 30 per cent. It is noteworthy that in Bulgaria and Czechoslovakia the average income of the highest paid women (professional women) trails the income of men from the lowest income stratum (unskilled male workers). Moreover, male administrative and clerical workers fare quite well in comparison to male professionals, whereas female administrative and clerical workers lag behind. This may be attributed primarily to the fact that the majority of women in this stratum are simple administrative employees, whereas the majority of men are medium-level engineering and technical personnel.

Changing skill requirements pose another difficulty for the tariff system. A rapidly expanding national programme for general education and

Table 8.3. Wage differentials between occupations: Centrally planned economies, 1965-80: Industrial employees (wage of manual workers = 100)

	Poland[1]		Czechoslovakia[2]		Hungary[3]	
	Engineering and technical	Administrative and clerical personnel	Engineering and technical	Administrative and clerical personnel	Engineering and technical	Administrative and clerical personnel
1965	164[4]	107[4]	135	86	155	96
1970	150	103	135	86	151	96
1971	148	102	133	86	150	97
1972	146	101	131 (119)[6]		85	148
1973	144	100	120		142	92
1974	141	97	119		144	93
1975	130[5]	94 89[5]	117		140	117[7]
1976	131	89	118		139	117
1977	132	88	116		136	117
1978	132	87	116		135	115
1979	129	85	115		136	115
1980	129	86			137	117

[1] Monthly net wages in socialist industry. [2] Gross wages. [3] Net wages including social insurance premiums in state industry (up to 1974) and in socialist industry (since 1975). [4] Monthly gross wages. [5] New classification. [6] Technical-management personnel. [7] Non-manual workers.
Source: G. Kertesi and G. Kővári, op. cit., p. 54.

training combined with increased mechanisation and automation of the work process is producing a progressively more skilled workforce, which in turn is being allocated to higher grades in the tariff scales. For example, during the 1960s and 1970s, there was what may be termed "grade creep" in the tariff system of the USSR – that is, an increase in the share of persons in the higher grades. In 1962, the share of industrial workers in the highest grades (IV-VI) was 33.2 per cent; by 1979, this proportion had risen to 45.6 per cent. The other CPECs have experienced similar trends.

At the same time, mechanisation has not been extended to all sectors of the economy and certain jobs are bound to remain predominantly manual. These are often associated with arduous working conditions, and those performing them tend to remain in the lowest grades. It has been noted that there is competition among enterprises for workers to undertake such jobs, pushing up incomes. But where higher pay is used to palliate difficult or dangerous working conditions and jobs with lack of inherent work value, it is not those who are producing the best results who are rewarded, but rather those who have been convinced by the pay system to undertake non-prestigious work. The wage structure can be further complicated by higher regional coefficients for jobs in new areas of development in the USSR (for example,

in Siberia and the Far East). To attract workers and to reduce labour turnover in these difficult work environments, regional coefficients and increases for seniority in the same enterprise can as much as double the tariff rate.

The setting of and achieving production norms (an integral part of the wage system in CPECs) raises more problems. New equipment and technologies are often introduced faster than general branch norms are revised. Earnings are thus increased by the significant over-fulfilment of unduly low norms. Such low norms also contribute to the tendency of labour hoarding mentioned earlier. Efforts are being made to overcome these problems by the widespread use of more technically sound norms.

Finally, the relative pay position of engineers and other technical cadres seems to have suffered. For example, between 1940 and 1979 workers' wages in the USSR increased 5-6 times, whereas those of technical cadres rose by only 3 times. Following a revision of the tariff system in the mid-1960s the average pay of engineers equalled workers on the highest grade of the tariff scale, and technicians' pay was equal to workers in grade IV. In 1980, wages of engineering and technical personnel were only 114.6 per cent of wages of workers in industry and in construction they were only 102.7 per cent. In 1970 these proportions were 136.3 per cent and 134.7 per cent respectively.

Table 8.3 presents data from 1965 to 1980 for Czechoslovakia, Hungary and Poland on relative wage ratios for manual workers, administrative and clerical staff and engineering/technical personnel. They show that in the long run wage differentials have narrowed, with a considerable fall in the relative wage advantage of engineering/technical personnel.

Experimenting with new wage systems

Developing a system of remuneration that copes with these problems is a daunting task. Its basic requirements have been outlined by the 1986 edition of the programme of the Communist Party of the USSR:

"Payment according to work done remains the principal source of working people's incomes during the first phase of communism. The system of wages and salaries must be improved constantly so that it fully corresponds to the principle of payment according to the amount and quality of work done, with due account of the conditions and results of work, stimulates the upgrading of workers' skills and labour productivity, and promotes better output quality and the rational use and saving of all types of resources."

Various alterations to the tariff system are being experimented with in the different countries to cope with this complex situation.

The factors in job evaluation have been modified. A new draft job evaluation scheme drawn up in Poland in 1985, for example, has added under the factor "complexity of work" new subfactors such as "creative thinking" and "skill", while under the factor "work arduousness" a new subfactor relating to "psychic stress due to low prestige of work" is being actively debated.

In Hungary, the classification of jobs in each grade now takes account of five degrees of working conditions rather than four. Revisions had to be made to the tariff system in 1976 and 1981 because the best workers soon reached the ceiling of their wage scale. In 1984, a new category had to be added to the existing five, for those workers with exceptional skill, versed in several trades and with long vocational experience.

Wage rates have been increased in Hungary since 1984, the upper limits by 25 per cent and the lower limits by 10 per cent. (The minimum wage had already been raised by 35-40 per cent in 1977 and the ceiling by an average of 30 per cent.) With a view to attracting young well-educated entrants to the labour force, the starting rate for those with a university or college education has been raised by 40 per cent. The new tariff system also makes it possible for the basic wage rates of those performing outstanding, particularly technical, activities to rise faster than before.

Researchers in the CPECs are increasingly arguing for greater flexibility in the tariff system to make it more responsive to the changing needs of the economy and the evolving composition of the workforce. There is a particular need for the tariff system to take account not only of the qualification on the basis of which grade allocations are initially made, but also of the work done once the worker is in the job. Suggestions for achieving this include increasing wage differentials, providing special allowances for professional competence and expanding the list of specialist grades. An important goal in this process would be to improve the pay of engineers and technicians, as well as their social prestige.

Policy-makers are of course aware of these problems, and have done their best to overcome them. In addition to payments from the material incentive fund, savings in the wage bill in the USSR can be used to provide bonuses to engineering and technical personnel (up to 30 per cent of their basic wage) and to designers and technologists (up to 50 per cent) for achieving high skill levels. New regulations governing the tariff system in Bulgaria, introduced in 1979, contain measures to compensate highly skilled workers and supervisory staff by aligning their wage rates to the category above in the same occupation. In Romania, a 1984 Decree provides for the payment of special allowances to outstanding workers and technical personnel for innovatory work.

In a series of wide-ranging experiments initiated in the USSR in 1984, enterprises have been accorded greater leeway in the use of the tariff system. The enterprises participating in the experiment have the right to pay higher rates, to workers employed in key jobs and for the acquisition of more skills. Thus workers in grade IV can receive up to 16 per cent, workers in grade V can receive up to 20 per cent, and those in grade VI can receive up to 24 per cent more than the corresponding wage rate. Enterprise directors also have the right to pay highly skilled engineers, technicians and certain categories of white-collar workers up to 50 per cent more than the basic rate. The experiment already seems to have met with some success, since a similar, although lower, series of increments have been allowed for these grades in enterprises that are not participating in the experiment.

More generally, attempts to improve the relative situation of scientific and technical staff have had mixed results. In Bulgaria and Romania, their remuneration was higher in absolute terms, and rose faster than wages in industry during the 1980s. In Czechoslovakia, the increase in wages for scientific workers was slightly below the average, but their absolute level remained above it. Despite slight increases in the remuneration of scientific workers in the USSR in 1982-83, their average wage was about 97 per cent of those in industry. In Poland, sharp rises in wages during the 1980s widened the existing gap between industrial and scientific workers in favour of the former.

It has been argued that by its very nature the tariff system has a difficult role in motivating and rewarding work. The revision of tariff scales, a massive exercise that can take place only infrequently, is financed by the state budget. Increases in tariff scales are provided to a whole branch, a region or a professional group; as such, these increases cannot be seen as having been won by a particular worker or collective. Therefore, some experts think that self-managed collectives should play a major role in fixing wages, with the rate of average wage increases as well as total volume of resources being centrally fixed, but with individual wage determination left to the enterprise. A more far-reaching idea that has emerged out of the debate between academics and practitioners on the tariff system in Hungary has been that of assigning only the upper limits of the tariff system as a directive.

4. Adapting enterprise wage systems

The axiom, "from each according to his capacity, to each according to his work", far from necessarily leading to any egalitarianism, implies a system in which pay is linked to performance. The preceding discussion has shown the extent to which all issues relating to pay in the CPECs revolve around the question of somehow reconciling this principle with that of improving the living standard of the population as a whole and avoiding what would be considered unacceptable earnings differentials by the majority of the working class.

This section will concentrate mainly on the trends in the CPECs from an initial situation of reliance on traditional piece-rates for linking pay to performance to one of using more global collective methods for raising productivity.

Individual piece-rates

Piece-rates were used extensively at the beginning of mass industrialisation. However, such systems, where the reward is proportional to the degree of fulfilment of work norms, and in particular progressive piece-rate systems, where the rate of change of earnings gradually increases with growth in performance, tend to push average wages beyond plan targets if over-fulfilment is high. One of the reasons for the comprehensive wage reform in the USSR between 1957 and 1961 was that the widespread use of progressive piece-rate systems had produced problems at the enterprise level. As a result of weaknesses in standard setting in establishments, it had become possible to earn a high bonus relatively easily, thus increasing the proportion of incentive pay in the pay packet.

The effect in terms of uncontrolled wage costs in the whole economy was considerable. The response of the central authorities was to consolidate most of the piece-rate components of the pay packet into basic rates and then to make sure that the norm for each job was set in such a way as to relate the now consolidated basic pay with the norm. This was done because, if grade rates are a sufficiently high proportion of the total pay under variable reward payment systems, then it is possible to exercise greater control over the growth of wage fund expenditure and the productivity represented by the norms than if a large proportion represents earnings from incentive pay administered locally.

As a result of the reform, the number of industrial workers on piece-work fell and the proportion of basic pay (tariff rates) rose. It currently represents from 70 to 90 per cent of the total pay packet. Thus, the Soviet wage reform represented a move towards reducing the incidence of individual piece-rates, especially of the progressive kind. Also, where individual piece-rates survived, the aim was to reduce the proportion of incentive pay in the pay packet. At the same time, the process of technical norm-setting was accelerated to strengthen control over "wage drift" and "erosion of norms".

Data for all the CPECs show trends similar to that of the USSR, in that the proportion of piece-rate workers in the economy was reduced by the beginning of the 1960s from the very high earlier levels. Since that period, the available figures show that the proportion of piece-rate workers has remained comparatively stable in these countries. At the same time, there has been a marked shift from simple time wages to time wages plus a bonus, and from simple piece-rates to piece-rates plus a bonus.

Group forms of incentive payment

There have also been important moves towards group and establishment-wide forms of incentive payment, parallel with policies of increasing as well as *reducing* pay in accordance with performance. The system of work in brigades is perhaps the most well-known in this connection. There were almost 1.5 million of these brigades in 1983 in the USSR, covering over 56 per cent of workers in industry. (In Bulgaria, approximately 85 per cent of industrial workers are currently organised in brigades.) The brigade is a collective which enters into a contract with enterprise management to deliver a finished product for a specified sum, which it distributes among its members. The wage bill is calculated according to the skill levels of the brigade members, who include time-workers, piece-rate workers as well as technicians, engineers and salaried employees. The brigade receives a premium if it surpasses the target, and suffers reductions if the target is not met. Premiums are paid both for results and for savings in labour costs and raw materials. The wage bill is distributed among brigade members according to skill grade and time worked, with a limit of a specified percentage of the relevant tariff rate. To promote individual initiative and responsibility within the brigades, each worker is accorded a "coefficient of labour participation", which regulates his earnings upwards or downwards, the tariff rate being guaranteed. The coefficient is determined by criteria such as quality of work, technical competence, innovative work methods, rate of rejects and so on, and fixed at the end of each month by the brigade leader after consultation with the brigade council, or at a general assembly of the brigade.

The labour participation coefficient may be applied in different ways for distribution of earnings, depending on the decision of the brigade council. Usually, bonuses are distributed according to the coefficient, while the wage bill is distributed on the basis of tariff rates. However, the total wage bill may also be distributed according to the coefficient.

There have been recent experiments in the USSR to extend the system of the collective contract from the level of the brigade to that of workshops and entire enterprises, as well as to introduce uniform principles of remuneration for all categories of personnel within a particular collective (piece-rate and time-rate workers as well as engineers and technicians). The results of these experiments will be interesting in pointing possible directions for overcoming some of the rigidities of the tariff system.

In Poland, a "complex task contract" is a signed agreement between a group of workers and the enterprise management, specifying the work to be done and time limits. If the work is finished before the specified time, a premium may be paid, provided the quality of work is satisfactory. This method has become widespread in building and more recently in other industries. In Bulgaria there is a similar system in operation, termed "global piece-work", where the contract specifies norms for expenditure of raw materials, fuel and energy as well as of output and time. The bonuses are distributed amongst members of the work team according to their wage grades. In a new type of brigade system being experimented with in a large engineering enterprise in Czechoslovakia, the individual wage rates, wage supplements and incentive bonuses of the brigade members are left intact. The group payment is limited to a "collective fund" given for savings in manpower, materials and energy.

Since 1982, Hungary has developed a new form of contract work known as "economic work partnerships within the enterprise". These are organised as a kind of autonomous "undertaking" from amongst the employees of an enterprise or co-operative, and are paid out of the enterprise's operating costs, and not from the wage bill. Originally, they were initiated in part to make use of underutilised capacity, to produce goods and services that were in short supply (including the production of components required by the enterprise). In practice, they have tended to be used more for overcoming labour shortages and bottlenecks in production. Peculiar aspects of these work partnerships include the fact that they are made up of workers who are also supposed to fulfil their normal work roles in the enterprise, who continue to receive wages from the wage bill, and whose earnings are much higher than other workers in the enterprise. In 1985, they were estimated at 18,000 in number, with a membership of 200,000 workers. Similar organisations have arisen in Bulgaria.

Recently, such partnerships have been the subject of considerable debate and some criticism in the CPECs. They may give rise to inequities vis-à-vis other workers who are not members – and it is usually the more skilled and competent ones who are chosen to join these partnerships. Furthermore, the members often have to economise on their efforts during normal working hours in order to carry out the second task which is far more remunerative. This has led some enterprise managers to abandon the use of these arrangements.

Incentives for managers

At the same time, a concerted effort has been made in all the CPECs to motivate enterprise managers to adopt more ambitious plans and implement them efficiently by linking managers' earnings to performance of the enterprise. In Hungary, a 1976 Decree provided for a bonus of up to 30 per cent of the basic annual salary of managerial staff, depending on the profitability of their enterprise. It also provided for an additional payment of 10-20 per cent of their salary on the basis of an evaluation of their individual activities over the year. The evaluation takes account of efforts to improve access to local and foreign markets and to utilise manpower effectively. In Bulgaria, managers and other high-level staff can receive up to 50 per cent of their basic salaries as bonuses; however, if certain criteria relating to quantity and quality of work are not met by the enterprise, they stand to lose up to 20 per cent of their salaries. In Romania, a 1983 Law relates the payment of management and supervisory staff to the results obtained by their subordinate units.

Incentives from the enterprise social consumption fund

There are recent signs that policy-makers would like to add some motivational aspects to the ever-increasing proportion of income flowing from the enterprise social consumption funds. The experiments undertaken in the USSR since 1984 to improve the management and organisation of the economy have included attempts to strengthen the direct relationship between the scale, level and quality of social services provided to workers by the social consumption fund and the results of their collective work. The basic size of the fund is increased in accordance with each percentage point increase in labour productivity or in profits. In 1987, this system is scheduled to be adopted by all industrial and transport sectors and by all branches of the national economy by the end of the 12th Five-Year Plan (1986-90).

Such a shift in policy may be in recognition of the fact that payments from the enterprise social consumption fund increasingly tend to play a role that is closer to that of basic wages. They often serve to attract and retain labour, and to promote skill development through training programmes. In this sense, the enterprise social consumption fund may be regarded as supplementing the social policy of the State, designed to provide employees with services that are difficult to obtain in the open market. It has also been pointed out that people often prefer, in return for higher productivity, to receive scarce goods (holidays, housing, pre-paid tourist packages and so on) than a monetary bonus which sometimes cannot be spent because certain consumer goods are unavailable. While the official policy, as reflected for example in the new 1986 edition of the programme of the Communist Party of the USSR, continues to allocate an egalitarian and social function to the enterprise social consumption fund in the years ahead, enterprises may well use their own funds in a more pragmatic nature.

Overcoming labour shortages

Wage-policy measures to overcome labour shortages in the CPECs have already been mentioned. This continues to be an important goal, especially in view of the need for structural adjustment to "intensive" economic development. One of the first experiments to defeat labour hoarding was begun in a chemical plant in the USSR in 1967. Any savings in the wage bill by reducing the number of workers could be used to raise the wages of the remaining workers. This principle was extended to other enterprises. Recently, in the construction of the "East-West" gas pipeline from the Tyumensk region to the Western frontiers of the USSR, a fixed standard wage was set per kilometre of pipeline commissioned from the main construction unit. The workforce comprising this unit was allowed to decide its own size and composition. The decision was to reduce the number of workers to one-third, and this smaller work unit laid 200 kilometres of pipeline per year as opposed to the 45 kilometres per year before introduction of the incentive scheme. The wage bill declined by 25-30 per cent whereas individual wages rose by 30-50 per cent. A similar experience in the Byelorussian railways was considered sufficiently noteworthy to be included as an example in the report of the central committee of the Communist Party of the USSR in 1986. A saving in the wage bill resulted from identification of a total of 12,000 superfluous jobs, and the remaining workforce received a 20 per cent increase in their wage rates. The workers affected by the restructuring are provided with various alternatives in training and other jobs, at the same pay.

Other types of wage policy measures have been taken in the CPECs to promote labour market adaptations to economic requirements. For example, a series of incentives were introduced in Poland in 1979 aimed at inducing scientific higher-educated, especially technically qualified persons to move to small towns. These include a monthly income supplement, monthly travel expenses for family visits and an installation loan. In the same year in Czechoslovakia, additional incentives were provided to redundant workers to take up jobs where there were manpower shortages. Those who did so were given a "recruitment allowance" for contract periods of up to five years, the maximum amount being up to six times the previous monthly wage.

Another method of overcoming labour shortages is encouragement to retired persons to return to work. State administrative bodies in the USSR adopted a series of measures in the 1960s and 1970s which helped boost the total number of pensioners working from 3 million in 1970 to 7.3 million in 1980. This trend was even more accentuated in those areas experiencing acute shortages. For example, in the Russian Soviet Federated Republic, the number of working pensioners increased by 48 per cent during the 1981-85 plan period. In Czechoslovakia, Hungary and Poland, retirees are allowed to work part time without any cut in pensions. In sectors with labour shortages, they can work full time and collect both pensions and wages.

5. Conclusion

The CPECs are squarely faced with the contradiction between one consideration of equity, namely that of removing existing inequalities of earnings and raising the incomes of the lowest paid and those most in need, and other considerations of equity which imply differences in pay linked to differences in work and performance. On the whole, it appears that the countries under consideration have all tended to

varying degrees and, at least until recently, to place greater weight on the first consideration of equity at the expense of the second. This has led to a progressive process of what has variously been termed "levelling" or "egalitarianism" – a compression of differentials and the granting of relative earnings advantages to those employed in manual occupations in heavy extractive, processing and manufacturing industry. At the same time, these industries have seen a decline in new job creation while demographic variations and a rapid increase in general educational standards have resulted in substantial employment creation in the tertiary, so-called non-material sphere.

Similarly, wage policy has been used to achieve certain goals – at least until recently – of macro-economic efficiency in terms of economic growth, productivity and low rates of inflation. But this has been at the expense of other macro-economic criteria and of allocative and operational efficiency at the sectoral and enterprise level, manifested in labour hoarding and shortages, unrealistic production targets, inefficient work or production methods, the production of poor quality goods, and inadequate supply of consumer goods or poor adaption to consumer needs.

In trying to resolve these problems policy-makers in the CPECs have implemented several distinct modifications to wage policy. They have sought to give more wage autonomy to the enterprise through changes in methods of wage-bill determination and distribution, emphasising, for example, more qualitative (profit and value-added) as opposed to quantitative (gross output or sales) success indicators, and by allowing wage increases if enterprises can find the funds from their own resources. Different means of stemming the compression and stimulating a widening of differentials have been pursued, especially for higher-educated new entrants, for managers and for scientific and technological staff, which circumvent or revise the rigid tariff system. An important vehicle for doing this is group payment systems and in particular, work brigades, in which workers decide among themselves how to reward labour input and performance and where earnings vary upwards and downwards according to performance. This form of work organisation is expected to play a growing role in resolving the conflict between equity and efficiency considerations in the CPECs.

Bibliographical note

This report is based on internal papers written by various ILO departments. It has drawn on a wide range of ILO work as well as a variety of outside sources, including research reports and publications of other international organisations. Some of the chapters are based on specially commissioned studies or ILO working papers which can be obtained from the ILO's Publication Branch. Most of these include extensive bibliographies. Selected sources are listed in the following bibliographical notes for each chapter.

Selected sources – by chapter

Chapter 1

Data on trade, remittances and capital flows are taken from various IMF sources. Much of the discussion on the economic context draws on a background document prepared for the ILO tripartite preparatory meeting on employment and structural adjustment (Geneva, 1987). The box on remittances is based on an internal ILO paper.

The section on employment is largely an overview and much of the source material is noted for other chapters, especially chapters 4 to 6. Data on employment and unemployment are taken from the ILO's *Year Book of Labour Statistics*. A study by Jamal and Weeks (1986) provided information on urban areas in sub-Saharan Africa. References to China are based on internal ILO material, while the subsection on Latin America draws on Tokman (1986), for adjustment policies, and Jatobá (1986) on trends to more casual wage employment during the 1980s.

The section on skill development makes use of a number of individual country studies by the ILO and other researchers, including mission reports by ILO staff. The discussion on vocational training in the formal sector and much of the source material is based on a World Bank discussion paper by Psacharopoulos (1986). Two other World Bank discussion papers, one on SENA by Jiménez and Kugler (1986) and the other on experience in sub-Saharan Africa (Auerhay, Romain, Stoïkov et al., 1985) also provided valuable background data. Information on training in the informal sector is drawn from various ILO publications and reports: an ILO study on French-speaking African countries (Maldonado et al., 1984) and on two CINTERFOR reports by Ramírez Guerrero (1985 and 1986).

The section on labour relations is largely based on ILO internal reports prepared by the regional advisers in labour relations for Africa, Asia, Latin America and the Caribbean.

Chapter 2

The section on employment draws mainly on a specially commissioned study by Newell and Symons (1987a) and an article by van Ginneken (1986). The discussion on trends in hours of work uses ILO data, backed up by statistics from the OECD. More detail on many of the developments can be found in ILO's *Conditions of Work Digest* (1986) which contains a detailed summary of legislation, examples of collective agreements, an extended annotated bibliography and a glossary. The section on collective bargaining draws extensively on work of the ILO's Labour Law and Labour Relations Branch. The source material for the section on social security comes largely from information collected by the ILO's Social Security Department, supplemented by published statistics for individual countries. The box on the new Japanese pension scheme is based on information from the Japan Pension Schemes Research Foundation (1985). Country developments in labour relations and social security are documented in the ILO's *Social and Labour Bulletin*.

Chapter 3

Chapter 3 draws extensively on two specially commissioned studies, one by Antosenkov (1986a) on the USSR and one by Kertesi and Kövári (1986) on the other CPECs. The section on employment and labour productivity uses statistical information from recent issues of the Economic Commission of Europe's *Economic Survey of Europe*, and various country sources. It also draws on internal ILO papers and on a wide variety of original country sources. Hethy (1986) provides a useful review of developments in Czechoslovakia, the USSR and Hungary.

The section on workers' participation is based on a number of studies, including Hethy (1986), an ILO review of worker participation (ILO, 1986), and on original country sources (mainly from the USSR).

The section on social security draws largely on information collected by the ILO's Social Security Department.

Chapter 4

This chapter is principally based on three ILO World Employment Programme working papers written by Jamal and Weeks (1987) on Africa, Ray (1987) on Asia and de Janvry, Sadoulet and Wilcox (1986) on Latin America. The country data for *Africa* are taken mainly from World Bank and FAO sources. The debate on economic policies in Africa can be said to have been launched by the World Bank's 1981 report on sub-Saharan Africa. Since then there have been numerous analyses of the African crisis, with all shades of opinion expressed. The African viewpoint is presented in the Lagos Plan of Action, published by the Organisation of African Unity in 1980.

Additional sources for *Asia* are Rajamaran's study (1985) on India and Rudra (1982) on West Bengal. The box on China uses material from the *Beijing Review*, the *China Agricultural Yearbook* and the *Statistical Yearbook of China*. The box on the Republic of Korea draws on studies by Ban, Mun and Perkins (1980) and Mason (1980). Sources for the section on Latin America include Klein (1984) and de Rezende (1985).

Chapter 5

Chapter 5 has drawn on a large number of country studies and research reports by ILO staff and others.

The labour surplus model of development was initially formulated more than three decades ago by Arthur Lewis (1954) and later elaborated upon by Ranis and Fei (1961 and 1964).

The discussion on wage levels uses data from an ILO study by Lecaillon et al. (1984) and a World Bank study by Squire (1979). The section on the level of wages from regular employment makes use of articles by Taira (1966) and Thompson (1986), among others.

Data on trends in minimum wage fixing for the period 1966 to 1977 can be found in Starr (1981) and later information is contained in Volume 1 of the *World Labour Report* (1984). The experience of Latin American countries regarding minimum wages is documented in PREALC (1985).

The discussion on wage restraint and stabilisation policies makes use of another PREALC study (1983) which looks at the relationship between real wages and unemployment in Latin America.

The section on inter-industry wage differentials draws on Papola and Bharadwaj (1970) and Macarthy (1984). Sources for the section on inter-occupational differentials include Taira (1966), Berg (1969), Gregory (1974) and Gunter (1964), while the discussion of public/private differentials makes use of the IMF study by Heller and Tait (1983) and Abdin et al. (1983).

Chapter 6

This chapter draws on a very wide range of country studies by the ILO, other international organisations and academic researchers. A full list of references is contained in a paper by Standing for the ILO's World Employment Programme, to be published in 1987. However, a few – not already cited as sources for tables – may be mentioned here.

Use has been made of studies by Harriss (1982 and 1985) on Coimbatore, India, Penouil and Lachaud (1986) on French-speaking Black Africa, Perlman (1976) on Rio de Janeiro, Standing (1983) on Malaysia and Rodgers (ed.) (forthcoming) which includes chapters by Pollack on Costa Rica, Jatobá on Brazil, Evers on Indonesia and Bardhan on West Bengal. A 1983 World Bank working paper by Lipton contains an extensive analysis of disadvantage in developing country labour markets. Bromley and Gerry (eds.) (1979) includes a wide range of studies on casual working in Third World cities. The plight of labour circulants is documented in Standing (ed.) (1985) while experience of urban migration in developing countries is collected in Goldscheider (ed.)

(1983). An ILO study edited by Rodgers and
Standing (1981) looks at the causes, functions and
consequences of child labour, documented extensively
in an earlier ILO review of the situation edited by
Mendelievich (1979).

Chapter 7

The section on wage levels and employment makes
use of economic analyses and data from the OECD
and the Commission of the European Communities.
A detailed rebuttal of the view that high real wages
cause unemployment is put forward by the European
Trade Union Institute (1985).

A number of studies are cited in the text in the
discussion on wage adjustment and wage flexibility.
This section also draws on Newell and Symons
(1985).

The box on concession bargaining in the United
States is based on Flanagan (1984), various reports
on wage developments by the Bureau of Labor Statistics (various issues), Ruben (1981), and Gay (1984).

The box on Australia is based on ILO internal
reports and government publications.

The section on public/private differentials draws
on work by the OECD (1982) as well as individual
country sources, while that on male/female pay
differentials makes use of Paukert (1984 and 1986).

The section on pay systems makes use of the ILO's
review of payment by results systems (1984a) and a
variety of country sources. The discussion on financial
participation and profit-sharing, inter alia, uses
information from Remus (1983).

Chapter 8

Basic source documents on the economies of the
CPECs are the UN Economic Commission for
Europe's annual economic survey, the ILO's *Year
Book of Labour Statistics* and the CMEA *Statistical Yearbook*. These have been supplemented by national
statistics. Wage developments in the CPECs are also
documented in the ILO's *Social and Labour Bulletin*.

Chapter 8 draws on a number of special studies,
notably work for the ILO by Héthy (1985), Mikheev
and Ray (1985), Kertesi and Kövári (1986) and,
concerning the USSR, Antosenkov (1986a). Other
sources include Gomberg and Sushkina (1983),
Kheifets (1983) and Bunich (1981).

The section on adopting enterprise wage systems
uses data contained in the ILO's report on payment
by results (1984a).

Selected sources

Abdin, R., Bennell, P., Fajana, O., Godfrey, M. and
Hamdouch, B. 1983. *A world of differentials: African pay
structures in a transnational context*. London, Hodder and
Stoughton.
AFL-CIO Committee on the Evolution of Work. 1985. *The
changing situation of workers and their unions*. Washington,
DC.
Aganbegian, A. 1986. *Make the economy more responsive to
innovations*. Moscow, Novosti.
Antosenkov, E.G. 1986a. *Employment and labour productivity in
the USSR*. Monograph prepared for the ILO, Moscow;
mimeographed.
—. 1986b. "Regional aspects of labour force development", in *Social and Labour Bulletin* (Geneva, ILO), No. 2,
p. 317.
Auerhay, J., Romain, R., Stoïkov, G. et al. 1985. *Institutional development in education and training in sub-Saharan
African countries*. World Bank discussion paper,
Education and Training Series, Washington, DC.
Ban, S.H., Mun, P.-Y. and Perkins, D.H. 1980. *Rural development*. Studies in the modernisation of the Republic of
Korea. Cambridge (Mass.), Harvard University Press
for the Council on East Asian Studies.
Berg, E.J. 1969. "Wage structures in less-developed coun-
tries", in A.D. Smith (ed.): *Wage policy issues in economic
development*. London, Macmillan.
Bromley, R. and Gerry, C. (eds.). 1979. *Casual work and
poverty in Third World cities*. Chichester, John Wiley and
Sons.
Bruno, M. and Sachs, J. 1985. *Economics of world-wide stag-
flation*, Cambridge, Mass., Harvard University Press.
Bunich, P. 1981. "Wages as an economic incentive", in
Problems of Economics (New York, Armonk), May 1981.
Bureau of Labor Statistics. *Current wage developments*.
Washington, DC, US Department of Labor, various
issues.
Chan-Lee, J., Coe, D.T. and Prywes, M. 1987. "Micro-
economic changes and macro-economic wage
disinflation in the eighties", in *OECD Economic Studies*
(Paris), Spring 1987.
Chokine, A. 1984. "Sotsialnaya spravedlivost i
raspredelenie dokhodov", in *Molodoi Kommunist*
(Moscow), No. 9.
Clark, R.O. 1984. "Collective bargaining and the econ-
omic recovery", in *OECD Observer* (Paris), July 1984.
Coe, D.T. 1985. "Nominal wages: The NAIRU and wage
flexibility", in *OECD Economic Studies* (Paris), Autumn
1985.
Craig, C., Garnsey, E. and Rubery, J. 1983. "Women's pay
in informal payment systems", in *Employment Gazette*
(London, Department of Employment), Apr. 1983.
Economic Commission for Europe. 1987. *Economic survey of
Europe in 1986-87*. New York, United Nations.
Estin, S. and Wilson, N. 1986. *The micro-economic effects of
profit-sharing: The British experience*. Centre for Labour
Economics, London School of Economics.
European Trade Union Institute. 1985. *Flexibility and jobs:
Myths and realities*. Brussels.
FAO. 1986a. *Production Year Book*. Rome.
—. 1986b. *Worldwide estimates and projections of the agricul-*

tural and non-agricultural population segments, 1950-2025. Rome.

Flanagan, R.J. 1984. "Wage concessions and long-term union wage flexibility", in *Brookings Papers on Economic Activity* (Washington, DC). Vol. 1.

Gay, R.S. 1984. "Union settlements and aggregate wage behaviour in the 1980s", in *Federal Reserve Bulletin* (Washington, DC), Dec. 1984.

Ghai, D. 1987. *Successes and failures in African development: 1960-82.* Geneva, ILO; paper prepared for the Seminar on Alternative Development Strategies in the Light of Recent Experience, organised by the Development Centre, Organisation for Economic Co-operation and Development, Paris, 28-30 Jan. 1987.

van Ginneken, W. 1986. "Full employment in OECD countries: Why not?", in *International Labour Review* (Geneva, ILO), Jan.-Feb. 1986.

Goldscheider, C. (ed.). 1983. *Urban migrants in developing nations, patterns and problems of adjustment.* Boulder, Colorado, Westview Press.

Gomberg, I.A. and Sushkina, L. 1983. "Basic directions of wage differentiation in industry", in *Problems of economics* (New York, Armonk), Mar. 1983.

Gregory, P. 1974. "Wage structures in Latin America", in *The Journal of Developing Areas* (Macomb), July 1974.

Grubb, D., Jackman, R. and Layard, R. 1983. "Wage rigidity and unemployment in OECD countries", in *European Economic Review* (Amsterdam), Mar.-Apr. 1983.

Gunter, H. 1964. "Changes in occupational wage differentials", in *International Labour Review* (Geneva, ILO), Feb. 1964.

Harriss, J. 1982. "Character of an urban economy: Small-scale production and labour markets in Coimbatore", in *Economic and Political Weekly* (Bombay), Vol. XVII, Nos. 23 and 24.

—. 1985. "Our socialism and the subsistence engineer: The role of small enterprises in the engineering industry in Coimbatore, South India", in R. Bromley (ed.): *Planning for small enterprises in Third World cities,* Oxford, Pergamon Press.

—. 1986. "The working poor and the labour aristocracy in a south Indian city: A descriptive and analytical account", in *Modern Asian Studies* (London), Apr. 1986.

Havasi, F. 1984. "Further development of the system of economic control and management in Hungary", in *Acta Oeconomica* (Budapest), No. 3-4.

Heller, P.S. and Tait, A.A. 1983. *Government employment and pay: Some international comparisons.* IMF occasional paper, No. 24, Washington, DC.

Héthy, L. 1985. *Pay systems in Eastern Europe.* Budapest, mimeographed.

—. 1986. "New developments in collective forms of work organisation in socialist countries", in *International Labour Review* (Geneva, ILO), Nov.-Dec. 1986.

ILO. 1984. *Payment by results.* Geneva.

—. 1986a. "Flexibility in working time", in *Conditions of Work Digest,* No. 2, 1986.

—. 1986b. *Workers' participation: A voice in decisions, 1981-85.* Geneva.

—. 1987. *Tripartite preparatory meeting on employment and structural adjustment* (Background document). Geneva.

Jamal, V. and Weeks, J. 1986. *Rural-urban income trends in sub-Saharan Africa.* Geneva, ILO; mimeographed.

—; —. 1987. *African agricultural crisis and rural incomes.* Geneva, ILO; mimeographed World Employment Programme research working paper; restricted.

de Janvry, A., Sadoulet, E. and Wilcox, L. 1986. *Rural labour in Latin America.* Geneva, ILO; mimeographed World Employment Programme research working paper; restricted.

Japan Pension Schemes Research Foundation. 1985. *National system of old-age, disability and survivors' benefits in Japan.* Tokyo.

Jatobá, J. 1986. "The labour market in a recession-hit region: The north-east of Brazil", in *International Labour Review* (Geneva, ILO), Mar.-Apr. 1986.

Jiménez, E. and Kugler, B. 1986. *An economic evaluation of a national job training system: SENA.* World Bank discussion paper, Education and Training Series, Washington, DC.

Kertesi, G. and Kövári, G. 1986. *Real wages in Eastern Europe.* Monograph prepared for the ILO, Budapest; mimeographed.

Kheifets, L. 1983. "State regulation of wages", in *Problems of economics* (New York, Armonk), July 1983.

Klein, E. 1984. "El impacto heterogéneo de la modernización agrícola sobre el mercado de trabajo", in *Socialismo y Participación* (Lima), No. 30.

Korolev, M. 1987. "Ladachi perestroiki statistiki", in *Vestnik Statistiki* (Moscow), No. 4, pp. 3-12.

Krishnamurti, J. 1984. "Changes in the Indian workforce", in *Economic and Political Weekly* (Bombay), 15 Dec. 1984.

Lecaillon, J., Paukert, F., Morrisson, C. and Germidis, D. 1984. *Income distribution and economic development: An analytical survey.* Geneva, ILO.

Lewis, W.A. 1954. "Economic development with unlimited supplies of labour", in *The Manchester School of Economic and Social Studies,* Vol. 22, May 1954.

Lipton, M. 1983. *Labour and poverty.* World Bank staff working paper, No. 616, Washington, DC.

Macarthy, P.G. 1984. *Consumer prices, real wages, the long-run structure of wages, inter-industry wage differentials and the long-run equalisation of wages in 19 Latin American countries.* Social Science working paper No. 64, Paisley College of Technology.

Maldonado, C. et al. 1984. *Emploi, apprentissage et accumulation de capital dans les micro-enterprise urbaines en Afrique francophone.* Geneva, ILO; mimeographed.

Mangum, G.L., 1984. *On the job training in small business: The state of the art.* Salt Lake City, Institute of Human Resource Development; mimeographed.

Mason, E.S. et al. 1980. *The economic and social modernisation of the Republic of Korea.* Cambridge (Mass.), Harvard University Press for the Council on East Asian Studies.

Mendelievich, E. (ed.). 1979. *Children at work.* Geneva, ILO.

Mikheev, S. and Ray, R. 1985. *Remuneration in Eastern Europe.* International Institute of Labour Studies Research Series, No. 82, Geneva, ILO.

Newell, A. and Symons, J. 1985. *Wages and employment in the OECD countries.* Discussion paper, No. 219, Centre for Labour Economics, London School of Economics.

—. 1987a. *Mid-1980s unemployment.* Discussion paper No. 283 (London, Centre for Labour Economics).

——; ——. 1987b. "Corporatism, laisser-faire and the rise in unemployment", in *European Economic Review* (Amsterdam), June 1987.

OECD. 1982. *Employment in the public sector.* Paris.

——. 1985. *Employment outlook.* Paris.

——. 1986a. *Labour market flexibility.* Report by a high-level group of experts to the Secretary-General (the Dahrendorf report), Paris.

——. 1986b. *Flexibility in the labour market: The current debate.* Paris.

Organisation of African Unity. 1980. *Lagos Plan of Action for the economic development of Africa, 1980-2000.* Addis Ababa.

Papanek, G.F. 1975. "The poor of Jakarta", in *Economic development and cultural change* (Chicago), Oct. 1975.

Papola, T.S. 1983. *Women workers in an Indian urban labour market.* Geneva, ILO; mimeographed World Employment Programme research working paper; restricted.

—— and Bharadwaj, V.P. 1970. "Dynamics of industrial wage structure: An inter-country analysis", in *The Economic Journal* (London), Mar. 1970.

Paukert, L. 1984. *The pay differential for women: Some comparisons for selected ECE countries.* Paper prepared for the UN-ECE Seminar on the Economic Role of Women in the ECE Region, Vienna, 15-19 Oct. 1984.

——. 1986. *Male and female earnings differentials in industrialised and developing countries.* Paper prepared for the ILO.

Penouil, M. and Lachaud, J.-P. 1986. *Le secteur informel et le marché du travail en Afrique noire francophone.* Geneva, ILO; mimeographed World Employment Programme research working paper; restricted.

Perlman, J.E. 1976. *The myth of marginality: Urban poverty and politics in Rio de Janeiro.* Berkeley, University of California Press.

PREALC (Programa Regional del Empleo para América Latina y el Caribe). 1983. *Empleo y salarios.* Santiago, ILO.

——. 1985. *Beyond the crisis.* Santiago, ILO.

Psacharopoulos, G. 1986. *To vocationalise or not to vocationalise? That is the curriculum question.* World Bank discussion paper, Education and Training Series, Washington, DC.

Rajamaran, I. 1985. *Returns to labour in developing country agriculture: India.* Geneva, ILO; mimeographed World Employment Programme research working paper; restricted.

Ramírez Guerrero, J. 1985. *Informe sobre los programas de formación para el sector informal urbano en Venezuela.* CINTERFOR, Montevideo.

——. 1986. *Informe sobre los programas de formación para el sector informal urbano en Colombia.* CINTERFOR, Montevideo.

Ranis, G. and Fei, J.C.H. 1961. "A theory of economic development", in *American Economic Review* (Nashville), Sep. 1961.

——. 1964. *The development of the labour surplus economy: Theory and policy.* Homewood, Illinois, Irwin.

Ray, S. 1987. *Returns to rural labour in Asia.* Geneva, ILO; mimeographed World Employment Programme research working paper; restricted.

Remus, J. 1983. "Financial participation of employees", in *International Labour Review* (Geneva, ILO), Jan.-Feb. 1983.

de Rezende, G.C. 1985. *Price of food and the rural poor in Brazil, 1960-80.* Rio de Janeiro, Brazil, Instituto de Pesquisas.

Rivera, R. and Cruz, M.E. 1984. *Pobladores rurales.* Santiago, Chile, GIA.

Rodgers, G.B. (ed.). *Trends in urban poverty and labour market access.* Geneva, ILO, forthcoming.

——; and Standing, G. (eds.). 1981. *Child work, poverty and underdevelopment.* Geneva, ILO.

Ruben, G. 1961. "Industrial relations in 1980 influenced by inflation and recession", in *Monthly Labor Review* (Washington, DC), Vol. 10, No. 6.

Rudra, A. 1982. *Extra-economic constraints on agricultural labour: Results of an intensive survey in some villages near Santiniketan, West Bengal.* Bangkok, ILO-ARTEP.

Schott, K. 1984. *Policy, power and order: The persistence of economic problems in capitalist States.* London, Yale University Press.

Selunin, V. and Hanin, G. 1987. "Lukavayá Tsifra", in *Novy Mir* (Moscow), Feb. 1987.

Sheehan, P.M. 1974. "Wage indexation: Solution or stimulus to inflation?", in *Australian Bulletin of Labour* (Bedford Park), Dec. 1974.

Squire, L. 1979. *Labour force, employment and labour markets in the course of economic development.* World Bank staff working paper, No. 336, Washington, DC.

Standing, G. 1983. *Migration in Peninsular Malaysia.* Kuala Lumpur, EPU-ILO.

——. (ed.). 1985. *Labour circulation and the labour process.* London, Croom Helm.

——. 1987. *Vulnerable groups in urban labour processes.* Geneva, ILO; mimeographed World Employment Programme research working paper; restricted.

Starr, G. 1981. *Minimum wage fixing: An international review of practices and problems.* Geneva, ILO.

Taira, K. 1966. "Wage differentials in developing countries: A survey of findings", in *International Labour Review* (Geneva, ILO), Mar. 1966.

Thompson, A.G. 1986. "Work incentives and the efficiency of internal labour markets", in *Journal of Industrial Relations* (Sydney), Mar. 1986.

Todaro, M.P. 1976. *Internal migration in developing countries.* Geneva, ILO.

Tokman, V. 1986. "Adjustment and employment in Latin America: The current challenges", in *International Labour Review* (Geneva, ILO), Sep.-Oct. 1986.

Weitzman, M.L. 1984. *The share economy.* Cambridge, Mass., Harvard University Press.

World Bank. 1981. *Accelerated development in sub-Saharan Africa: An agenda for action.* Washington, DC.

——. 1984. *Toward sustained development in sub-Saharan Africa.* Washington, DC.

——. 1986a. *Financing adjustment with growth in sub-Saharan Africa, 1986-90.* Washington, DC.

——. 1986b. *World Development Report.* Washington, DC.